An Ounce of Prevention

Navigating your way through Damage Control and Crisis Response

By Dr. Allan Bonner, MA, MSc, DBA, LLM, MScPI (Cand.)

Also by the author:

Doing and Saying the Right Thing:
Professional Risk and Crisis Management

Media Relations

Speaking, Writing and Presenting in SOCKOs®
Strategic Overriding Communications & Knowledge Objectives

Political Columns
Behind the Scenes with Powerful People

Tough Love at the Table
Power, Culture and Diversity in Negotiations, Mediation and Conflict Resolution

Political Conventions
The Art of Getting Elected and Governing

An Ounce of Prevention

First printing, November, 2010

Printed and bound by Motion Creative Printing Inc., Carleton Place, Ontario, Canada

Published by Sextant Publishing, Edmonton, Alberta, Canada

Printed in Canada.

ISBN 978-1-926755-02-1

For educational or institutional discounts or for information
about seminars and speeches, please contact:

Sextant Publishing, Edmonton, Alberta, Canada

or

www.allanbonner.com
1-877-484-1667

CONTENTS

Preface v

Foreword vii

Introduction xi

CHAPTER 1 1
Risk: What are the Chances? 2

CHAPTER 2 9
Crisis Management 10

CHAPTER 3 49
Resource Rooms 50

CHAPTER 4 69
Communicating about Risk and Crises 70

CHAPTER 5 101
Media Relations 102

CHAPTER 6 151
Making Public Remarks 152

CHAPTER 7 173
If your Crisis Requires Negotiation 174

CHAPTER 8 183
Witness Preparation: Testifying as a Skill 184

CHAPTER 9 193
Legislation 194

CHAPTER 10 199
Policy 200

CHAPTER 11 213
Victims 214

CHAPTER 12 219
Specific Threats 220

CHAPTER 13 239
Running Simulations 240

Appendix 1: Learning from Past Disasters 247

Appendix 2: Is a Crisis a Failure of Security? 257

Appendix 3: Public Participation in Crises—a Prerequisite for Effective Disaster Management 263

Appendix 4: Why Risk Communication? 269

Appendix 5: Witness Preparation 277

Appendix 6: Post-Traumatic Stress Disorder and Crises 299

Appendix 7: Apologies 307

Endnotes 311

Bibliography 313

Preface from the Publisher

Allan's book *Tough Love at the Table* (Sextant Publishing, 2008) deals with conflict resolution. He begins the first chapter with the sentences: "Disputes are thieves. They rob us of time, energy and money. Disputes can even lead to death. Preventing disputes and resolving them quickly is imperative."

Those sentences could have been about risks and crises.

It is a cliché of modern times that we are experiencing more crises than ever before. They last longer and have deeper effects. There are many reasons for this: instant communication, 24-hour news, a better educated population, workplace rights and so on.

I live in a jurisdiction with one of the most controversial energy projects in the world: the Alberta oil sands. Criticism from environmental protesters and Hollywood stars triggers multi-million-dollar PR responses from the Alberta government. That's a crisis affecting all taxpayers and workers. It also affects energy users in the United States.

I live in a country that spent a billion dollars hosting the G20 and G8 meetings. We were on the world's stage briefly, regrettably with images of vandalism and clashes between police and protesters.

The principles in Allan's new book would have reduced or eliminated both problems. His notion of risk management long before an event, and the sound principles of crisis management if a problem does occur, could have saved money, jobs, image and injury. In fact Allan was interviewed for news programs about the G20 meetings and argued that they could be held on a military base, at the UN in New York or even on a floating facility ringed with security.

This book is in keeping with Sextant Publishing's commitment to fostering intelligent discussion of important public-policy issues. But it goes a step further. This is also a prescription for staying safer, protecting property, saving lives and maintaining a positive reputation.

Long before a crisis hits, the checklists, diagrams and tables will ensure that organizations are better prepared. The companion DVD, containing many dozens of these tools, can be divided up among crisis managers to assemble a several-hundred-page plan from scratch in short order.

Your crisis plan can benefit from the many case studies in this book. Allan has chosen some in which he was involved, some that are very well known, a few obscure ones—but all with serious lessons to teach. He also tackles the controversial issue of Post-Traumatic Stress Disorder, the very difficult task of negotiating with stakeholders, risk communication and the aftermath of many crises—the public inquiry.

I'm pleased that the principles of effective risk and crisis management that Allan uses for his private clients can now be accessible and affordable for all organizations, regardless of size, need or budget.

K. J. (Ken) Chapman
Sextant Publishing
Edmonton, Alberta

FOREWORD

I'm not sure if I should credit luck, chance, thought or hard work for my now being in the crisis-management business. The main thing I knew in my early career as a journalist was that spokespeople needed clear, newsworthy messages to get booked on and to thrive on my radio and TV programs. Most didn't have clear messages, and it was a mystery to me why. Within a couple of years of starting my media training business, I was training responders who went to the Valdez, Alaska oil spill and people in the chemical industry reacting to the tragic release in Bhopal, India.

Following these events, my clients asked me to conduct crisis simulations to test their abilities to respond to unexpected events. I designed and delivered oil spill, sour-gas explosion, fire and chemical release simulations in four jurisdictions on both coasts of North America. The companies mobilized hundreds of responders.

The simulations did their jobs and revealed that corporate crisis plans wouldn't work in real events. So I was asked to write a crisis plan that would fill in the gaps. I had hoped to find a template in a library or with an industry association. I didn't. I'll never forget writing the crisis plan from scratch—for about two weeks at my dining-room table. I kept thinking up what tasks would be required— especially the ones that had not been handled well during the simulations I ran. This was the beginning of my philosophy of concentrating on capabilities, not job descriptions or causes.

After this great professional-development experience, I worked with peace-keepers in Cyprus, ran an earthquake simulation in Tokyo and participated in military war games. I also conducted tabletop simulations with a broad range of public and private-sector organizations on five continents. About half of my time over the past twenty-five years has been spent responding to incidents as they happened. I get calls that begin with:

- Police are on their way to charge an employee with theft. Will you come to …?
- A camera crew is on the lawn of a facility that emits nuclear radiation …
- A TV network is doing a one-hour exposé in ten days …
- A national newspaper will be exposing a same-sex sexual-harassment case in the morning …
- A town will be gobbled up by the big city nearby in a week …

All these experiences caused me to enrich this document every time my colleagues and I re-wrote it for new clients. My other priceless professional development experience began on a trip to the U.K. My wife, public broadcaster Lorna Jackson, handed me information about Leicester University's postgraduate programs in Risk, Crisis and Disaster Management. I had been toying with the idea of studying risk and crisis management in the faculties of environmental studies or public policy. With Leicester, I found a comprehensive curriculum: 2,000 pages of reading, lots of books, six 4,000-word essays to write and a 20,000-word dissertation. We studied quantitative risk assessment, the history of jurisprudence, risk engineering, crowd control, systems theory and dozens of crisis cases. The interesting thing about the cases is that they were not the usual ones we study in North America. I was reading about Walton Town Centre, the Happy Valley Racecourse Fire, King's Cross Underground, the Iranian Embassy hostage-taking, Flixborough, the Commercial Union bombing and so on.

British Prime Minister Benjamin Disraeli once said all crises are the same. He might have been exaggerating, but there are lessons to be learned from *any* event. There's little difference between the fires that have occurred in theatres in Montreal (Laurier Palace) and Chicago (the Iroquois), nightclubs in Boston (the Coconut Grove) and Rhode Island over a period of about 100 years. They all featured locked exit doors, stampedes and crushes of patrons, flammable materials and so on. How people behave, responders react, lawyers sue, media report and courts rule are often common to all events.

My experience at Leicester caused more rewrites of this crisis plan. I added case studies, bullet points and the most important aspects from my essays and research. I owe Leicester a debt of gratitude. I know that readers can't access the Scarman Centre for the Study of Public Order (SCSPO) documents I studied, but I want to acknowledge the comprehensive and inspirational character of the curriculum materials at Leicester. You can access Leicester papers on the university's website and can listen, read and watch more through my other books, CDs and DVDs, which are outlined at the back of this book.

The best way for readers to turn this into their own crisis plans is with the companion DVD. The most exciting part of the DVD is the 80 or so pages of charts, tables, lists and documents that you can customize for your particular situation. You can also send the DVD to sites around the country or the world for local customization. The task of filling in the tables can be spread among multiple employees. One person can take responsibility for collating the results and looking for anomalies, economies of scale or problem areas. The DVD also contains some video clips for private study. Together, this book and the DVD are the most powerful tools to put a plan in place, revise it regularly, test it and respond to a crisis if needed. I hope they're not needed.

A version of this work is available in French. Une version de cette œuvre est disponible en français.

Allan Bonner
Lord Beaverbrook Hotel
Fredericton, New Brunswick, Canada
Summer, 2010

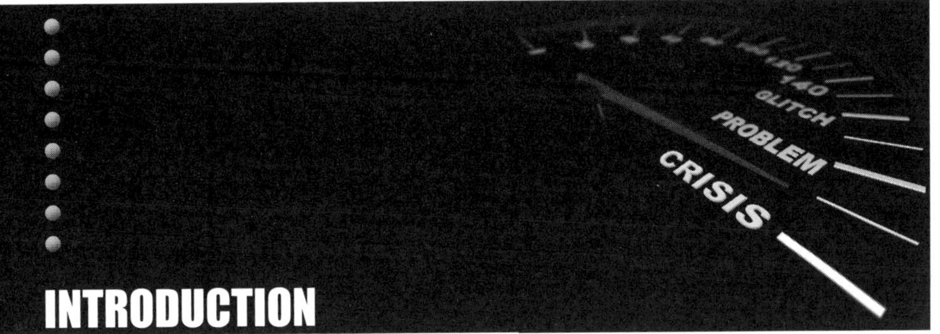

INTRODUCTION

An organization must recognize the need to be as prepared as possible for crises and controversies. This book, and the companion DVD, are templates to use in preparing both corporate and site-specific crisis-management plans. The DVD contains charts, tables, lists and text that you can modify to suit your needs (see the description at the end of this book and the icon throughout). Your organization must commit itself to regularly reviewing, testing and modifying these plans.

Effective crisis management maintains the integrity and activities of your enterprise. An effective plan reduces uncertainty, lowers risk and liability, and helps you return to normal conditions. The well prepared organization is committed to a communications policy that is honest, timely, open, accurate and consistent.

Your communications goals are as crucial to address as the physical components of an event. Your organization must not only do the right thing but *be seen* to be doing the right thing. Poor communication often makes people think the worst, and people who think the worst of you can make your crisis more costly.

I should say a few words about terminology. Terminology doesn't keep anyone safer, so I will keep my comments brief. I advocate classifying crises to let responders know how serious the event is, what equipment to deploy and perhaps how long the event will last. But a crisis is also in the eyes of the beholder. A crisis can call the integrity of people and organizations into question and even destroy them. Business, government and the academic community don't all use the same terms or even use terms consistently. Does an *event* lead to a *crisis*? Are there *emergencies* within *crises*, and without response, does a *crisis* lead to a *disaster*, or can a disaster happen all at once? These are good and interesting questions, but they don't take the place of getting on with crisis planning and response.

Then there are the terms that describe the people who plan and execute crisis response. In many companies this person is called the loss-prevention manager. Some call the activity risk management, business-resumption planning, contingency planning or business-continuation planning. Sometimes the person holding this title is a lawyer, engineer, communication specialist, HR manager, insurance professional or has another background or skill. In this book I mainly use the terms 'risk manager' and 'crisis manager' to describe all these people who prevent and respond to crises. This book is for all those who have to write and update a crisis plan, reduce risk, plan a simulation or report to a board on risk, including reputation management or risk by any other name.

While on disclaimers, I'll add one about some of the case studies in this book. I recount some of the cases I've handled over 25 years. I've used traditional ethical means (journalistic and academic) to protect the identities of my clients, so no inference should be taken from references to locations, gender or organizations, since some or all may have been altered for privacy reasons.

Crisis managers must deal with the irony that the news media, governments and others often know more about the crisis than the corporate officers do. Furthermore, at a time when an organization most needs extra efforts and loyalty from its employees, this group may be the last to find out crucial information about their own plant. Thus one of your organization's goals must be to create understanding and support among various internal and external stakeholders.

It's often extremely difficult or impossible for stakeholder groups to become familiar with an organization during times of crisis. Moreover, if there are ambiguities or fact gaps, these leave considerable leeway for innuendo or suppositions coming from a variety of adversarial parties.

Crisis-management and communication-skills training should be woven into your existing health, safety and environmental-compliance training-programs. You can then test the effectiveness of this training with simulations and drills. One way to develop skills is to learn lessons from others. In these pages you will see references to dozens of real-life events. If the Happy Valley Racecourse fire or King's Cross Underground fire aren't familiar, please Google or visit a library to find out more. I've just included enough about some case studies to whet your appetite or illustrate a particular point.

The advice in these pages doesn't take the place of issue management, media training, simulations, polling or any other element in the public-affairs functions. Nor will this book take the place of existing guidelines or policies within your organization. You will need to adapt and modify the advice that follows to suit your local and organizational needs. Many sections can serve as guides to produce a comprehensive policy.

Naturally the use of this book implies no warranty against the negative effects resulting from a crisis or negative results of any kind following communication or any other action with stakeholders. Full and final responsibility for all actions rests with the staff of organizations to whom such responsibilities are assigned.

A Ticket to Ride

In the summer of 2001, I was in Los Angeles with an organization that rented private jets. I was putting senior executives through simulated crises to see if they'd be prepared for challenging issues—crashes, theft, air rage, drug and alcohol abuse, narcotics smuggling, prostitutes in private planes, etc. People with lots of money do funny things with planes.

Company spokespeople were gamely explaining that private-plane rental offered confidentiality and convenience. I countered with concerns about security and safety. This questioning went on until we hit a telling area of inquiry.

"What will you do if someone rents one of your planes to fly it into the White House?" asked one of my trainers in a simulated interview.

"That wouldn't happen," the company spokesperson assured him as if comforting a child who was afraid of the dark.

"How can you be so sure?" we pressed.

"Well, first of all, they'd lose their deposit." The spokesperson was searching for more ways to state what for him was the obvious. "And they'd kill themselves!" he added triumphantly.

My client's spokesperson was a former military officer. His excellent military training was actually creating danger for him and his company. Many well trained people see problems only through their particular prisms. Academics call this phenomenon the use of heuristics, paradigms or world views. Sometimes it's just plain ego.

My client had to keep rich clientele happy and safe. The planes needed maintenance, well stocked bars and minimal administration at private airports. It took a shift in thinking for him to view high-class customers as a potential threat.

I informed the company's senior team that there were thousands of people around the world who might be willing to die to harm America, to make a political point, or to exorcize a mental demon. Tens of thousands of other people might fund such an operation, we told him.

We also reminded our client that a light plane had once landed on the White House lawn. What's more, an ultra-light plane had landed in Red Square, and a World War II bomber had crashed into the Empire State Building—then the tallest in New York. At least one person had tried to hijack a plane to crash it into the White House.

We recommended some rudimentary security measures that were not yet in place in the private-airplane rental business. These included requiring passengers to produce identification, keeping a passenger list and filing the plane's flight plan.

A little more than a month later, the world changed when two commercial jets destroyed the World Trade Center in New York City. It took the news media a few hours, but reporters eventually began asking questions about the security arrangements at small airports that rent private planes. My client received many calls and was one of the few in general aviation with something of substance to say.

A while later, the client took a moment to call and say they were pleased to have been through the tough questions long before they were needed.

CHAPTER 1: RISK AND CRISIS

Event: *9/11, World Trade Center, New York City*

Date: *11 September 2001*

Summary: *The terrorist group al-Qaeda coordinated suicide attacks on the US. They hijacked four airplanes, crashing two into the World Trade Center Towers, another into the Pentagon and a fourth (probably destined for the White House or the Capitol) near Shanksville, Pennsylvania. Some people trapped in the World Trade Center walked up stairways to the roof hoping for helicopter rescue, but the door was locked. Emergency responders' radios were incompatible. Hundreds of responders were killed or injured. The popularity of President George W. Bush and New York Mayor Rudy Giuliani soared. The Patriot Act was passed. Sikhs wearing turbans were assaulted and one killed. There was a firebombing at a Hindu temple. The invasion of Afghanistan and Iraq followed.*

Result: *2976 victims, 19 hijackers dead, 6,000 injured, incalculable counter-terrorism costs. The US war on terror and stronger anti-terrorist laws in many countries. Incalculable financial cost, but direct rebuilding-cost was perhaps in excess of $30 billion with another $30 billion in lost GDP in New York alone. 18,000 small businesses were destroyed or displaced. 31.9 million square feet of Lower Manhattan office space was damaged or destroyed. Negotiation and fighting over rebuilding the site and a memorial to victims lasted more than a decade.*

Lessons Learned: *The apparent and confessed mastermind of the 2001 attack was involved in the 1993 World Trade Center bombing and related to the lead bomber in that attack. The event could have been predicted, since the same building had been bombed before and there had been numerous airplane hijackings and bombings in the US and of US installations around the world. White House perimeter security is breached regularly, even as late as under the Obama administration.*

The day of the event, Cold War responses were still in place with military scanning and reactions tens of thousands of feet up in the air and out over the Atlantic, but not 500 feet up and north over the Hudson River.

When you build the world's tallest building, you build risk into the system.

Risk: What are the Chances?

People and organizations should consider themselves 'put on notice' that they will experience a crisis or disaster. Before the Exxon tanker ran aground, there had been numerous oil spills in Valdez, Alaska. A nuclear accident similar to the one at Three Mile Island had occurred some months before in the Tennessee Valley Authority. Product tampering happens weekly in North America, and yet the Tylenol, Pepsi, Perrier, Ball Park Frankfurters and other incidents show that many companies fail to heed the weekly warnings.

> *"I cannot imagine any condition which would cause a ship to founder. I cannot conceive of any vital disaster happening to this vessel. Modern ship building has gone beyond that."*
>
> ***— Edward J. Smith, Captain of the Titanic***

After reading of countless similar incidents in the history of crisis management, it's easy to become unsympathetic to managers who are bedevilled by crises and disasters. Using case studies of past incidents to transfer knowledge from one system or incident to another is an excellent beginning. Knowledge gained through case studies can improve organizations' 'safety cultures'.

Organizations, like people, have personalities. An organization's culture or personality can be identified by its attitudes, values, beliefs and norms. This might help predict problems, types of response required and abilities available. All organizations have a safety culture as an aspect of their corporate personalities. Some cultures ignore or welcome risk. Some workers in mining or the construction industry are known as 'hot dogs'—risk-takers. It's sometimes hard to get them to slow down and work more safely.

In some organizations, safety is front and centre. There's a joke in Wilmington, Delaware that everyone in the suburbs knows who works at a certain company. They know because those are the people mowing their lawns with safety boots, eye goggles, earplugs and perhaps even hard hats. Signs promoting safety are so prevalent in this one company that employees chastise each other for not holding handrails on stairs and for walking too quickly in halls. Maybe they forget the cardiovascular benefit of not holding the handrails, proving that there's no free lunch.

So, as you construct a crisis plan and response capability, consider what your organization's safety culture is. How will responders behave? Will they be in danger? Is there an acceptable trade-off between that danger and the safety they create by their actions? Better yet, what actions can you take now to make safety a more important aspect of your organization's culture? An effective safety culture might display itself in preventative maintenance, a more alert workforce or reporting unusual occurrences or dangerous practices. You might be able to harness dozens of eyes, ears and hands in your organization and reduce losses of all types.

Identifying the risks to your organization doesn't have to be 'rocket science': any risk and/or crisis manager can access the Internet to review historical case studies of crises in comparable industries, climates, geographical locations, political scenarios, and so on. At minimal cost you can find video documentaries on every conceivable crisis. Reaching out and communicating with other similar organizations (for example, with a unionized workforce or one with a specific type of process or equipment) can give a 'heads-up' to the potential crises.

To read more about learning from past disasters, please see Appendix 1: "Learning from Past Disasters."

What is a Crisis?

A crisis can mean many things to many people. I've worked for CEOs who felt that appearing in a news report was a crisis. On the other hand, when I worked for the world's longest-serving mayor, I had the impression that he felt not getting his name in the papers was a crisis. The accounting-department might think that any unforeseen expenditure is a crisis, but a manager might think instead that a crisis is the inability to spend money on short notice to accomplish unforeseen but vital objectives.

A good starting-point may be to put a few definitions on the table. Crises are "situations requiring a rapid response"[1] or, more precisely, "a serious threat to the basic structures or the fundamental values and norms of a social system."[2] Some define a crisis as "the onset of disaster."[3]

As a first step to defining a crisis for your organization, you need to examine the intensity, type, duration and likelihood of any potential crisis. This examination will also enable your management to gauge the intensity and duration of crisis that your organization can endure and ask important questions. How will the media, government, regulatory bodies, protest groups, legislators and other stakeholders view the organization's crisis? How will perceptions and actions differ, depending on whether you are the cause of the crisis or the victim? How will matters change if the crisis is a natural or weather event or if there's a human cause? What might competitors or pressure groups do to take advantage of your organization during a crisis?

As a general rule, an organization that is prone to a crisis is public, governmental, high-profile, with a celebrity CEO, in an important industry or in a field with a history of controversy. The crisis may be triggered by events thousands of miles away that make the news and then put you under scrutiny.

For a further discussion of the crisis concept and the role of security, see Appendix 2: "Is a Crisis a Failure of Security?"

Causes of Crises

Situations leading to crises often include one or more of the following elements:

- Loss of life
- Near loss of life
- Panic
- Moral offences
- Weakness or vacillation
- Labour/management difficulties
- Public or private investigation
- Product recall or failure
- Legal or financial difficulties
- Customer service failure
- Other media-attracting reports
- Product tampering
- Acts of God
- Terrorism
- Conspiracy
- Bribes
- Misuse of public funds
- Crime
- Fires or explosions
- Health, safety or environmental problems
- Perceived disregard for public health, safety or environmental protection
- A System Failure

Levels of Crises

A fire is not a crisis for a fire-fighter—it's another day at the office. A fire in a plant with oxygen tanks stored in it is a different level of crisis from one in a plant made of non-combustible materials.

Effective crisis management often requires you to categorize crises by intensity and duration. While it is difficult to set hard and fast rules or establish mechanical processes, site-specific plans should attempt to distinguish between the potential levels of crises.

One popular concept is to categorize levels of crises, such as Level I, Level II and Level III.

> *"[The] disaster must not be seen like the meteorite that falls out of the sky on an innocent world; the disaster, most often, is anticipated, and on multiple occasions."*
>
> ***— P. Lagadec (1982)***

A rule of thumb could be to anticipate the duration and the degree of impact on air, water, ground, humans and other living organisms. For example:

- a Level I crisis would probably last one day and have no short- or long-term health effects on humans, no mortality among wildlife and little or no impact on air, water or ground beyond government regulations or guidelines.
- a Level II crisis is harder to define but would last more than one day and at least have ambiguous effects on humans, wildlife and the environment.
- a Level III crisis would last more than several days or, if corrected within the first day, would be reported on for more than several days and would involve death or near death to humans, death or long-term health effects to wildlife, protracted remediation and potential ongoing environmental impact or speculation about such potential impact.

The decision to place a crisis at the highest level then triggers a series of activities such as procuring assets and marshalling responders. This requires each facility and organization to come to terms with its capabilities, and that's a great part of pre-crisis management. Your plan- and site-specific documents should help responders assess the nature and intensity of potential crises.

Effects of Public Inquiries and/or News Reports

Public inquiries or reports about an incident can cause it to move from Level I to Level II or even Level III, even though the physical components remain unchanged.

Effective crisis management therefore involves factoring in public perception and communication. An effective crisis manager tries to view the crisis from the perspective of the outside world.

It is important to recognize that the crisis itself may look quite different to each of the media, government, public and other stakeholders. Moreover, one group's attitudes or actions may have a big effect on what others do. For example, when the public demands action, politicians often act whether action is required or not. This can escalate your crisis. The most effective antidote to this situation is usually the repeated dissemination of meaningful, helpful, timely, newsworthy information. Material should be given to those who will comment on and respond to your crisis and to groups with a special need to know. In Chapter 4, "Communicating during a Crisis," you will find information on the SOCKO™ communication system that will enable you to make informed responses and, to some extent, control the discussions you are bound to have during a crisis.

Risk and Crisis

Discussion Points:

1. What's the worst-case scenario for you?
2. How will you categorize levels of crisis for your organization?
3. What events have there been in your organization's history?
4. What events have similar organizations handled?
5. What environmental, labour-relations, libel and other laws will govern your response and eventual settlements with others?
6. What are the trends in other jurisdictions?
7. How do others, especially critics, view your organization and its operations?
8. Are there organized critics in your community or on the web?
9. What's on social networking-sites?
10. What's in the archives of radio, TV and print media?

Response, Not Causes

My friend the late Charles Gaines was second on the scene at the Oklahoma City bombing. The deputy fire chief responded to a call and drove to the back of the Murrah Federal Building. He thought he might be at a false alarm, because the building looked just fine.

Then he went around the front and found that most of the façade had been hollowed out as if by a giant ice-cream scoop. His first thought was that a light plane had hit the building.

> *"There are no alternatives which have no risk."*
>
> ***—S.L. Derby and R.L. Keeney (1981)***

When Chief Gaines realized that there had been an explosion, his mind raced through the fact that his department had no plan to deal specifically with such a large explosion, but it did have a plan to deal with tornadoes. He quickly realized that a tornado could have scooped out the front of a building and made it look just like what he was seeing. They know how to respond to tornadoes in Oklahoma and got to work.

One lesson I took from my many conversations with Chief Gaines (including ones in Dubai, Ottawa and Toronto) is that the cause doesn't really matter as much as your response capability. Whether the Murrah Building had been damaged by a plane, tornado, gas-main explosion, terrorism or earthquake, the response would have been much the same—triage, putting fires out, first aid, evacuation and so on.

Fire-fighters and police sometimes become targets themselves. Snipers and secondary explosive devices can be a real danger. But for the most part, responding is more important than wondering what might have triggered the event.

CHAPTER 2: CRISIS MANAGEMENT

Event: *Hurricane Katrina*

Date: *23-30 August, 2005*

Summary: *The storm began over the Bahamas, strengthened in the Gulf of Mexico, then weakened before hitting land for the second time on the morning of August 29. The worst damage in New Orleans occurred when the levee system failed, with many failures after the hurricane had moved inland. Eighty per cent of the city was flooded. It was among the strongest, deadliest and costliest storms in US history. The federal agency FEMA was criticized for slow response, as was President George W. Bush. The President declared an emergency on August 27, two days before the hurricane hit land. There has been controversy about why certain parishes were not evacuated under the emergency declaration, and critics blame FEMA, the governor and others. Many private facilities could not evacuate because buses, ambulances, taxis and rental cars were scarce. Thousands of people had lived in trailers for years. About 1.2 million people on the Gulf Coast evacuated either under a mandatory order or voluntarily.*

The City of New Orleans designated the Superdome sports stadium as a "refuge of last resort." Its roof was compromised, as was the waterproof membrane. There were four deaths in the Superdome from natural causes, one drug overdose and one suicide. There may have been a homicide in the Convention Center. More than 46,000 troops were eventually deployed. About 300,000 refugees went to Texas—35,000 to Houston. About 5 per cent had criminal records with 22 per cent involving violent crimes. Homicides in Houston went up 23 per cent with 29 murders involving displaced Louisianans. Governor Blanco of Louisiana wouldn't allow Homeland Security to take over operations, saying that her state's National Guard could cope.

The affected area was about the size of the United Kingdom, and three million people were without electricity.

Result: *1836 confirmed dead, 705 missing, about $90 billion in damage. Nine refineries closed and 30 oil platforms were damaged or destroyed. Between 18 and 24 per cent of America's oil and gas production was affected for the six months following. It was the largest evacuation in US history. Some insurance companies stopped insuring homes in New Orleans.*

Lessons Learned: *The Army Corps of Engineers had designed inadequate levees. The Superdome was designated to handle 800 people and 30,000 showed up. The New Orleans Civic Center was not designated as an evacuation centre, but 25,000 people showed up. Some offers of help from other countries were refused. New on-line communication was vital during the event, as was old-fashioned AM radio. Cellphones were knocked out for several months.*

A city should be able to clothe, house and feed its citizens in emergencies. Why couldn't truckloads of supplies have been delivered to the Superdome and other sites? Why shouldn't city bylaws have required adequate supplies of food at arenas, hotels and convention centres? Why couldn't the city be evacuated? One news story featured university students who drove into New Orleans to rescue a few victims. Why couldn't others have driven in or out? Why couldn't fit people walk out?

Amazingly, just one month later, Hurricane Rita raised many of the same questions as it damaged New Orleans again and also hit parts of Texas.

New Orleans was the largest peacetime evacuation in North America, surpassing the Mississauga, Ontario train derailment that forced 200,000 from their homes on November 10, 1979. There were no deaths in Mississauga. A fireball rose almost 5,000 feet in the air and could be seen 200 kilometres away. The evacuation was spurred by worry over styrene, toluene, propane, caustic soda and chlorine at the site.

Crisis Management

Security is dedicated to identifying and managing risks. It is sometimes referred to as 'operational readiness.'[4] This implies not merely prevention but the ability to deploy when things are happening. Mitigation involves both managing and reducing risks, not necessarily eliminating them. It is inevitable that some risks remain. Crises will occur, and they must be managed.

The centre of the following diagram represents an event that could trigger a crisis. This might be a fire, spill or release to the atmosphere. It could be a natural or weather event. It could be news reports or statements in the legislature that harm your reputation.

Crisis-Management System

Note that Claims, Communication, Remediation and Support for Responders will often overlap.

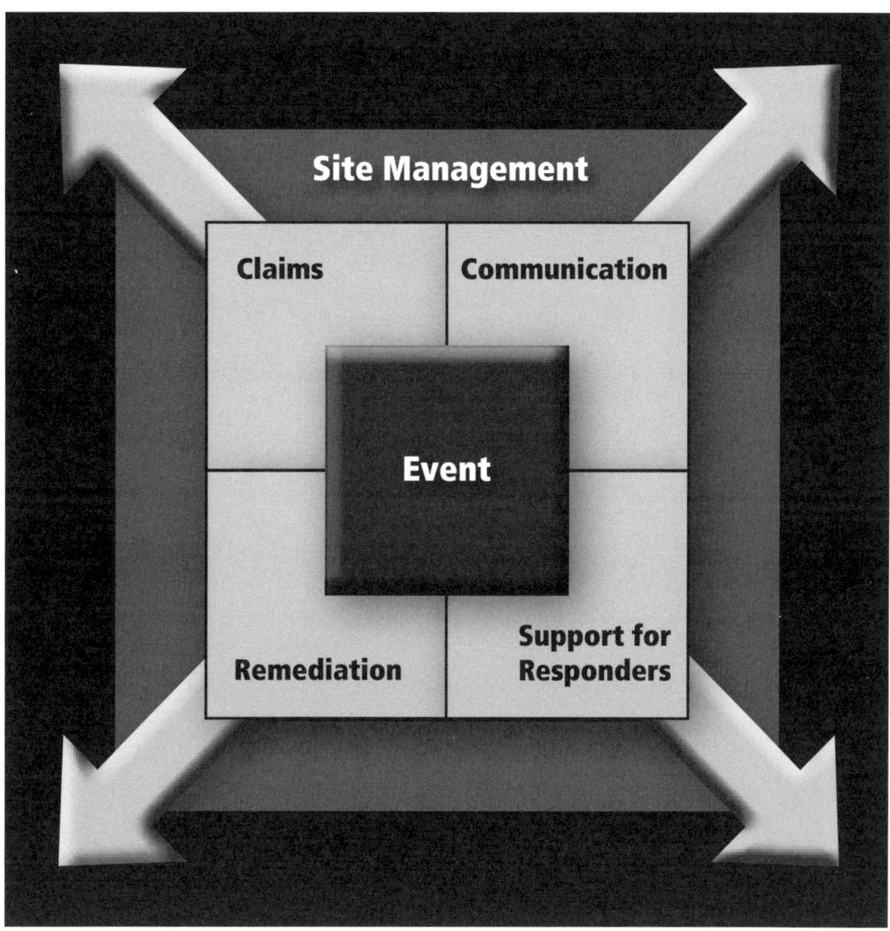

All activities within the quadrants surrounding the event need to be activated as soon as possible. The event should trigger a virtually instantaneous effort to remediate at the site. The initial response may be pulling a fire alarm, evacuation, deploying safety gear or other steps.

Those who are charged with remediation require support—food, clothing, shelter, response equipment and other materials.

At the same time with these efforts, a communication system needs to be triggered, so that your good name is protected with all significant third parties—legislators, regulators, suppliers and others.

Working with outside insurers and legal counsel, your organization's officials will be responsible for claims by affected third parties. This work may go on long after the actual incident has been addressed.

The area outside the quadrants, entitled "Site Management," refers to logistics and security to ensure safe and efficient operations at the site of an event. The extreme outside area, entitled "Crisis-Management System," refers to head office or a remote team that provides support, guidance and direction to the site team.

Your plan should address who will head the team that responds in each quadrant. The plan should also divide up tasks to insure that procurement and activities begin immediately and progress in tandem, not one after another. Tasks must be allotted to both internal and external responders, and there must be a mechanism to ensure they are accomplished.

The forms, checklists and tips included throughout this book and in the companion DVD will help you prepare for this.

Making Decisions

Crises are lessened or prevented by action, and action often springs from decisions. The effective crisis-management team must be willing and able to make tough decisions. There are many considerations in the decision-making process. The team must be able to distinguish between an urgent situation and one that is only important. The members may be empowered to make a decision but not be responsible for carrying it out. Team members may be obliged to take action by laws but be unsure of how to interpret the laws or how to resolve apparent conflicts between laws. Actions may require approval by regulators who disagree on a course of action or fail to reach a decision.

Typical decision-making identifies options, weighs anticipated outcomes, implements a trial decision, examines actual outcomes and reassesses options. The process is then repeated. Some decision-makers make their jobs easier by exaggerating positive or negative outcomes to reduce choices. Others exaggerate the difficulty of implementing certain courses of action. However, eliminating options simply to make the decision process easier is dangerous. While an 'either/or' decision is much simpler to debate, it may ignore many viable options.

In a crisis decisions have to be made quickly. You'll be explaining your decision to the courts, victims, media, shareholders and others for years to come. But there's another reality: many responders don't make decisions at all—they act. Medical, fire, police and other emergency responders are trained to take action, not ponder alternatives. They thought about alternatives during hundreds of hours of training, and a crisis is a time for action.

But if there are competing elements, you're best to simplify the decision you need to make. When there are two courses of action and elements such as the degree of difficulty, cost and expected outcome are similar, then they cancel themselves out, as in algebra. What might remain is the number of people needed to implement the decision or the time it would take. You can then choose the option requiring the fewest people or the shortest time. If every possible course of action costs about the same, or the cost is unknown, then the cost should not be discussed when each option comes up. Some people like to complicate matters by repeatedly pointing out "We don't know the cost" or "We'll be spending $X," but if this is true for every option, then it is irrelevant. A crisis is no time to be discussing irrelevancies.

In most oil spills we know that the environmentally soundest approach is to leave most of the oil alone. Oil is a naturally occurring product, made up of decomposed living matter, half of which is biodegradable and with little or no toxicity (keep in mind that toxicity varies with dosage over time, and so most everything is toxic if you ingest too much too quickly). Half the oil evaporates within about six hours of a spill.

One of the best options is to burn the spill while the combustible 'light ends' (toluene, benzene, etc) are still present. But permission to burn may have to come from more than a dozen local, state, provincial and federal agencies with some authority over the matter—your co-decision-makers, if you like. Meanwhile the news media will want to cover your response activities, and it will be hard to tell reporters that you're waiting for spilled oil to biodegrade. Some rocky beaches are better off if left alone and not washed with high-pressure hoses that kill living things under the surface. You will have tough, competing interests in your crisis.

In other cases, decision-makers may refuse to act. In one oil-spill simulation we ran for the Coast Guard, no one in that organization had the authority to burn the spill or spray dispersants on it. They consulted environmental and other government officials, but no one would take the necessary decisions. With the option to burn only remaining open for about six hours, the decision had to be made fast, or the option would no longer exist. In the end, no one would decide, and the question went right up to the head of the national government. The two-day simulation was over before we heard back.

Much is made of expert opinion and how to access the best and latest data. But great work has also been done on so-called 'lay information' and how it can be valuable too. Local citizens, farmers, indigenous people and others may have valuable information. How to seek out local and lay information during an event is a challenge. The right decision and decision-making strategy is often found in unexpected places. Intuition plays a role. There are stories of trapped fire-fighters deciding to take highly unorthodox actions with little information and yet saving lives. Information gained from local residents long before an incident can also save lives. Gut feelings and the hair on the back of your head can lead you to the right decisions too.

How do you get good instincts? Perhaps some instinct is God-given or involves chance, but it may also be the fruit of studying and practising. I'm not sure, but I am certain that reading case studies, drills, simulations and speaking with others who have 'been there' helps.

Decision Planning

All possible decisions should be made long before a crisis occurs and removed from crisis-management activities.

Are indemnification agreements in place? Will procurement contracts help or hinder in retaining labourers?

When I'm discussing crisis plans with clients, I often point out the window to a construction site and say that in the right kind of crisis you'll be walking over there and asking every available worker to cross the street to your site at the end of their shifts to work for you at double their hourly wage. If you put a complex contract in front of 'can-do' people like this, many will just walk away. If you want people to have certain types of insurance, you might want to figure out how to put that in place quickly or have it already in place.

On the issue of physical assets, identify which ones you can procure and stockpile right now. Which ones can you put on order for automatic delivery in times of crisis? Having extra office supplies on hand is obvious. Having a manual typewriter in case of power failure is less obvious but not expensive. The principle is to have a little more inventory and a little less 'just-in-time' delivery.

Alternative supply-chain and delivery routes that can use different modes of transport won't hurt. I have a client who brings truckloads of products from South America through the US and into Canada. As he and I were looking at a map of North and South America, I immediately pictured line-ups of trucks at border crossings delaying delivery and annoying customers. My client told me stories of hundreds of trucks lined up at the US-Mexico border behind a trucker suspected of having drugs aboard. My advice was to use air and boat transport to bypass every border he could to avoid these slow-downs.

Another client—this one in the offshore-exploration business—has a deal with the nearest, largest hotel on land. A conference room is reserved 24 hours a day, 7 days a week. This is where the company will meet with worried family members or the media in case of crisis. The hotel still rents out the big meeting-room to other customers but tells them that they might have to leave on ten minutes' notice.

Why not have food, supplies and even workers automatically show up if a crisis occurs? If there's no crisis, you can give the food to a food bank or homeless shelter. You might want to be very careful with the criteria by which heavy equipment, counter-terrorism squads and psychological counsellors start arriving, but you still probably want to list how to find these items and people anyway.

When you remove all possible decisions from your actual response, you will act with more speed. You will also make better decisions, because you made them long before the event. During the actual event you'll be experiencing trauma or at least the 'flight-or-fight' response. When you're in this state, you are genetically programmed to start 'thinking' with your old, reptilian brain, the amygdale. This walnut-sized object sends messages to the muscles quickly but doesn't process complex information well. It's getting you ready to stand and fight or run away. It also cuts off the smart, thinking part of the brain—the neo-cortex— and prevents it from sending signals to the body. Hence the 'blank mind' we've all experienced when we're nervous.

Researchers call the kind of decision-making that's most effective during a crisis Naturalistic Decision Making or NDM.[5] This doesn't really involve thinking but rather taking action. NDM is typical among fire-fighters and medical responders. They arrive on a scene and start clearing rubble, dousing flames with water, taking vital signs and so on. They keep taking action until there is no more action to take. They might have to pause and think whether the building they are entering is stable or whether moving an injured person will cause more injury, but then they start taking action again. Police and the military have to pause a little more often to consider whether there are snipers, booby traps and so on, but they use a lot of NDM as well.

Isn't it better to think and make decisions with the bigger, newer, smarter part of the brain? This works best long before the crisis or long after. I advise thinking and deciding beforehand.

Obstacles to Good Decision-Making

- Lack of preparation
- Hidden agendas
- Personal vested interests
- Manipulation
- Miscommunication
- Different terminology
- Variations in interpersonal skills
- Enforcing rank or status and weighing votes or opinions
- Parties refusing to be accommodating
- Protest without explanation: "I just don't like it!"
- Hurt feelings affecting judgment
- The flight-or-fight response

The Crisis-Management Team

The make-up of a Crisis-Management Team will differ from organization to organization. It may also differ within the same business for different crises. But many duties need to be assigned in advance. Certain people and roles need to be designated in advance as well.

While the chief executive, president and/or board chair must be present and available to communicate on behalf of the organization, s/he will not always head the Crisis Management Team. That requires superior interpersonal skills and patience, and in some organizations special expertise may be more important than the general management function the top person performs in non-crisis times.

Members of the team should include officials responsible for financial affairs, human resources, marketing, investor relations, government relations, legal and medical matters, communications, security and risk. Most or all of these duties can be assigned in advance. When a crisis occurs, the senior manager of the affected division, site or region should be a member and perhaps even the head of the team.

The Crisis-Management Team will need a variety of tools and facilities with which to manage the crisis. Suitable rooms should be designated in advance both on and off site and should be available on short notice. Choosing and maintaining your off-site assets may be crucial, because your crisis may involve an event that makes your facilities unusable. You should compile a checklist of materials like the one found under "Crisis-Management Team Situation Room" (see "Resource Rooms") and regularly update it.

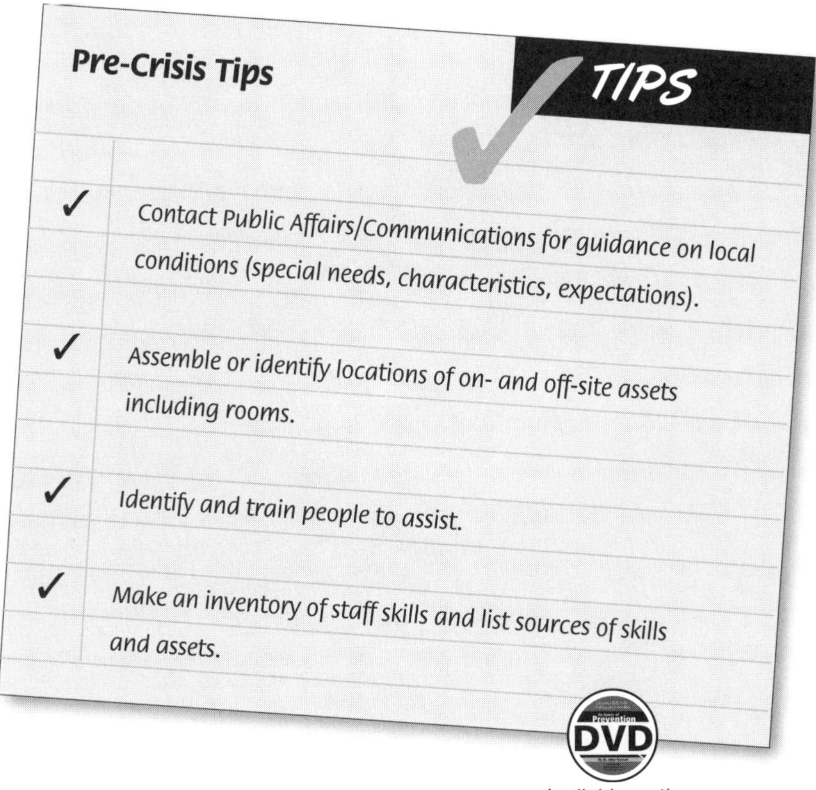

Crisis Management

Discussion Points:

1. What decisions can you make ahead of time?
2. Are there stumbling-blocks to decision-making (money, assets, people) that you can reduce or eliminate?
3. Who should be on the Crisis Management Team?
4. Who should lead the Crisis Management Team?
5. Should the team leader or team composition change if the cause changes?
6. Can customers, suppliers or other stakeholders provide some off-site assets during a crisis?
7. Can local schools, churches and public buildings be used in a crisis?
8. What role can your workers' homes play?
9. Can your workers work from home?
10. Can stockpiles of crisis-response materials serve other useful purposes in normal times?

Toner Before Crisis

I'm always excited about reading crisis plans for clients. I enjoy them the way I enjoy a good novel. I visualize the prescribed response, the assets listed and the glitches that can occur—as I do when reading Tom Clancy, Ian Fleming or Michael Crichton.

On this occasion, I had to wait a little to enjoy my reading.

This company had 2200 pages of crisis plans for 18 locations on five continents—and those were only the ones in English. It took 17 hours to download them from a secure website.

Worse, some sections were numbered and some lettered. Some used Roman numerals. Some used capital letters and others lower case. It became very difficult to distinguish among page number 1, letter l, Roman numeral I and so on. Some sections were in Word, others in Word Perfect and still others were PDFs.

I imagined the company having a crisis in several jurisdictions at the same time and needing their written plans, protocols and policies. The crisis would be either much worse or over by the time the plan was downloaded and collated—provided they had several replacement toner cartridges on hand.

Crisis-Management System

Maintaining an Enterprise during a Crisis

A crisis doesn't have to be widely reported or spectacular to do significant harm to a business. An otherwise insignificant event – or even a rumour – could make it impossible to receive or ship goods, operate equipment or perform other vital functions. Site-specific crisis-management plans should address a broad range of potential situations that could hamper the ability of the enterprise to operate effectively. This section addresses many of the needs that arise both in corporate headquarters and in satellite or regional locations. Sharing operational details can be invaluable during a crisis. Pre-planning can identify additional capabilities you might need.

Organizations and their regional locations should have plans in place to safeguard vital records and proprietary information. The Human Resources Department should list secondary skills available in the workforce and have a system in place to maintain continuity of management in the event of sudden death or departure. The departure of staff could be a result of a positive event, which then triggers a crisis. What if a key person or group wins the lottery and retires?

Shut-down procedures should include systems to continue the enterprise if some aspect is impaired or fails. Agreements with suppliers, customers and even those in similar businesses may allow your enterprise to continue in otherwise trying times.

When your activities are interrupted, various third parties need to be informed—first off, employees and their families, beginning with those on the next shift. You may need to contact several government, regulatory, licensing and other agencies. Suppliers, customers and others will need information, especially if your event is going to disrupt your relationships with them. It is also wise to establish crisis-oriented financial procedures and alternate banking-capability. Likewise you may require alternate data-processing and stakeholder communication.

Here are a series of forms designed as guidelines to help you prepare to continue to run your enterprise even in the midst of a crisis. The most important of these forms are also found on the companion DVD, where you can customize them to your own requirements. You can also make our own forms and lists to handle situations unique to your organization.

Division or Location Information

For an organization to assist its locations in a crisis, head office must have access to activities, assets and conditions at local facilities.

The following forms should be filled out and copies filed both locally and at head office. They should be updated annually or oftener if circumstances warrant.

Business Information

Organization Name________________________________ Division ____________________

ASSET	DETAILS
Describe principal activity performed at facility	
No. of vehicles	
Types of vehicles	
Property size in acres or sq. ft. or metres	
No. of Building(s)	
Size of Building(s) in sq. ft. or metres	
Types of items produced	
No. of items produced	
Volume of material processed	
No. of people served	
Value of production	
Hazardous materials on site:	[ ] Yes [ ] No If yes, describe:
Is facility operated under licence or permit?	[ ] Yes [ ] No If so, Type of license/permit: Year Issued: Issuing agency:
Year facility opened	
Previous Owner	
Major modifications and year	
Past incidents, month and year	

Customize on the Companion DVD

Human Resources Data

Key Personnel

Organization Name					
Name of Division	Address		City	Province/State	Postal/Zip Code
	Tel:		Fax:		
NAME	**TITLE**	**HOME PHONE**	**CELL PHONE**	**ALTERNATIVE**	**EMAIL**

Customize on the Companion DVD

Employee Information

<table>
<tr><td colspan="5">Organization Name</td></tr>
<tr><td rowspan="2">Name of Division</td><td>Address</td><td>City</td><td>Province/
State</td><td>Postal/Zip Code</td></tr>
<tr><td>Tel:</td><td colspan="2">Fax:</td><td></td></tr>
</table>

SHIFT	NUMBER OF EMPLOYEES	SALARY	HOURLY

DVD

Customize on the Companion DVD

Human Resources Data-Management Information

Organization Name				
Name of Division	Address	City	Province/State	Postal/Zip Code
	Tel:	Fax:		

MANAGERS					
TITLE	NAME	ADDRESS	PHONE	HOME	CELL
Manager					
Assistant Manager					
Operations Manager					
Safety Manager					
Technical Manager					
HR Manager					
District Manager					
Regional Manager					
Marketing Manager					

DVD

Customize on the Companion DVD

Crisis-Management System: Maintaining an Enterprise during a Crisis

Discussion Points:

1. What information is missing from the operational readiness forms?
2. How will we discuss operational readiness with employees and mobilize them for secondary tasks should a crisis occur?
3. Is all emergency contact information for employees current and accurate?
4. What special assets or skills do we need to keep the operation running off site?
5. What skills or assets will bring operations to a halt if they are absent?
6. Where are the bottlenecks in the supply or delivery chain?
7. How much redundancy in the supply or delivery chain can we afford and justify?
8. Ask workers for their input on how to keep the enterprise running off site or with supply or delivery problems.
9. Can you find retired workers from your organization or others to call on in times of crisis?
10. Can you house, feed and move workers around your sites or off site if need be?

Site Management

While the corporate plan is designed to provide a framework that you can use to create local, division or regional plans, you will need to take a variety of factors into consideration in order to create an appropriate document. Among the considerations will be:

- Climate
- Degree of risk
- Proximity to transport and communication systems
- Political milieu
- Historical or public interest in the plant
- History of the plant

- Geographical location of the plant
- History of interest in the industry, materials produced or parent company

Efficiently managing a crisis site will be among the most challenging aspects of your response. The procedures to be followed, expertise required and physical assets needed will vary widely. Site management will be affected by evacuation; contamination to air, water or ground; the range of outside agencies and responders involved (police, fire, federal, provincial, state and municipal officials); and the insurance, legal and other implications.

Furthermore, you will find it an enormous challenge to manage the number of people and groups who wish to interact in some way at the site. Politicians, reporters, citizens and aggrieved parties will all want to visit or tour the site.

Death will pose special challenges for all. No life or professional experience can adequately prepare anyone for death. Very few people can predict how they or others will act when faced with it. The deaths of children and responders are particularly traumatic. A crisis manager should have access to qualified counsellors to help employees, responders and others through the trauma. Significant traumas may not occur until some weeks after initial exposure. It is not unusual for relatives or friends of the deceased to want to visit the scene to have a meaningful personal interaction with the site. All these individuals and circumstances must be well managed and planned.

Multiple deaths also present unique problems. Many more responders are needed to handle the increased workload. Triage centres, body identification and morgues require highly skilled functions. Pre-arranged agreements with undertakers and others can be in place long before an event, so that these responders will arrive automatically if deaths occur.

Appropriate local officials should be consulted to customize plans. In remote locations, you may need to pool expertise with others and arrange for experts to be flown in if a crisis hits. Brainstorming and creativity can help ensure your plans mesh with those of other relevant organizations.

The following chart shows some of the activities that might be required simultaneously during a crisis. Activities begin with the senior manager at the site, who must gather enough facts, and have an adequate list of activities to begin several simultaneous actions.

The diagram assumes that the manager has access to at least five delegates. These might even include the Crisis Management Team leader, the CEO, chair, president, and general manager. The point of using the term 'delegate' here is not to suggest that these functions are subordinate to the senior manager at the site but rather to specify the number of functions that are needed simultaneously for effective crisis management.

As soon as the highest level of crisis is declared, logistical support must begin. This includes such routine tasks as booking hotel rooms, ordering food and ensuring transport and communication systems are available. There must also be a system to handle visiting dignitaries, board members and the media who arrive at head office, regional offices and the crisis site itself. Legislators and regulators need to be notified. At the same time, the delegate will be summoning all internal and external responders, perhaps through a phone tree (see following form) to remediate the site. Until the incident is contained, the response team must perform its tasks while it is working with various outside responders.

Meanwhile, a well prepared company will also require various internal and external spokespeople. Telephones will need to be staffed 24 hours a day to respond to public and media inquiries. Volunteers will have to be dealt with courteously and their expertise used. There needs to be communication with customers, suppliers and others. In a large enough crisis, the media can tie up dozens of spokespeople simultaneously, as can victims, family members and members of the public.

At the same time, the crisis team will need to communicate with employees, neighbours, branch plants, the board, suppliers, customers and many others.

Incident

Delegate 1	Delegate 2	Delegate 3	Delegate 4	Delegate 5
Logistics	Responders	Spokespeople	Public Affairs – Agencies, EMO Government	Senior Management
Food	Phone Tree	Training	Media	Employees
Facilitators	Response Team	Messages	Checklist: when reporters arrive or call	Neighbours
Perimeter Security	Liaison with outside responders – fire, police		News Conference	Branch plants
Transport	Incident containment		Follow-up Phone, fax, in person	Selected govt. officials & agencies
Communication	Retired employees			Board members
Retired Responders	Neighbouring suppliers			Suppliers
	Co-agreements with managers			Customers

Phone Tree Sample

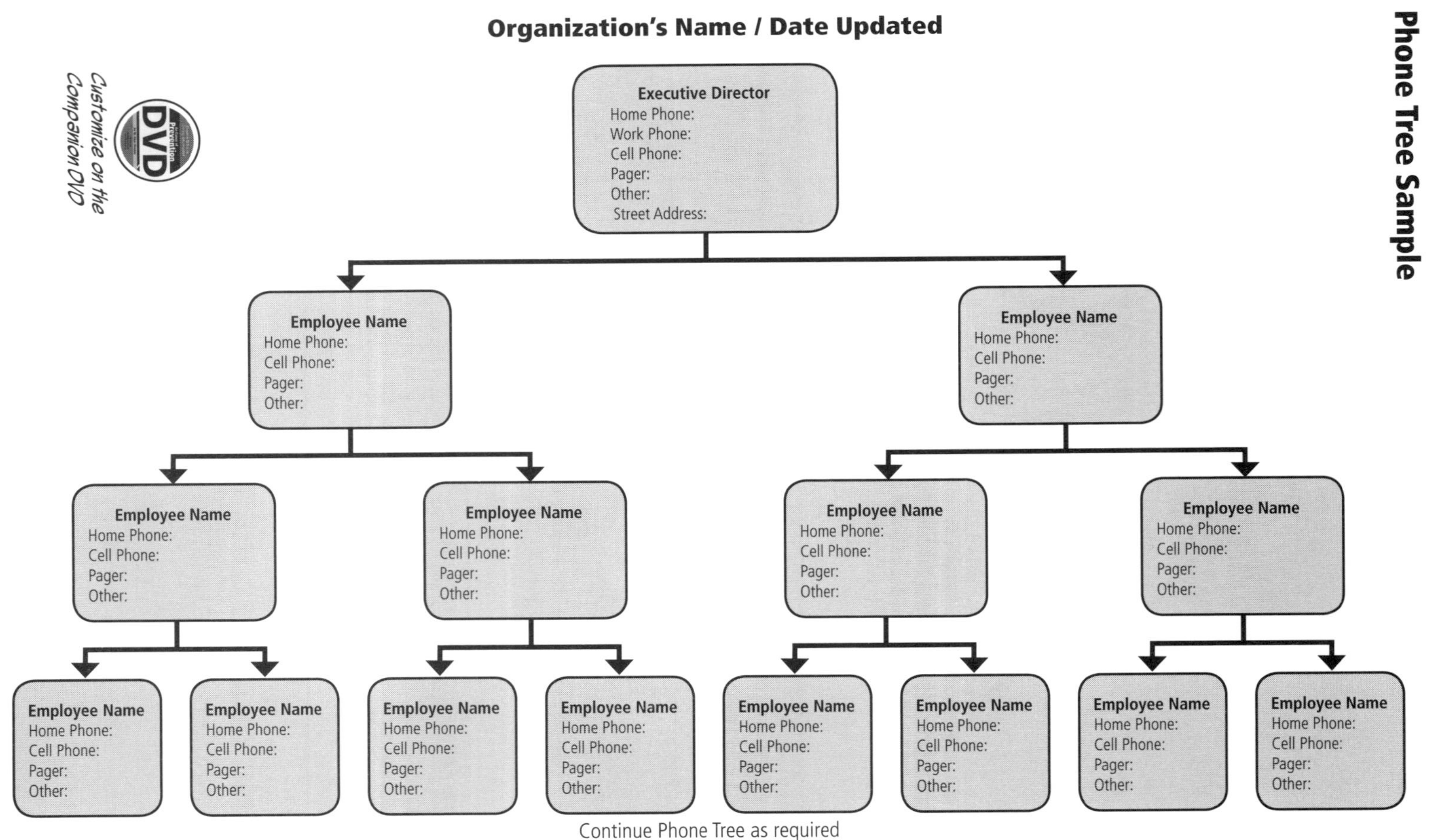

Employee Crisis Skills Inventory

A wide variety of skills may be required to address a crisis. While all needs cannot be accurately predicted, it may prove vital to assess the secondary skills and assets available to you. An inventory should be kept using the following form, so that people and assets can be called upon quickly. There should be a similar inventory of physical assets on hand.

EMPLOYEE CRISIS SKILLS INVENTORY			
Skill	**Person**	**Contact Info**	**Date Confirmed**
Knowledge of emergency response policies	example: John from shop floor	000-000-0000	
	example: Mike from IT	000-000-0000	
	example: Sam from Accounts	111-111-1111	
First aid training	example: Joe from Sales	000-111-0000	
	example: Ron from maintenance	111-000-1111	
Knowledge of how to implement emergency plans			
Knowledge of emergency facilities			
Knowledge of operations, technologies, systems etc			
Knowledge of past experience with emergencies			
"Knowledge of general experience of others who have dealt with emergencies"			
Media training			
Crisis management training			
Languages (list)			
Physical assets (snowmobile, 4 wheel drive, etc.)			
Security / law enforcement background			
Media relations			
Other			

DVD

Customize on the Companion DVD

Perimeter Security

Maintaining perimeter security is often confused with effective event management. You can prevent access to a site but still have a crisis on your hands. You can even make a crisis worse by providing great perimeter security—by assaulting people who try to cross your property line, for example. But it's still quite difficult to manage the communications component of an event effectively without proper perimeter security. Reporters will arrive on the scene of an emergency quickly and want immediate access. This access should be professionally managed and only denied if it will interfere with remediation or present serious risk to the safety of the reporters or others.

One effective type of perimeter security involves creating several perimeters, one inside the other, each designed so that the closer one gets to the site of the incident, the more stringent the measures in place become. An outer perimeter should be established around the whole crisis site to keep out all visitors except those who have some business within. Once visitors enter this outer perimeter, they then have to re-establish their credentials, or give reasons why they should be allowed further in, at each successive perimeter. Each designated area within the larger perimeter will have its own perimeter security. The immediate crisis site may have the tightest security possible.

Visitors may have a legitimate reason to be in the crisis-management centre yet not be allowed access to the actual site of the emergency. Then access will be granted to the outer perimeter, the crisis-management centre perimeter, but not to the perimeter surrounding the site of the emergency. Similarly, those who have access to the Media Work Centre will have crossed two perimeters but may not be allowed into the crisis-management centre or the actual site of the emergency.

The News Conference Room (see "Resource Rooms") should be secure and feature a sign-in and accreditation process. It should be maintained around the clock. This will be especially important when you are using hotels and other off-site venues. Similarly, the crisis-management or operations centre should be within the outer perimeter and have its own security system.

Security personnel and outside police forces must be informed that your organization wishes to interact with reporters openly and quickly. Pictures may be taken from public roads and sidewalks at all times and at most times from gates and reception areas.

Security personnel should treat reporters respectfully and gently, assuring them that a public affairs/communications person will be notified of their request for information as soon as possible and will treat this as a high-priority function.

Effective ‘point-to-point’ security comes into play when a vehicle or person requires security while moving on roads, on sidewalks, in hallways and so on. A security ‘advance’ team leapfrogs ahead of the subject. One security person stations himself at the next point in the subject’s path where the subject will be forced to turn or stop or where the line of sight is obstructed (corner, crossroads, doorway). At each new point the subject does not proceed until security signals that the way is clear. Be sure to consult local police and other professionals before executing your security plan.

Perimeter Security

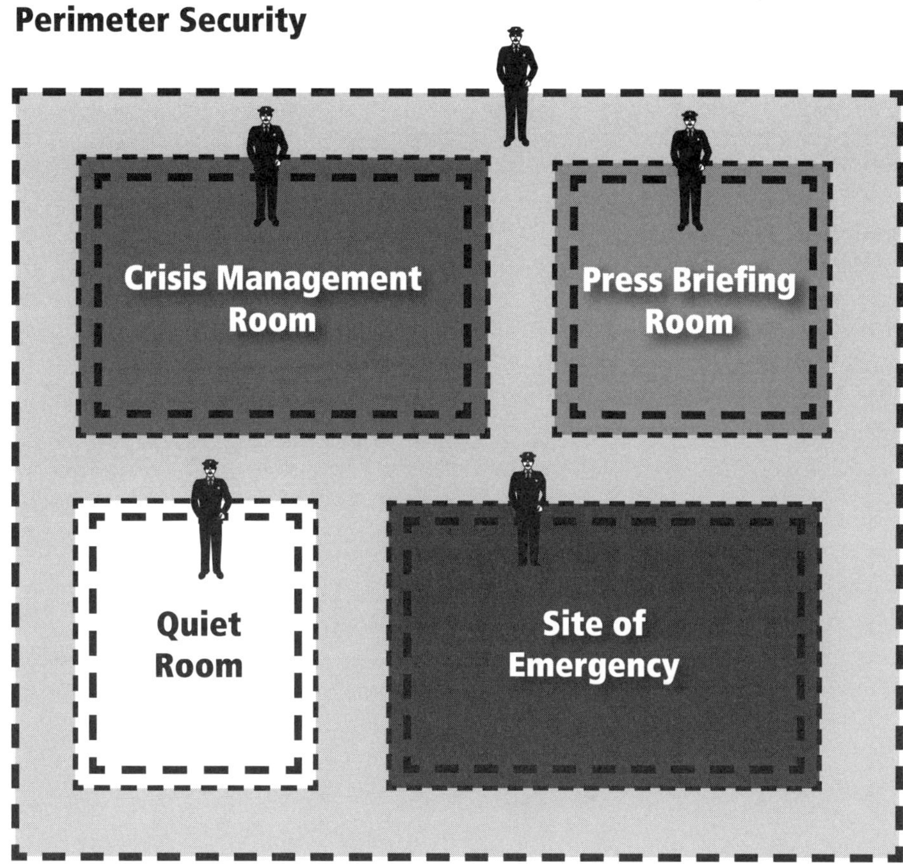

Crisis Perimeter Security Checklist

TASK	RESPONSIBLE	SOURCE	COMPLETED
Contact Public Affairs/Communications for guidance.			
Brief all security people regarding goals and communication procedures.			
Survey site with security for obvious locations media will visit and unique challenges.			
Survey route to/from airports, hotels, site, legislatures and other venues.			
Survey potential off-site venues for unique challenges (parking, access, exits etc.).			
Provide training as needed.			
Identify appropriate entrances and exits for reporters to use.			
Identify with security an unobtrusive way to create a combination of site pass and press credential.			

DVD

Customize on the Companion DVD

TIPS

Tips for Security Personnel Dealing with Reporters

DO

- ✓ Introduce yourself, politely.
- ✓ Ask what information or access reporters need.
- ✓ Relay requests to Public Affairs/Communications and tell reporters you are doing so.
- ✓ Get back to reporters with the status of request quickly and often.
- ✓ Allow reporters to operate equipment (take pictures) within reason.
- ✓ Keep calm and cool: de-fuse confrontations.
- ✓ Good relations with reporters and their safety are of primary concern.
- ✓ Explain how your procedures are for the public and their safety.
- ✓ Reporters will use creative means to gain access—expect this and remain calm.
- ✓ Chat with reporters in a friendly manner without speculating about the event.

DON'T

- ✓ Do not touch reporters.
- ✓ Do not touch or confiscate equipment unless there is a clear and present danger (ie. explosion).
- ✓ Do not put hand in front of camera lenses.

Available on the Companion DVD

Site Management

Discussion Points:

1. What measures do you need to take to create a secure perimeter at your site?
2. What outside help do you need to maintain a secure perimeter?
3. Are there retired police or security people you can call on in a crisis?
4. Where are the best vantage points for reporters to take still pictures and video of your site?
5. Are there assets you'll need to maintain perimeters, such as fencing?
6. Which employees live closest to your site and thus can be on scene first?
7. Which employees own assets you may need to employ in a crisis, such as boats, snowmobiles or four-wheel-drive vehicles?
8. Which employees can billet others in a crisis?
9. Are there nearby facilities such as churches, schools and theatres that you can use in a crisis?
10. Have you discussed your plans with other local responders, organizations and officials?

External Responders to your Crisis

Viewing the public as *de facto* first responders simply acknowledges what is a reality in many disasters. Even if the public do not respond in any official, organized or meaningful way, they are present. A member of the public is often the one who reports the incident by various means, including yelling for help, dialling emergency numbers, flagging down emergency vehicles or directing responders. This is a distinct role that the public play, separate from their other roles as victims, relatives and so on.

The public are usually orderly and do not display the cliché responses of shock and panic. They usually respond well and quickly before official responders arrive. Individuals often function better than organizations do. The public can be a valuable resource during disasters.

In the King's Cross Underground (subway) fire in London, one passenger alerted the ticket office of the danger. Another passenger made a second report to London Transport (LT) staff a few minutes later. A third passenger shouted warnings to other passengers, alerted police and pressed the STOP button on the escalator. The official inquiry into the disaster noted that in one 14-day period in the month before the fire, there were 463 verified and unverified cases where the public notified LT staff of problems with the escalator. LT staff ignored most of these reports. Rather than ignore the public, it would be better to educate staff and responders to the value of information that the public may have.

However, there are dangers in untrained but enthusiastic response. Moving the injured can cause further injury, particularly spinal damage. Reporting a fire is one thing, but trying to fight it is another. Throwing water on electrical fires can electrocute responders and bystanders. Spraying water on an oil fire can spread the flames. Some combustible materials create invisible flames and the danger of inhaling white-hot air and walking into the flames.

In the Sakhalin Island earthquake of 1995, many of the lay responders trying to assist actually moved large pieces of debris into the eventual path of the official response vehicles. Despite their good intentions, they probably hampered response.

In natural disasters, emergency services themselves can be disabled. In the Sakhalin incident about two thirds of the local police officers and medical personnel were killed and many others were injured. Lay response can be the first and, occasionally, the only response possible.

'Extending' organizations emerge when community resources are called on to perform non-traditional roles in a disaster. These groups take on unusual tasks using their existing expertise. A mining-company knows how to move earth and rock and thus can clear debris. The armed forces are used to following orders and getting tasks done despite difficult circumstances. 'Emergent' groups are ones that didn't exist before the disaster but are formed to tackle tasks new to them. These might include volunteer search and rescue, first aid or meal preparation. This is seen in oil spills, when local fishing-boats serve as water taxis ferrying workers and gear to where they are needed. Besides the bystanders who respond by chance, many other members of the public will belong to one of the above groups and thus can be recruited as *de facto* responders.

Admittedly the world has become more specialized with a greater division of labour. Professionals may rightly cite the need for specific training and equipment to deal with crises. The correct stance on how valuable lay response can be depends on the person, the disaster and other factors. Both the trained professional and the lay person need to be heard and involved. Training for unofficial responders can develop more skills and thus a more effective response.

You can read an extended discussion of this issue in Appendix 3: "Public Participation in Crises."

Preparing for External Responders

One of the most perplexing difficulties in any emergency is determining who is in charge. Smooth interaction between various responders and agencies not only makes for a quicker and more efficient response but can also limit damages after the event. Confusion at the site of an emergency among various responding groups will add fuel to claims by aggrieved parties.

I ran a simulation with one of the big three auto-makers. The scenario was a paint fire late on a Friday afternoon. There were a couple of injuries—at least one serious. As we worked through systems and reactions, I discovered that the plant's fire brigade would have begun fighting the fire after hearing an automatic alarm. The plant manger would have been called to the scene by either the alarm, the guard at the gate or someone in the paint shop. I wondered if people on the scene would have had the presence of mind to call the plant manager.

My larger worry was who would call the city fire department if the fire got too big for the internal fire brigade. It turned out it was going to be the guard at the gate, with the plant manager assessing the event. I pictured the manger and the guard having a meeting about the severity of the fire while looking at injured or even dead workers through clouds of smoke and flame. I doubted they'd have the presence of mind to make good decisions under those circumstances. They might not even remember they had to make the decision. They might be overcome with smoke themselves.

I advised the auto plant to have their fire alarm ring through automatically to the city fire department. The client protested that this could annoy the city if there were false alarms. They also said they'd have to negotiate this arrangement with city officials, and it might not be possible. Ironically, I had several oil and chemical clients down the road who had just this kind of arrangement with their city fire departments. Most of the time, the fire department would arrive to find they were responding to a false alarm. Fire-fighters would then wave to the guard at the gate and return to the fire station. I'm not sure if they were compensated, but when seconds count and fire-fighters who arrive early can save lives, negotiation and even payment to the city is worth it.

Organizations should know the roles of outside agencies in their neighbourhood, inform them of site-specific plans and modify those plans to mesh with local procedures. Local agencies should be involved in drills and simulations.

Community Resources

A wide variety of philanthropic and community-oriented groups can assist in times of crisis. They provide everything from refreshments and blankets to emergency shelter. Organizations should apprise themselves of such groups and regularly update phone numbers, addresses and the types of assistance available (see Community Resources Contacts chart following.)

The Red Cross traditionally helps to register people at evacuation centres. The Salvation Army often supplies food and drink to emergency responders. Other groups supply people and vehicles to transport the injured, assist on triage teams and help the disabled. A variety of other groups in individual communities may perform other tasks. Site-specific plans should list these groups and their contact people. Plans should also list facilities such as recreation halls, churches, service clubs and other such buildings that can be used as evacuation centres and emergency facilities.

Individuals

In an emergency, many civic-minded individuals will wish to volunteer their services. You should see their offers of support as an opportunity to generate or maintain goodwill. Each caller should be treated with respect and an inventory of volunteers maintained. It is vital to acknowledge these kind offers. Thank-you letters after the event are a way to enhance your organization's reputation. These volunteers should be referred to the community support groups mentioned above, because those groups have the expertise to manage them. (see the Volunteer Resource Chart following).

If you need direct assistance from volunteers, you should have them sign an indemnification agreement like the one following. Locations should use the form, vetted by counsel, to protect themselves from lawsuits in the event of injury.

Crisis sites attract thrill-seekers and imposters. Tactfully ensure that the people volunteering are who they say they are. Reporters will impersonate victims to gain access to secure areas or morgues, and the homeless will impersonate victims to get out-of-pocket settlements or access to shelters.

If you refuse or decline offers of volunteer help, the people and groups you shun may criticize you in the media. Using some volunteers is, at the very least, good PR.

Community Resource Contacts

AFFILIATION	CONTACT NAME	ADDRESS	OFFICE PHONE	ALTERNATIVE	EMAIL
Example: Red Cross					

DVD

Customize on the Companion DVD

Volunteer Resource

NOTE: Refer volunteers to appropriate third parties.

NAME OF ORGANIZATION	TYPES OF ASSISTANCE	PHONE NUMBER	ADDRESS
Example: The Red Cross Society	Evacuation, shelter management, handling phone calls	XXX-XXXX	XXXX Dundas St. West

DVD

Customize on the Companion DVD

Indemnification Agreement

Name: ______________________________

(Print; last name first) ___________________

Address: ____

Telephone: ___________________________

Office: _________________ Home: Alternate: ________ Occupation: ________________

Skills: ____

Next of Kin, Address and Phone: ____

I, ____, am participating in the activities of
(Name of volunteer)

___________________________________ purely as a volunteer and acknowledge that I have
(Name of assistance organization)

not been requested to participate in these activities by _________________________________
(Company/Organization)

nor am I supervised in any manner by _______________________________or its employees.
(Company/Organization)

Accordingly, I agree not to make any claim or demand against ____________________________ and its employees for any losses, injuries, damages *(Company/Organization)*

or expenses that I may incur in the course of my participation in the activities of

____, and I further agree to hold
(Name of assistance organization)

__________________________________ and its employees harmless from [and indemnify them
(Company/Organization)

against] any loss, injury or expense that I may so incur. I understand and agree that this statement relates to losses, injuries, damages or expenses howsoever they may arise and whether or not they result from the negligence of ___________________________________ or its employees.
(Company/Organization)

I, _______________________________, agree to hold __________________________________
(Name of volunteer) *(Company/Organization)*

and its plant(s) and/or operating-companies harmless from [and indemnify them against] any injury I may incur in performing my duties as a volunteer.

Signature of Volunteer ____

Date, time of enrolment ____

Enrolling official (name & signature) _______________________________

Vetted by counsel (name & signature) _______________________________

Customize on the Companion DVD

Tips for Managing Assistance

- ✓ Contact Public Affairs and Legal Department for guidance and support.
- ✓ Establish and maintain list of third party volunteer groups.
- ✓ Meet third party groups regularly.
- ✓ Distribute list of third party volunteer groups to all those with public contact (gate, security, phone, site).
- ✓ If volunteers are to be used, have indemnification agreement signed.
- ✓ Alert third party groups that individuals will be referred.
- ✓ Refer all those possible to third party groups (Red Cross, St. John's Ambulance, Salvation Army, etc.)
- ✓ Thank each caller offering assistance.
- ✓ Take all names, addresses and phone numbers and pass on volunteer registration forms to Public Affairs.
- ✓ Write a letter of thanks to each group and person after the crisis.

DVD

Available on the Companion DVD

External Responders

Discussion Points:

1. What groups are there in the vicinity that you could call upon for assistance?
2. Are there any groups/individuals who might be problematic volunteers?
3. Can you access people with religious and cultural information that you may need?
4. What existing organizations can you call on in a crisis?
5. What new organization might you need to form to respond to an event?
6. What equipment and assets might you need?
7. Where can you procure unusual assets?
8. Is there any training for volunteers that you can do now in the community?
9. Are there assets you can stockpile now?
10. Can you implement training-programs quickly in a crisis?

VIP Visits

While not responders, VIPs who visit a crisis site will influence the outcome. VIPs from all levels of government, agencies and non-governmental organizations often deserve access and full briefings and will become news sources for the media after their site visits. How you handle a VIP visit during an event becomes a mark of how well you have handled the entire crisis. A simple plant tour that goes off the rails can set a tone for future regulatory or legislative hearings, media coverage and relations with other stakeholders. These visitors can become allies or adversaries, depending on the outcome of their tour.

Personnel at the event site must be alert to the likelihood of such tours. Plans, assets and information will make VIP visits more successful. Things can get particularly bad if visits by politicians do not go smoothly. Imagine the local politician contradicting your official spokespeople or saying you're not providing adequate information. What if security at the gate causes friction? You'll be dealing with that politician and staff during the aftermath of your event, so you want the visit to help build positive relationships.

TIPS

VIP Visitor Tips:

- ✓ Never leave visitors (also non-VIP) alone.
- ✓ Where appropriate, plan a full itinerary of meetings and activities, make their visit productive and interesting.
- ✓ Meet visitors at airports or pre-arranged landmarks.
- ✓ Offer the visitor food and non-alcoholic refreshments.
- ✓ Insist on five minutes of quiet time before any visitors meet the media.
- ✓ Try to allow visitors to enter the site/building without encountering the press.
- ✓ Have a one-page written brief for visitors and ensure there are a few moments to answer any questions before the visitor meets reporters.
- ✓ Remember conversations on hand held devices are not confidential—others may be listening. Be cautious of discussions in public places including taxis.
- ✓ Alert switchboard, security, gate, reception and others to treat visitors as a priority.

Available on the Companion DVD

Crowds can present unique problems during VIP visits. Many politicians will arrive with their own staff, who will perform crowd control and media-relations functions, but the site must still be prepared. Routes to and from sites and buildings must be surveyed for the most efficient options. When crowds are unavoidable, four members of the security staff members must be detailed to usher the VIP through the crowd (see "Perimeter Security"). These people should not wear hard hats or push people but provide a gentle shield in front of and behind the VIP. All parties should keep moving slowly until they reach their destination.

VIP Visit Checklist

TASK	RESPONSIBILITY	COMPLETED
Consult Public Affairs/Communications and or government phone books for guidance on local VIP groups and conditions such as media interest and political engagement with the company, staff etc.		
Consult government lists and phone books.		
Compile a list of significant third-party groups, advocates, professors and other opinion- leaders.		
Maintain issues file of material significant to these third parties.		
Survey site for suitable entrance and exit points, washrooms.		
Designate alternative entrances and exits.		
Designate quiet room on site for VIPs.		
Review procedures with gate, security, switchboard and other entry points.		
Gather information on visitor(s): phone number, name, title, riding, district, party, organization, committees, etc.		
Unique needs of visitor: disability, religion, dietary, cultural, etc.		
Issue identification: visitors' interest, historical positions, probable questions/concerns.		
Obtain all needed safety equipment and distribute to visitor(s).		
Check and comply with customs/border regulations.		
Comply with checklists for category of visitor (politician, organization official, third party).		
Routes for VIPs to take.		
Crowd control/security.		
Liaison with political staff.		
Directions, itinerary.		
Follow-up calls, thank-you notes and follow-up letters.		

DVD

Customize on the Companion DVD

Checklist for Politicians' Visits

ACTIVITY	RESPONSIBLE	COMPLETED
Obtain contact numbers, including local office and Executive Assistant/Chief of Staff.		
Alert officials on site if a visit is planned.		
Place visit on all status boards in Public Affairs room if it should be publicized.		
Decide on timing of media notification, if at all.		
Keep the politician's office informed regularly.		
Local officials of similar rank should write a letter of thanks for the politician's interest and visit.		
Provide staff with possible questions reporters may ask as well as local positions on same.		
Alert all possible contact points, including gate, security and switchboard.		
Provide transport if requested.		

Customize on the Companion DVD

Checklist for Third-Party Visits

Many different individuals or organizations (professors, lobby groups, citizens' groups, industry associations, etc.) will consider themselves affected parties with a right to receive information or to have their opinions heard. All should be treated cautiously but with respect. Some guidelines follow.

ACTIVITY	RESPONSIBLE	COMPLETED
Obtain and analyze literature, documents, research papers, clippings used or endorsed by third parties.		
Determine questions or positions third party may have.		
Prepare organization positions or responses.		
Alert all possible contact points including gate, security and switchboard.		
Decide on timing for notifying media.		
Circulate among reporters to determine level of interest and possible questions		

Customize on the Companion DVD

VIP Visits – Materials and Services Checklist

SITES MAY SCALE DOWN LIST DOWN OR IDENTIFY WHERE ASSETS CAN BE PROCURED

ASSET/INFORMATION	SOURCE	RESPONSIBILITY	COMPLETED
Briefing-book			
Food			
Maps			
Plant and building plans			
Directions to off-site venues			
Hand-held devices			
Internet and email access if possible			
$20.00 small change for phones and vending machines			
Wind-up flashlight for night reading			
Coveralls			
Safety gear (glasses, hard hat, shoes, gloves)			
Winter or rain gear			
First-aid kit			
Phone numbers			
Transport			
(taxi - never a limo)			
Hotel			
Medical services			
Drug store			
Alternative transport (4 WD, helicopters, boat, snowmobile)			
Dry cleaners (minor repairs)			
Security			

DVD

Customize on the Companion DVD

Discussion Points for VIP Visits

1. What government or political VIPs might wish to visit the site?
2. Are there supportive government or political officials we want to visit the site?
3. With whom should we start building stronger and better relations in case of crisis?
4. Do we know enough about non-governmental organizations that may voice opinions about an event we experience?
5. Do we know enough about legislators and regulators who will be involved in the aftermath?
6. Have we built alliances with third-party experts who might speak in our favour during an event or influence VIPs?
7. Who in our senior management needs to visit the site of a crisis?
8. What can we learn from rehearsing a VIP tour on short notice?
9. How long does it take us to execute a thorough briefing on our activities or location?
10. Can we procure alternative transport by air, water, ground, rail, private vehicle and so on?

But What did I Just Swallow?

In the middle of the night, on the West Coast, the proverbial little old lady awoke in some discomfort. She grabbed for her familiar over-the-counter pain reliever. She fumbled with a few items on her night table, got some water, took the tablets and went back to sleep.

The next morning the lady began tidying up. She noticed several scattered tablets on the floor, some of which didn't bear their familiar logo. She wondered what she had taken during the night.

She strolled off to the drugstore, presented the pharmacist with the mysterious pills and asked him what they were. He didn't know but gave her a new bottle of her favourite brand.

She called the manufacturer's toll-free number to ask if they would take a sample of the tablets and tell her what was in them. The company sent her a new bottle of tablets without explanation.

In ten days, the little old lady had two new bottles of pills for her trouble but was no closer to an answer to her question of what she had taken in the middle of the night. Her next call was to an advocacy journalist at a national network. This story had all the elements needed to get on the air—a compelling victim, a West Coast focus, a classic David and Goliath tale, a tight-lipped company and memories of the Tylenol poisoning-case, in which seven people died horrible deaths when someone tampered with that pain-relief product.

The journalist sent the pills to a lab for analysis. Then he made a stand-up broadcast from the company headquarters. His script spoke compassionately about the little old lady's fears and indignantly over the company's lack of response to her and to him. He created drama and mystery about what might have been in the bottle and, by inference, what might be in millions of bottles in the marketplace.

The punch line of the journalist's dramatic item involved telling the little old lady that the mystery pills were a generic, differently marked tablet with the same ingredients as her usual ones. Most probably she had mixed up the contents of her own bottles and hadn't noticed.

The lady got her answer and free tablets. The viewers were entertained with a short, dramatic story.

The only loser was the multinational company, with 100 years of brand equity at stake. It was operating against generic, over-the-counter products without patent protection. So the main thing it was selling in the marketplace was brand recognition, brand equity, quality control, reputation and the sum of its marketing-efforts over ten decades.

That seems worth protecting a little more vigorously.

CHAPTER 3: RESOURCE ROOMS

Event: *Volcanic Eruption, Krakatoa, Sunda Strait between Sumatra and Java*

Date: *27 August 1883*

Summary: *Thought to be extinct, the volcano on the island of Krakatoa erupted with such force that it caused a 120-foot tidal wave. Five cubic miles of rocks flew 17 miles in the air. The shockwaves circled the earth seven times. The mountain, which had been 3,000 feet high, sank into a crater on the ocean floor 800 feet deep. Up to 100 miles away, people were kept awake all night by the noise. The water in the Sunda Strait was 60 degrees hotter than normal. People up to 3,000 miles away in Australia and the US heard the final explosion, although the sound took four hours to reach some destinations. Some people in Borneo were reported to have been so frightened that they jumped off cliffs. The air in Great Britain, 10,000 miles away, reverberated with shockwaves. The three-foot tsunami travelled at 350 miles per hour and hit land at Cape Horn, 5,000 miles away. The dust created red sunsets around the world for two years. They were so intense that Connecticut fire-fighters were called out on several occasions to put out what some people thought were fires. Seven feet of pumice floated on the sea near Krakatoa for months. Five months later, ash washed up on Madagascar beaches.*

Result: *Between 36,000 and 80,000 dead.*

Lessons Learned: *Beyond nature's power, this is one of the first times in recorded history that we learned we were all breathing the same air and occupying the same sphere in space. This attests to the environmentalists' contentions and to German sociologist Ulrich Beck's concept of the 'risk society' in which we all bear the burden of risk.*

Resource Rooms

Crisis-Management Team Situation Room

A crisis-management situation room may be the place where the team assembles for weeks at a time. When arranging for such a room, you need to take account of the technical, communications, security and human needs of the team. You must make every effort to ensure that a 'siege mentality' does not take over. Interaction with outsiders, media monitoring and regular breaks can help. What follows is a partial list of materials that should be readily available to set up a well outfitted situation room.

Situation Room - Materials & Services Checklist

LIST	SOURCE	RESPONSIBILITY	COMPLETED
Additional telephone lines			
Speaker phone			
Flip chart			
Coloured markers, bristol board			
Tape, thumb tacks			
2 TV sets			
2 programmable VCRs			
3 AM/FM radios			
Audio & video cassettes			
Dubbing wires			
Organizational charts			
Annual reports			
HR & company data			
Building plans			
Maps re: site, evacuation			
Clerical support			
Runners/messenger			
Catering			

DVD

Customize on the Companion DVD

Public Affairs Room

Whoever is managing the relationship with reporters and others may need to occupy an on- or off-site workroom for weeks during a crisis. The room needs to be set up quickly and be run smoothly. Rotating Public Affairs staff need to be briefed on what has gone on during the previous shift or in the few days before their arrival.

These rooms can be confusing and messy places when filled with people, paper, phones and TVs. Standard operating procedures will lessen confusion and increase efficiency.

Six-hour shifts are ideal for those staffing the office. Relief staff should rotate in on a staggered basis so that only one or two new staff join at one time. Shifts must overlap by at least 15 minutes to allow for orientation and briefing.

Public Affairs Room

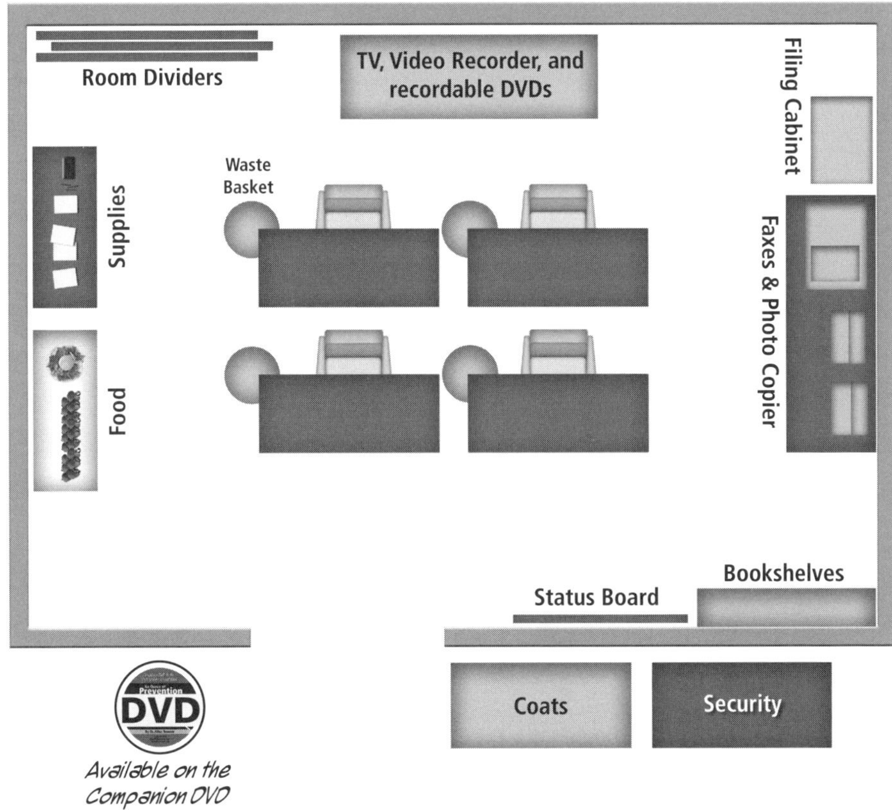

DVD

Available on the Companion DVD

Meetings should be kept to a minimum. Rotating staff can be brought up to date with the Public and Media Update form and by reading into the latest written material such as news releases. Occasional calls for silence in the room will allow all to hear announcements about new developments from team members.

Public Affairs Desk

Each Public Affairs desk should be similarly configured, as in the following diagram. Newly arriving staff should feel comfortable and familiar with the surroundings and not have to search for assets or information.

Three-ring binders with tabs dividing them by day and perhaps subject must be kept to maintain a record of all public data issued or dealt with by the organization. Electronic versions of information on computers or hand-held devices may be preferable. The appropriate desks should have all press releases, opening statements to news conferences, media clippings or transcripts, statements by spokespeople and so on logged. Government and media contact lists and information opportunities lists must be kept as well. Blank copies of the Record of Contacts Made by Media form (see "Speaking with the Media" in Chapter 5 below) should also be available in large numbers for easy tracking and recording.

Public Affairs Room - Materials and Services Checklist

SITES MAY SCALE LIST DOWN OR IDENTIFY WHERE ASSETS CAN BE PROCURED

LIST	SOURCE	RESPONSIBILITY	COMPLETED
3 organization phone books			
3 provincial/federal phone books			
International Communications Directory			
Association directory			
White & yellow pages for affected and major cities			
City directory (various relevant)			
12 room dividers			
4 desk and chair sets			
10 cardboard filing cases			
File folders, hangers & storage boxes			
Lockable steel filing cabinet			
Coat rack & hangers			
White board			
Garbage bags (20)			
Photographs of spokespeople & site (8 x 10, black & white)			
Cardboard box for chronological newspaper storage			
Fact sheets			
Style book			
Media & Government lists			
50 carbon message pads			
2 telephone answering machines			
2 Thesauruses			
2 French/English/Spanish dictionaries			
Paper shredder			
Speaker phone			
Flip chart with pads and markers			
4 rolls scotch tape			
2 rolls masking tape, thumb tacks			
Asset/Activity			
2 TV sets			
2 programmable DVDs & video camera			
3 AM/FM radios with recording ability			
Wind-up radios with recording ability			
Audio CDs			
DVDs			

Customize on the Companion DVD

Public Affairs Room - Materials and Services Checklist *continued*

LIST	SOURCE	RESPONSIBILITY	COMPLETED
Dubbing wires			
Organizational charts			
Annual reports			
Human resources & other data			
Building plans			
Clerical support (to update all status boards)			
Catering			
Paper towel			
2 clocks -1 battery, 1 electric			
Gas generator, gas can & oil			
Battery operated lights			
3 ring binders			
Evacuation maps			
2 photocopiers (+ extra toner)			
3 fax machines (+ paper)			
Folding tables, chairs			
Manual & electric typewriters, ribbons, cartridges			
Paper - lined, typing, fax			
Press releases & fact sheets			
Letterhead, envelopes			
Cables, extension cords, power bars			
Cell phone, beepers, camera, discs, chips			
Waste baskets			
Clerical, messenger services, courier			
Audio recorder, adapter, 5 sets of batteries, all types of headphones			
Asset/Activity			
Notification sheets, checklists, phone lists, media directories			
Scissors, rubber bands, stapler, white out			
Public and Media Update sheet			
Paper clips, tape, markers, highlighters, pens, pencils, erasers, grease pencils			
Printer cartridge, computer paper, disks			
Computers, laser printers, modems			
Bullhorns			
Portable toilets (if needed)			

DVD

Customize on the Companion DVD

Media Contact List:

It is not difficult to create your own media contact list. They can also be purchased in print or electronic format. These lists change frequently and need to be updated regularly. Make sure that the lists you purchase contain all the information listed in the forms below – especially deadline times.

RADIO

Name of Reporter __________ Station __________ Dial __________ Type: [ ] AM [ ] FM

Address __________

City __________ Province/State __________ Postal/Zip Code __________

Email: __________ Telephone __________ Fax __________

Website: __________ Blog: __________ Social Networking: __________

News Director __________ News Broadcast Times __________

Station Format __________ Coverage Area __________

Notes __________

____

PRINT

Name of Reporter __________ Paper/Magazine __________

Address __________

City __________ Province/State __________ Postal/Zip Code __________

Email: __________ Telephone __________ Fax __________

Website: __________ Blog: __________ Social Networking: __________

Editor __________ Deadlines __________ Circulation __________

Coverage Area __________

Notes __________

____

TELEVISION

Name of Reporter __________ Station __________

Dial __________ Call Letters/Channel __________

Address __________

City __________ Province/State __________ Postal/Zip Code __________

Email: __________ Telephone __________ Fax __________

Website: __________ Blog: __________ Social Networking: __________

News Director __________ News Broadcast Times __________

Station Format __________ Live Coverage Capability: [ ] Yes [ ] No

Coverage Area __________

Notes __________

____

DVD

Customize on the Companion DVD

Government Contact List

OFFICIAL	NAME	ADDRESS	OFFICE PHONE	HOME PHONE	CELL PHONE	EMAIL
Head of Government						
Principal Secretary						
Attorney General						
Environment Department						
Assistant in the Environment Department						
Local Politician						
National Politician						
"Medical Health Officer"						
Police						
Legislative Committee						
Cabinet Ministers						
Reeve/Mayor						
Clerk						
Councilor						
Councilor						
Councilor						
Councilor						
Councilor						
Councilor						
Fire Chief						
Other Fire Chief						
Police Chief						
Other Police Chief						
Other Officials						

DVD

Customize on the Companion DVD

Public and Media Update Form

NOTE: AN UPDATED COPY OF THIS FORM SHOULD BE POSTED ON THE STATUS BOARD IN ALL RESOURCE ROOMS AS WELL AS AT PUBLIC MEETINGS.

INFORMATION CURRENT AS OF: (INSERT DATE & TIME)	
LOCATION	**DATA**
Persons: Dead Injured Displaced	
Homes: Destroyed Damaged Estimated cost	
Businesses: Destroyed Damaged Estimated cost	
Public property: Destroyed Damaged Estimated cost	
Services interrupted or restored: What Where Duration	
Cultural policy	
Assets deployed	
Trade figures	
Causes determined: 1. 2. 3.	
Other	

DVD

Customize on the Companion DVD

Information Opportunities

A NOTICE OF INFORMATION OPPORTUNITIES SHOULD BE POSTED IN THE MEDIA WORK CENTRE AND PUBLIC AFFAIRS ROOM. AN EXAMPLE FOLLOWS.

EVENT	TIME	PLACE
example: Tour of Refinery Details	1:00 p.m.	Meet at Press Room
example: Availability - Dr. J. Smith (brief bio)	2:00 p.m.	
example: Signing ceremony	3:00 p.m.	See P. Jones hotel front desk

DVD

Customize on the Companion DVD

News Conference Room

A news conference room should be laid out as shown in the following diagram. Reporters should be greeted in a way that unobtrusively establishes whether they have a legitimate reason for being there and that their credentials are in order. Realistically, however, the media and public are unlikely to accept barring affected citizens from a quasi-public event such as a news conference. About the best that you can hope for is to obtain advance warning that third parties will attend. Remember, many legitimate reporters, especially freelancers and columnists, don't have official press credentials.

Reporters should pass through a progressively more stringent screening-process. Outside the entrance to the briefing-room there should be a table with background materials, followed by a security table for checking credentials, followed by a table at which each reporter signs in.

At the back of the room, a small platform or riser can be used for television cameras. This will provide a clear shot of the front of the room, over the audience. The cameras will also need a feed from the audio pool system.

At the back there should also be one table with refreshments and another for materials. The chairs should be laid out in theatre style, with a wide aisle in the middle and one on each side.

Speakers should be able to refer to Public and Media Update forms maintained in the Public Affairs Room, with maps, charts and other visual aids. The information table should hold the latest background material and news releases.

Provide room dividers in case few media people show up, so you can cut off corners and make the room smaller. Put out fewer chairs than you expect to need—the others can be stacked and brought out if required.

The speakers' table should have a floor-length cloth covering. Speakers should use pool microphones and be seated in front of a mid-blue curtain. There should be a rear entrance and exit, so speakers can avoid scrums if that's a goal (see "Managing Media" in Chapter 5 below).

Use a P.A. system only for groups of 30 or more. To gauge the correct room size, estimate the number of media people expected and add 20 per cent. This will accommodate bulky media equipment, coats and personal items.

Moderators and spokespeople must adhere as closely as possible to the protocol given in the section "Managing the News Conference" in Chapter 5 below.

In the event of a crisis, a variety of outside resources must be available quickly. The forms that follow (which you can customize on the companion DVD) should be updated annually to ensure that briefing-rooms, audio-visual equipment, food and outside consultants are known and available.

The appropriate site manager or crisis manager should pre-assign tasks to ensure that the organization or location is ready to conduct a news conference. The attached checklists must be regularly reviewed, updated and tested by locations.

Do not delay news conferences just because all these physical assets are not immediately in place. The most important aspect of any communication with reporters is the accuracy, timeliness and newsworthiness of the information conveyed. Your news-conference room can be upgraded as time goes on.

News Conference Room

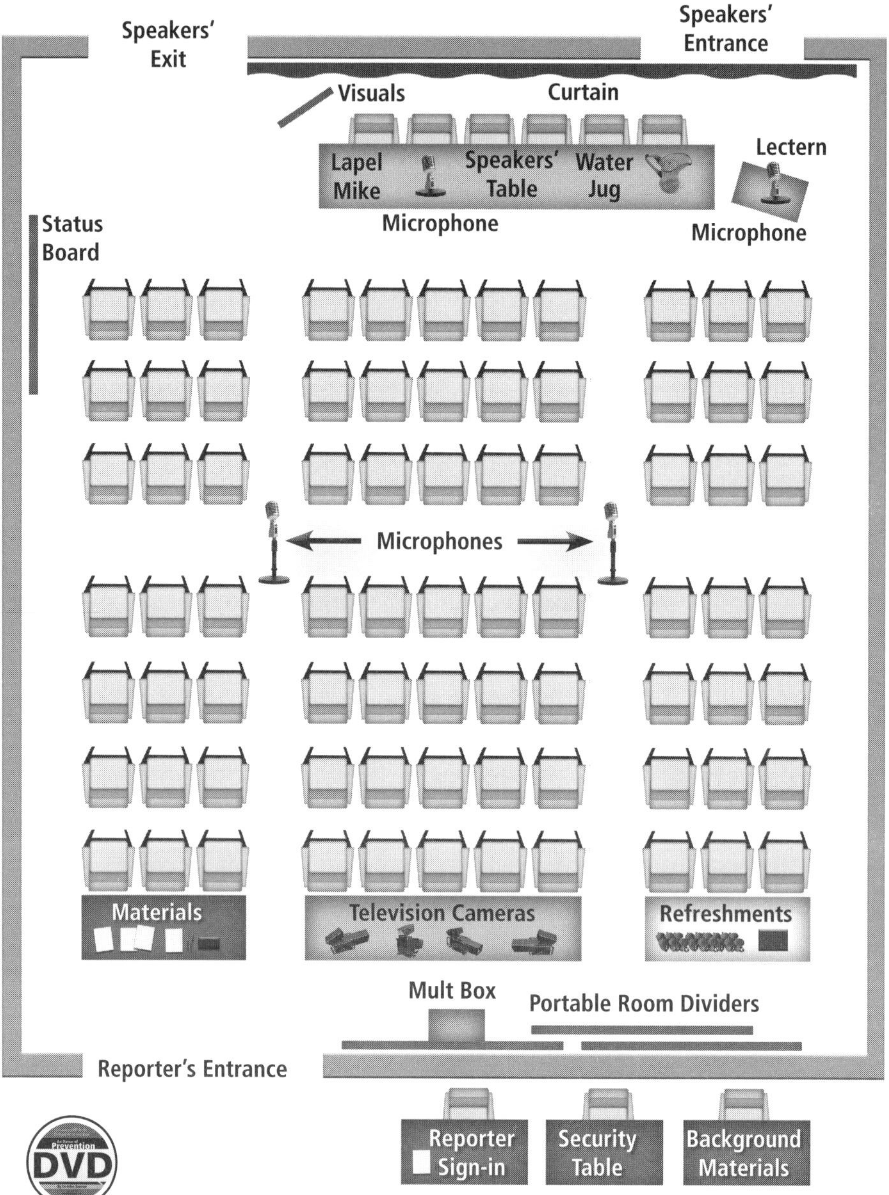

Speakers' Exit

Speakers' Entrance

Visuals

Curtain

Lapel Mike

Speakers' Table

Water Jug

Microphone

Lectern

Microphone

Status Board

Microphones

Materials

Television Cameras

Refreshments

Mult Box

Portable Room Dividers

Reporter's Entrance

Reporter Sign-in

Security Table

Background Materials

Available on the Companion DVD

News Conference Room – Materials and Services Checklist

SITES MAY SCALE LIST DOWN

ASSETS	SOURCE	RESPONSIBILITY	COMPLETED
6 - 8 ft. tables/20-50 chairs			
2 table cloths & curtains			
6 name cards			
Podium & lectern			
1 water pitcher & glasses (no ice)			
2 risers for TV cameras			
TV lighting (contact 3rd party supplier)			
Microphones			
Pool feed system (multi box-contact A/V supplier)			
Stock footage on 3/4" or Betacam			
Camera to record			
Maps/photographs/charts			
Visual aids (boom, shovel, etc.)			
Cover for visual aids (only with removable plastic)			
Easels/pointer			
PA system			
Audio recording capability			
20 DVDs / 20 CDs			
Status boards			
4 room dividers			
Sign-in sheets			
Background materials			
Portable toilets if needed			
Manual typewriter (in case of power failure)			
Memory Sticks			
Scanner			

DVD

Customize on the Companion DVD

Outside Resources

NEWS CONFERENCE ROOM		
Location:		Room No(s):
Addresss:		
City:	Prov./State:	Postal/Zip Code:
Contact:	Office Phone:	Home Phone:
Email:	Mobile:	Cottage:
URL	Alternative:	Fax:
Key Reporters		
Map and/or directions to site:		
AV EQUIPMENT		
Organization:		
Addresss:		
City:	Prov./State:	Postal/Zip Code:
Contact:	Office Phone:	Home Phone:
Email:	Mobile:	Cottage:
URL	Alternative:	Fax:
FOOD		
Organization:		
Addresss:		
City:	Prov./State:	Postal/Zip Code:
Contact:	Office Phone:	Home Phone:
Email:	Mobile:	Cottage:
URL	Alternative:	Fax:
LEGAL		
Organization:		
Addresss:		
City:	Prov./State:	Postal/Zip Code:
Contact:	Office Phone:	Home Phone:
Email:	Mobile:	Cottage:
URL	Alternative:	Fax:
PUBLIC RELATIONS		
Organization:		
Addresss:		
City:	Prov./State:	Postal/Zip Code:
Contact:	Office Phone:	Home Phone:
Email:	Mobile:	Cottage:
URL	Alternative:	Fax:

Outside Resources *Continued*

POLLING		
Organization:		
Addresss:		
City:	Prov./State:	Postal/Zip Code:
Contact:	Office Phone:	Home Phone:
Email:	Mobile:	Cottage:
URL	Alternative:	Fax:
ADVERTISING		
Organization:		
Addresss:		
City:	Prov./State:	Postal/Zip Code:
Contact:	Office Phone:	Home Phone:
Email:	Mobile:	Cottage:
URL	Alternative:	Fax:
VIDEO PRODUCTION		
Organization:		
Addresss:		
City:	Prov./State:	Postal/Zip Code:
Contact:	Office Phone:	Home Phone:
Email:	Mobile:	Cottage:
URL	Alternative:	Fax:
PHOTOGRAPHY		
Organization:		
Addresss:		
City:	Prov./State:	Postal/Zip Code:
Contact:	Office Phone:	Home Phone:
Email:	Mobile:	Cottage:
URL	Alternative:	Fax:

DVD

Customize on the Companion DVD

Media Work Centre

It is often desirable to offer reporters a room apart from the News Conference Room where they can work. This allows them to conduct their business while news conferences are being set up and planned. This room is especially useful when reporters need to be at the same location for more than a few hours. The room can be referred to as the Media Work Centre.

Ideally this room will be different from the News Conference Room, but the two functions may be combined if necessary. Signs should tell the media where to go, and if necessary a map should be handed out to reporters to direct them to the proper waiting-area. If the situation makes using your organization's facilities inappropriate, the media may be directed to a room off site, perhaps in a hotel.

Television equipment is valuable and takes up lots of room, so the facilities should be large and secure.

Although some small media outlets do not issue credentials to reporters, most news organizations do provide some form of identification. Such credentials should be checked and a record of contact with reporters should be maintained. A media contact form should be filled out by personnel staffing a table outside the door of the media room. When reporters are travelling to a remote location, their local hotel phone numbers or cell phone numbers should also be recorded.

Ideally, and during a prolonged stay, the Media Work Centre should provide as many reasonable amenities as possible to help reporters to do their jobs. Refreshments should be moderate. They should not take the place of meals, since this will present an ethical problem for many reporters.

The room should be visited every 30 minutes by a Public Affairs/Communications representative to gauge reporters' attitudes (see "Managing Media").

Media Work Centre – Materials & Services Checklist

EQUIPMENT	SOURCE	RESPONSIBILITY	CHECK
Flip chart, cork board notice boards (see "Public and Media Update" and "Information Opportunities")			
Desks, folding tables, chairs			
Waste baskets			
Status board			
Computers & portable information storage (CDs/memory sticks)			
Printers & appropriate toner cartridges			
Typewriter ribbons, manual & electric typewriter, fax, photocopier, toner cartridges			
Paper - lined, typing, fax			
Letterhead, envelopes			
Scissors, stapler, rubber bands, white out, staples			
Paper clips, tape, markers, pens, pencils, erasers			
File folders, storage boxes			
Coffee urn, contract with local food supplier for meals and light snacks			
Portable water, toilet, clock			
Podium, sound equipment			
Cables, extension cords			
Batteries, electrical power, generator, fuel			
Adapter, headphones			
Audio & video recording capability for live events and for radio & TV			
Television (cable & off air), radio - AM & FM			
Telephones - open, private & secure, hotline & mobile, silent beepers, extra SAT phones in case lines blocked			
Telephone answering machine			
Cameras, film			
Programmable video camera, player & DVDs			
Bullhorns, microphone			
Visual aids - graphs, charts of incident, location, effects, response, etc.			
Building / site floor plans			

EQUIPMENT	SOURCE	RESPONSIBILITY	CHECK
Maps re: evacuation routes, shelter location, emergency responders and equipment, specific site facilities, city, province			
Notification sheets, checklists, telephone contact lists, media directories, dictionary, thesaurus			
Photographs re: aerial view of sites, plant, facilities, equipment, systems			
Background materials			
Press releases, fact sheets			
Available transportation re: land, air & water carriers			
"All media – please report to ________" sign			
Sign-in sheets			
Blank press passes			
Hats/badges for easy ID of PR personnel			
Clerical/messenger services			
Clipping services			
Wire service			
Newspaper delivery			
Mingle - get to know reporters			
Update status board hourly			
OPTIONAL EQUIPMENT CHECKLIST			
Portable toilets			
Portable lecterns			
Multi boxes			
Extra microphones, speakers, power outlets, cables, connectors			
Sign-making kits			
Overhead projector			

DVD

Customize on the Companion DVD

Resource Rooms

Discussion Points:

1. What on-site rooms will we use?
2. What off-site rooms will we use?
3. Do we have appropriate stocks of materials on and off site?
4. Can we easily procure more stocks as needed?
5. Should some stocks be stored in responders' cars or homes?
6. Are there benefits to storing older items such as TVs, VCRs, computers, etc.?
7. What new technology is making our lists obsolete?
8. What old technology can we use if newer technology fails—HAM radios?
9. Do we have sufficient redundancy?
10. How often do we test equipment, systems and materials?

All Went Well, Except for the Dead People

A mainstay of the lecture circuit in crisis-management conferences is case studies of the Exxon Valdez *oil spill and the Tylenol headache-remedy poisonings.* Valdez *is usually taught to illustrate how not to handle a complex, rapidly escalating event. Tylenol shows how to handle things well.* Valdez *is even referred to in some college texts as among the worst handled crises in history with some of the most severe environmental impacts. Exxon is said to have been slow in responding. The Tylenol response featured swift action, withdrawing the product, 800 numbers for customer support, new packaging, a re-launch and contrite statements.*

I am intrigued at how the oil spill is handled, especially in the dispute-resolution courses taught at Harvard University.

Lawrence Susskind is a course leader in dispute resolution in the MIT-Harvard Public Disputes Program. He has written on the Exxon Valdez *oil spill, stating, "The residents, fishermen, local officials, and Native Americans ... would bear the brunt of the spreading oil."*

Susskind's book makes scant other reference to the readily available facts of the case. On March 24, 1989, the Exxon Valdez *oil tanker spilled more than ten million gallons of oil in Prince William Sound. At the time, the spill was about the thirtieth largest in history, and it now ranks well below sixtieth worldwide. The clean-up activity may have created an economic boom. Researchers found that 7.2 per cent of aboriginals reported medical conditions that they believed were related to the spill. Most were headaches. What, then, does Susskind mean by the "brunt"?*

It is interesting to contrast how Susskind treats Valdez *in his book with how his Harvard course treats the Tylenol poisoning case. Lecturers give the makers of Tylenol appropriate credit for recovering ninety-eight per cent of its seventy-five-million-dollar-a-year market through the rapid response described above. Yet they make no mention of the seven relatively young people who died horrible deaths and the many dozens of friends and loved ones who grieve their loss.*

The risk-management field may provide another perspective on the Tylenol cases (there were two). At the time there was a product tampering about every week in North America. Some risk managers might consider this ample warning of a loss-prevention problem needing mitigation.

Even if adequate compensation were paid to the family members, the process may have been unpalatable, and the psychological costs may have been high. From the standpoint of risk management and dispute resolution, Valdez *may have been handled more effectively than Tylenol.*

In the end, the modern practitioner needs a big toolbox to achieve success in more fields than merely on the balance sheet.

CHAPTER 4: RISK/CRISIS COMMUNICATION

Event: *TWA 800 Crash, Long Island, New York*

Date: *17 July 1996*

Summary: *About twenty minutes after takeoff, at about 14,000 feet, the Boeing 747 crashed into the water. The plane had spent double its projected lifespan—10 years—in the air. TWA and the plane had a good safety record. Some investigators settled on terrorism as the cause, in part because this was just a few years after the first World Trade Center bombing, the storming of the Branch Dividians' compound at Waco, Texas and the Oklahoma City bombing. One 'black-box' recording recovered by divers featured noises resembling those heard on other planes that had crashed as a result of bombs.*

The debris on the ocean floor was several storeys high, with many pieces of the plane being no larger than a football. Many miles of wire and cable made the site dangerous for divers. Microscopic testing was used to assess whether there was evidence of a bomb, missile or other cause. Optimization (one component performing multiple functions) and limited redundancy (few back-up systems) were potential causes. 'The socio-technical interface' is the technical term for pilot error or misreading instruments.

Other possible causes included design faults that might take years to uncover. Deregulation and competition led some observers to think airlines were skimping on safety and maintenance. The crash of a ValuJet DC-9-30 in May of 1996 put the policy of some airlines contracting out maintenance in the news.

The National Transportation Safety Board had fewer resources than intelligence agencies such as the FBI. NTSB simulations eventually found that the plane's air-conditioning unit underneath the centre fuel tank could have heated the fuel vapour beyond its flashpoint.

Recovery operations were based in a Coast Guard station on Long Island. A military officer in uniform volunteered to act as air-traffic controller and did so for a few days before authorities noticed incorrect insignia on his uniform and discovered he was an imposter.

Result: *All 210 passengers and 18 crew died.*

Lessons Learned: *The complexity of an air-crash investigation, especially at sea. Be aware of the vested interests that immediately try to influence an investigation. Inert gas can be pumped into the dead space of fuel tanks, and planes can be re-wired, to prevent sparks and explosion risk. Are passengers who want lower ticket prices partly to blame? With several agencies investigating a crash, it may be the one that decides first, has the most resources or is most influenced by perceptions that helps frame the findings. Who benefits if the cause is terrorism versus technical failure, versus commercial interests, versus pilot error?*

Communicating about Risk and Crises

Perception

Individuals have their own diverse views of risk, depending on their culture, the context and other factors (this is dealt in more detail in Appendix 4: "Why Risk Communication?"). There is no such thing as measurable, quantifiable risk. The person experiencing risk affects risk perception.

Ironically, as we live longer and become demonstrably safer, we worry more and more about risk. This may be because we know more about risk than ever before. Constant focus on making our cars, indoor air quality, children's toys, food and apparently everything safer may actually increase people's anxieties.

Our perception of risk changes depending on the circumstances and who is at risk. Asbestos risk in schools takes on a different dimension if it's in our own kids' school. Two factors are in play here: the personalization of the risk, and the fact that it affects children. We generally perceive risks to children as being much higher than they actually are.

Why is the risk of asbestos in schools more worrisome than the fear of fire, which asbestos can prevent? Maybe it's because of the dread of asbestos and the familiarity of fire. Why is cancer a dreaded risk, yet fear of skin cancer doesn't keep people out of the sun? Risks that attract high levels of attention in the news media are also perceived to be higher than they actually are. Maybe skin cancer doesn't get the media attention it deserves.

For some risk and crisis managers, an event may be another day at the office, but for regulators, politicians, the public and others it may be a calamity. The wise risk and crisis manager approaches an event from the point of view of the beholder, not just with the operational knowledge s/he has.

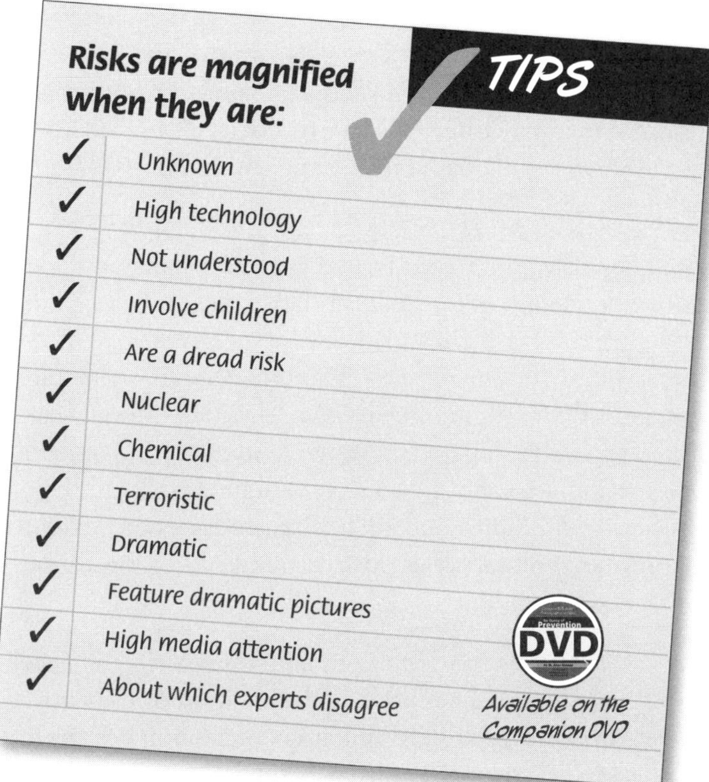

If people are to be persuaded to consider taking risks, they must be educated about the risk and assured that is it manageable. Risks are more acceptable when they are:

- Known
- Voluntary
- Controllable
- Familiar
- Human in origin
- Understood
- Natural, such as a weather event

Organizations interact with customers, clients and stakeholders through their goods, services and ideas. Customer and client interaction is also a distant-early-warning system, and your colleagues who are in regular contact with stakeholders can play a vital role in averting crises. Customers or clients who alert an organization to a problem with a product or policy are providing a valuable quality-control service. Complaints may also reveal problems in the physical plant, with workers, supervisors, suppliers, raw materials or a host of other matters. Concerns expressed about service may trigger a valuable human-resources, training, diagnostic or other function. Concerns about the ideas or positions that an organization asserts may offer an opportunity to glean free information that might otherwise only come from expensive polling, focus groups or élite interviewing.

Care should be taken to find out just what the customer is actually complaining about. In one case, a customer complained to a hotdog company that there was a razor blade in one of her dogs. The company reacted by withdrawing the product, issuing an apology that tacitly blamed worker sabotage and offering to replace any product that customers wished to exchange. These actions were premature. It soon appeared that the tampering was a hoax, probably designed to obtain free product or compensation. The company had created about a dozen copycat crimes, acrimonious labour relations and a huge bill for recalling, replacing and re-stocking product.

In another case, Dow Beer, which dominated the market in Quebec, Canada, was linked in media reports with the mysterious deaths of a few habitual beer-drinkers. No causal link was ever found, but the brewery withdrew all of its product and poured so much beer down the sewers that the streets were covered in foam. Customers assumed there was more of a link than science actually found, and the beer's market share plummeted overnight.

Tips Dealing with Complaints or Concerns

- ✓ Advertise your complaints procedure and invite comments.
- ✓ Have reception, answering services, security and others keep a record of and report all customer complaints.
- ✓ Be available to provide a human touch.
- ✓ Listen carefully to complaints.
- ✓ Establish a written policy for dealing with all customer complaints.
- ✓ Ask questions; probe for as much information as you can get.
- ✓ All complainants should identify themselves with a name or number for future reference.
- ✓ Suggest a solution or course of action.
- ✓ If you can't offer an immediate solution, explain what steps you will take.
- ✓ Contact the complainant regularly (often daily) with a status report even if there is no progress.
- ✓ Sincerely try to empathize.
- ✓ Ask for evidence in serious charges, but be polite.
- ✓ Record correspondence carefully; leave a paper trail.
- ✓ Live up to promises.
- ✓ Act as quickly as possible.
- ✓ Follow up.
- ✓ If you lose control of yourself, you lose control of the encounter.
- ✓ Dial you own toll free number occasionally, including in off hours, to test response.

DVD

Available on the Companion DVD

A Different Perspective

This diagram illustrates two perspectives on a release of hydrogen sulphide. Neighbours may naturally focus on the ultimate effects, i.e. death. A plant manager may focus on the actual effect and its short duration.

Effects of Exposure to Concentrations of Hydrogen Sulphide

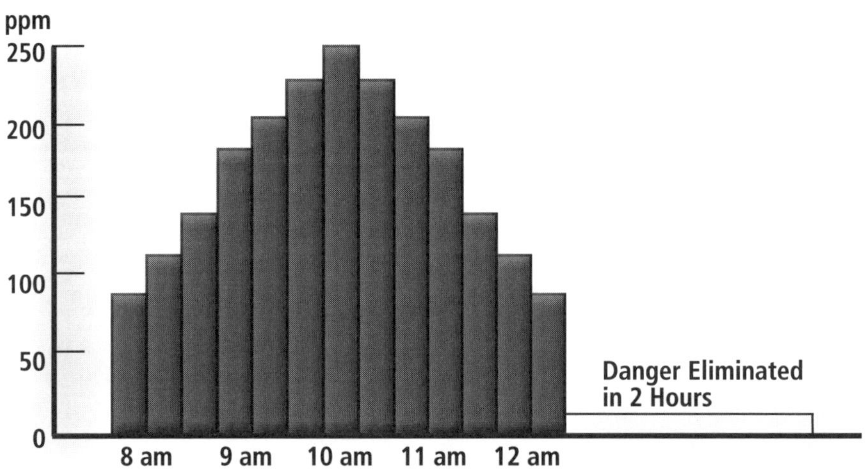

Health Effects	Intensity of Exposure
Rapidly Fatal.	>700 ppm
Fatal in 1 hour	500-700 ppm
May produces unconsciousness and death in 1 to 4 hours.	500 ppm
Produces headaches, drowsiness, (prolonged exposure many cause fluid accumulation in lungs).	200-300 ppm
Severe eye and respiratory tract irritation.	100-150 ppm
Marked eye and respiratory tract irritation.	50-100 ppm
Minimal eye and respiratory tract irritation.	20-50 ppm

DVD

Available on the Companion DVD

Framing and Signals

Does having to manage a crisis imply failure? Should you have been able to foresee the event? Perhaps. But you may not be able to predict all stakeholders' perceptions of risk and crises, so you may end up managing perception. How you frame your event and what signals you send can play very important roles.

There's no guarantee that communicating about risk will calm people down. It might just make them worry more. But I think that in our current public-policy environment, risk information is likely to get out, so I'd want to be in some modest control of the agenda. The risk communicator wants to be first to define whether the glass of asbestos is half full or half empty and whether a survival rate of 50 per cent means you've got a good chance to live or a good chance to die. That's framing or contextualizing. The person or group that frames an event first starts with a tremendous competitive advantage over all who come after and try to re-frame or describe it. It's like on Hallowe'en: saying "Boo!" to the kids is the easy part; getting across "There, there, it's just me under this mask" is much harder.

The frame through which you see an event could be the end result. Few people cared about polluting the waterways during the Normandy landing, because the larger frame was the liberation of Europe. But in a peacetime oil spill, the frame is the pollution of waterways. Responders may try to frame their activities in terms of their success in stopping the oil from flowing, but another frame is the use of toxic dispersants.

A 'signal' is a type of framing. You'll have more trouble if your event appears to be a 'signal' that a technology or industry isn't being well managed or that you've underestimated the risk.[6] All parents have had that sickening feeling when reading the news about a child who has disappeared or been killed. That's the signal that it can happen to us.

In industry, Three Mile Island was such a signal. There had been a similar near-event at another plant a few months before, but TMI was the straw that broke the nuclear industry's back, in no small part because of the added signal effect (or amplification) of the movie *The China Syndrome*. Events don't happen in a vacuum. The movie *As Good as it Gets* drew attention to practices in Health Management Organizations (HMOs), and after its release 50,000 people wrote emails and letters condemning HMOs. The movie *John Q*, in which a father takes hostages in a hospital to try to get his son a heart transplant, drew more attention to the fact that 40 million Americans lacked health-care coverage. A good risk and crisis manager keeps on top of popular culture as a distant-early-warning system to issues that may flare up.

Risk Rules

Risks that are known, understood and perceived as fair are more readily accepted than those that are mysterious and ambiguous. One way to make risks fair, known and understood is by comparisons, but some are better than others. Useful comparisons may be the same risk at two different times, comparisons with a standard, different estimate of the same risk and the effects of doing something versus not doing anything. Standards can come from local, province/state, national and international (World Health Organization) bodies as well as from the laws, rules and guidelines in other jurisdictions.

On the other hand, comparing a voluntary risk such as smoking a cigarette with an involuntary risk such as living near a chemical plant may seem to blame the victim and backfire. People jealously guard their freedom to act as they choose to, even when it harms them. It is counterproductive to compare what a company might be doing to its neighbours with what those neighbours are doing to themselves. Comparing smoking a cigarette with drinking a shot glass of tar and nicotine could work, because both are voluntary risks. Another effective strategy might be to compare a variety of similar risks over time and between several jurisdictions using credible third-party data. People will generally react well to evidence that the risk is diminishing over time.

Spokespeople should be ready to deal with a variety of statistics on the risk involved. You will usually be asked for a personal reaction to the risk (to you and your family) and should be ready to deal with this empathetically.

In describing statistical risk, be imaginative. For example, you can express parts per million to a lay audience as the equivalent of an envelope in a stack about eight miles high. You can describe a spill as having the impact of adding one bucketful of water to a swimming-pool. But remember, everybody can imagine how sickening a bucketful of sewage or oil could be in a swimming pool. Pick an image that explains but doesn't offend.

Generally, the public are much more willing to accept risks over which they have some control. Most people feel safer when they choose not to wear seatbelts than if forced to buckle up. People who drive their cars erratically still feel safer than they do as passengers in cars driven more safely. The actual danger or safety isn't as important as the individual's feeling of safety.

Try to present the risk as voluntary, familiar, non-memorable, controllable and not dreaded. Most people will perceive a risk occurring at a single location and time as higher than one dispersed over time and space. For example, a bus accident that kills 8 senior citizens and makes the news will focus people's attention on road safety more than reference to the 50,000 North Americans who die each year on highways. Dramatic pictures, especially in the media, make risk events more memorable. Control can come from giving people options for how to deal with the risk—diet, exercise, medical checkups and so on. For most people a dread risk means something like cancer, burning alive, AIDS, terrorism, nuclear exposure or chemical poisoning.

The more familiar and routine activities become, the less people fear them. I've had clients in Asia whose employees regularly go out on emergency-response calls during typhoons. They are used to typhoons and don't feel at great risk, while most North Americans would be terrified during a typhoon. Conversely, these people might feel at great risk during a snowstorm, but many North Americans would not.

Most people have a sense of their own cost-benefit trade-off in the risks in modern life. People should feel they are receiving their fair share of benefits to compensate for the risks they are taking. Very few people want to live with others' waste or close to a chemical plant—especially if it doesn't do them any good. Workers at the chemical plant will have their own perspective, based on familiarity and the pay they receive.

Neutral third-party data will enhance your credibility. People will want to know the characteristics, benefits and use of a particular risky substance. They will want to know the alternatives. A good risk communicator is ready to address such questions.

Three Pillars of Effective Risk Communication

Persuasiveness stands on three pillars: caring, knowledge and action. In our training-programs we ask participants to make a statement about their company or activities. We then ask them to give themselves a mark out of ten on each of the criteria caring, knowledge and action. Most participants give themselves modest marks—6s and 7s out of ten for a total of about 20. We then say that the bad news is that a passing mark is 25 out of a cumulative 30 on all three criteria. The good news is that it's remarkably easy to improve marks.

Consider the statement from a diplomat who says "My country is going to give $100,000 to each hospital in Mexico City." Does she care? Is she knowledgeable? Is she doing something about it? Marks would be low on all counts.

What if she revises her statement to be, "We're going to give $100,000 to each hospital in Mexico City to buy special masks to stop the spread of this virus"? Marks for caring go way up after just a few specific and descriptive words. Spokespeople are usually afraid to show caring, so we ask them simply to use the word 'care.'

So the hypothetical spokesperson can add, "Many viruses are spread through the air while patients, doctors, nurses and visitors speak to each other." Is she knowledgeable? Marks go way up. Does she have a degree in medicine? Who knows, and who cares? Knowledge need not be perfect and complete for credit to be given and marks to go up. Spokespeople are often afraid to say anything unless everything is known, but in breaking news stories, crises, controversies and risk communication this strategy is disastrous. By definition, very little is known in these cases. In a breaking story the gradual and sequential release of information is key.

Next the spokesperson adds, "And we've consulted medical specialists around the world to select the most durable and effective masks." Is she doing something about it? Marks go way up for having done her due diligence.

All the information about this virus in quotation marks above takes about 14 seconds to say. This is the length of a good clip on radio or TV, and perhaps the time that passes before an audience starts booing an industry spokesperson who is putting them at risk.

Story Power vs. Stats

Often audience members will react more positively to anecdotal information, even if the incident being cited is an anomaly. The persuasive power of a story lies in the fact that it did happen to at least one person. For example, a spokesperson for a chemical company may make 25 reassuring statements to a group of neighbours. Then one person may get up and say that his uncle used to live near a similar plant and he went bald at age 35. This person may point to his own full head of hair and ask why his uncle would be bald at 35 when all other family members have plenty of hair. The person may then show a picture of his bald uncle as evidence.

Most spokespeople are devastated by such a tactic. Even though the incident is an anomaly and statically irrelevant, it did happen to at least one person and a fixed time and a fixed place. There is probably no causal relationship, but this anecdote has enormous credibility.

Company officials must be armed with similar but contradicting anecdotes to survive. The least credible tool they can use in this case is dry and boring statistics. What might work is four empathetic statements, such as:

1) "I'm sorry to hear about your uncle's baldness."
2) "An unusual case of baldness in a family can be troubling."
3) "I can see you don't want the same thing to happen to you."
4) "I'd like to help put this issue in perspective."

Now you need four substantial statements:

1) "We study our workers' health and safety, and we actually have less baldness in our workforce than there is in the general population."
2) "If baldness isn't an issue with our workers and they're right in the plant, it stands to reason that it won't be an issue with people who live outside the plant."
3) "Our health and safety people have done studies that show no linkage between our plant and baldness. I'd be happy to get more information and ask them to take another look at the medical literature, to see if there's anything new since their last study."
4) "I'd like to discuss some of the ways people who live anywhere can avoid the effects of baldness—perhaps with sunscreen."

There are several important points here. I used the preposterous example of baldness because many industry executives dealing with the public will just dismiss something that they know has nothing to do with them. This is a mistake. If a citizen is angry, confused or fearful, you must deal with those effects, regardless of the cause. Then you may find opportunities to empower the questioner with actions s/he can take to reduce or manage the risk. There may be ways to make the risk fairer and better known. Showing action by doing more research, displaying caring by making empathetic statements and showing your knowledge of your organization's health and safety research will also help.

You may not convince that questioner. You may not get public support. But you may reduce the fear, convince at least some other audience members, reduce the opposition and gain public acceptance. It depends on the issue, but one thing is certain—it takes lots of effort and skill.

Trust

So the old adage that perception is reality often holds true for risk communication. However, an organization must not only be seen to be doing the right thing, it must also actually do the right thing—reality is reality as well. Building trust and credibility is vital. It will come as no surprise that many large companies don't enjoy the trust of their stakeholders. Those in media or investor relations often shrug this off, but it must be taken very seriously when risk is involved.

Two-Way Communication

All communication is becoming increasingly two-way. Not only is technology allowing this, but sociology is demanding it. The rights and freedoms that citizens are winning all over the world bring with them the right to communication and information. Risk communicators have to listen more and pay attention to perceptions. In some court cases, judges have awarded damages to people who *felt* at risk from electromagnetic

Tips for Risk Communication

TIPS

- ✓ Body language and non-verbal communication predominate.
- ✓ The visual overrides the verbal.
- ✓ Gestures and mannerisms are up to 75% of your impact.
- ✓ Reaction is a binary sort—good or bad.
- ✓ Lower your voice.
- ✓ Use eye contact—50-75% of your non-verbal impact.
- ✓ Sit up straight, lean forward a little.
- ✓ Keep both hands in full view.
- ✓ Gesture your palms at 45 degrees, below chest level.
- ✓ Do not use a podium.
- ✓ Dress one above the audience and one below your work peers.
- ✓ Keep your coat open.
- ✓ Arrive early.
- ✓ Stay late.

DVD

Available on the Companion DVD

fields. These people did not have to prove they *were* at risk, let alone prove actual damages. Judges listened and acted as if what they heard were true. Perhaps the judges were awarding compensation for the distress that living near high-tension power lines was creating, quite apart from whether that caused them any actual harm.

Special Considerations for Women

In many sectors, women are still judged by more exacting criteria and may have greater difficulty convincing parties in risk situations. Female risk communicators should:

- Stress résumés
- Cite data
- Use some technical jargon but explain it
- Add structure
- Use a more formal tone

Communicating about Risk and Crises

Discussion Points:

1. How do our stakeholders perceive risk in our industry or field?
2. How do we empower stakeholders?
3. What information will calm stakeholders' fears?
4. What risk comparisons can we make?
5. Do we have enough solid information to sustain a full evening public meeting?
6. What credible and independent third parties can we cite?
7. What alternatives do stakeholders have?
8. What alternatives do we have?
9. What specifically are we doing to reduce risk?
10. What measures can we put in place to frame risk issues favourably?

Communicating During a Crisis

Sóckō: n. acronym for Strategic Overriding Communications and Knowledge Objective.

1. A short, positive, sharp, memorable, honed, polished, true, unassailable statement.
2. A 'media-genic' clip or quotation on radio, on TV, or in newspaper stories.
3. A quotable quote with impact, often showing caring, knowledge and/or action lasting 20 seconds or less.
4. A rough equivalent to a headline, cutline or lead, best delivered after full rehearsal at least three times: e.g. "I have nothing to offer but blood, toil, tears and sweat";[7] "Ask not what your country can do for you; ask what you can do for your country";[8] "Just watch me...";[9] "Yes, we can!"[10]

Strategic Overriding Communications Knowledge Objectives

(SÓCKŌs™)

The SOCKO™ system is a series of techniques that help you communicate more effectively. SOCKOs™ help you identify your objectives and stay focused on them. You can apply this system to media and stakeholder communication, speech-writing and delivery and to meeting, time and reputation management. While the SOCKO™ system should be used across the organization in a wide variety of ways, the focus here is on crisis communication.

Each part of the acronym SOCKO™ adds something to the power and impact of the message. A message is *Strategic* because a spokesperson thought about it, practised and rehearsed it and gave serious consideration to what he or she hopes it will convey. *Overriding* reminds speakers that they need to be giving out the most important piece of information they can at all times. *Communication* refers to the difference between oral and written messages. Good oral communication features repetition, imagery, simplicity, brevity and clarity. *Knowledge* is reflected in facts, figures, history and dates. *Objective* refers to measurable behavioural objectives such as a positive headline in the newspaper, clip on a newscast, regulatory approval or court ruling in your favour.

SOCKOs™ are not designed for the eye but for the ear. That's why they are brief and to the point. They are not designed to be read like a memo but heard as part of a conversation.

Most people take their daily lives and activities for granted. When asked to describe what they do, why they do it and why it's important, they generally look and sound uncomfortable. Imagine how this discomfort can be magnified when a person or organization comes under public scrutiny.

A crisis is the wrong time for an organization to begin to think about what it wants to tell its stakeholders and neighbours about what it does, how and why it does it and why it's important. This information—together with everything else that can help convince the public that the organization is a responsible, caring, trustworthy and indispensable part of the community—needs to be identified beforehand and converted into SOCKOs™.

This must be done long in advance of an incident, because there's no time for this work while you're managing a crisis. If you never have a crisis, having compiled all this information will do you no harm. You can still use it as speech modules, briefing-notes, orientation documents for new employees, press releases and so on.

The SOCKO™ system has you codify your values, beliefs and accomplishments to enhance your reputation. These statements and records of achievement are then ready to go when you need them. SOCKOs™ keep you out of the weeds and minutiae.

SOCKOs™ are essential for media encounters, whether over the phone, in person, on camera, with a print reporter or on background with an editorial board. Appearances before legislative committees or in public forums with special-interest groups or customers also go better with SOCKOs™.

Special circumstances require special messages. You can use this format to make and rehearse new SOCKOs™ for new or challenging forums. Your SOCKO™ manual should be a living, working document.

SOCKOs™ are not secrets to be hidden away where no one will find them: they should be given as wide a circulation as is practical and kept where they can be found and used for easy reference. SOCKOs™ need to be reviewed and updated regularly.

SOCKOs™ are particularly useful in the early stages of an unforeseen situation that attracts attention. Media and public attention is most acute when the dimensions of a potential problem are unclear.

What happened? How many people are affected? Who's to blame? Who pays for the damage? Are you insured? How will this affect your future?

These are very likely the kind of questions you'll be faced with. And even though you probably won't have the answers, you had better have something to say, or you risk being portrayed as an organization that (a) hasn't a clue what's going on, and/or (b) doesn't care.

Armed with SOCKOs™, spokespeople can talk during a crisis about safety procedures, training and on-site emergency crews or about the organization's links to the local community.

For all these reasons SOCKOs™ should always be part of a crisis-management plan. They should also be backed up with fact sheets (see "Crisis-Management System: Maintaining an Enterprise during a Crisis" in Chapter 2 above). These fact sheets should deal with production figures; the work force; product information; details on potentially hazardous materials used, stored or transported in and out of the plant; pollutants; and any other key factors.

Let's take a closer look at the individual elements of a SOCKO™.

Strategic

In the communication process strategic thinking usually receives far too little attention. Few people stop to think of the effect their words may have before they say them. To have a strategic value, your message needs to be thought out, practised, rehearsed and given serious consideration. Can your message achieve a measurable result, or does it just fill up time?

Why don't we take as much care over the words we say as over the words we write? Oral communication must be polished, edited and rehearsed just as much as written communication is re-worked for clarity.

Overriding

Most people take in only a small fraction of what they hear. Memory is very weak. Speakers need to stay focused on the most important pieces of information they want to convey.

It helps if you picture an iceberg. Think of all the information and knowledge you'd like to convey in the irregular shape of an iceberg. The most important 10–15 per cent should be in the top—the part that sticks out of the water. The rest of the information should be there if you need it, but you need to focus on the information in the visible tip.

Imagine you are on a bus and a passenger says to you: "I notice from your briefcase that you're with XYZ Corporation. Didn't I read something bad about your company recently? What's going on?"

But before you can respond, your questioner signals the driver that he wants to get off. You have 10 or perhaps 15 seconds to tell that person the most important things you know about your organization.

Should your questioner decide to get off at a later stop, you'll have an opportunity to reinforce your message by delivering the next most important 10 per cent of your information, and so on.

Communications

There are vast differences between oral and written communication, and if you want to communicate effectively, you should be aware of them. Readers and listeners have different requirements. One of the biggest for listeners is the need for repetition.

If we read the same phrase or sentence over and over again in a book, we'd assume somebody had goofed in the editing-process. But when you rely on your voice to communicate, repetition is not only desirable but mandatory for your message to be clearly understood and believed.

Think how many times you re-read a section of print to see if you have grasped its meaning. However it's not so easy to interrupt a spoken presentation to ask the speaker to keep repeating a phrase until you have understood it. If you want your audience to understand the point you're making, don't be afraid to repeat it several times.

Another key to communicating, whether you are speaking or writing, is simplicity. Throughout history great leaders have used simple words and concepts to reach out to their audiences and move them to undertake momentous acts. Compare the speeches of Lincoln, Gandhi or Churchill to the pumped-up and pompous jargon you often hear on the news or in board of trade speeches.

Knowledge

Most of us are reasonably sure we know all we need to know about our organizations and activities. If we absolutely must have the exact number of employees or the amount and type of raw materials we import to make widgets and the number of trucks that pass through the plant gates every day, the answers are usually a phone call or email away.

But in a crisis, controversy or disaster you may not have time to go looking for the answers. Your questioners, critics and adversaries will not understand if you don't have basic factual information about your company or organization at your fingertips. The number of employees in the building at any given time, percentages of women and visible minorities, number of vehicles, annual sales, the number of annual fire drills—all these provide a living experience with your organization.

So make sure you have these basic facts ready today. Tomorrow may be too late.

Objective

The final O in SOCKO™ refers to the measurable, quantifiable, human, behavioural or tangible result that you want to achieve. This is your aim, your goal, your objective. Behavioural objectives in any forum can be seen and measured.

- What is your objective in a speech to community groups—applause?
- What is your objective at a meeting with legislators or regulators—heads nodding in the affirmative?

If you are dealing with the media, your objective is probably fair, and preferably favourable, coverage. You can help yourself by being aware of the various elements that can convey a story. For print media these include headlines, subheads, pictures, quotes and cutlines (captions). For broadcast media they include interviews (more likely clips or soundbites) background video and sound and narration. Various Internet applications, including blogs and social-networking sites, may use all these elements too.

The SOCKO™ Basics

The format to follow is:

Issue: (Not a question but a key word or short phrase to trigger a response)

SOCKO™ (The most important thing you can say on the topic)

Discussion: (Responses for when your audience engages)

Issue statements are designed to trigger stimulus response—message delivery. They need to be general enough to address any number of specific questions concerning that issue.

It doesn't matter if a question dealing with costs implies that something is too expensive, that you can't pay for remediation or even who will pay for it. Your cost ISSUE should contain a generic SOCKO™ that can respond to many of the questions dealing with cost. That doesn't mean you only need one SOCKO™ —you need many. Depending on the question, a discussion point may end up being at the tip of your iceberg and delivered first. You'll get multiple use out of SOCKOs™ and discussion points.

Once you've identified your ISSUE, you should decide which is the most important 10 per cent of the information you want to tell the world. This is your SOCKO™.

After that you can add four or five supporting discussion points that you can use to expand your answer when you respond to follow-up questions. This way, you make sure you have enough material to present and defend your case, no matter how rigorous the question. You also want more information at hand if the question is just, "Oh really?... Tell me more ... Are you sure?..." and so on.

SOCKOs™ should be as brief as you can make them. A single declarative sentence is much more effective than a paragraph full of adjectives and clauses. It's also easier to say and easier for your audience to understand.

Corporate Background

A good crisis plan will contain plain, understandable statements about activities, products, divisions and geographic zones of operation (see "Crisis-Management System: Maintaining an Enterprise during a Crisis" in Chapter 2 above). Be audience-focused. A spokesperson for a chemical company is probably better off saying it makes plastic car parts such as gear-shift knobs rather than saying it is in the rotomoulding business. You should glean and feature information that the company is especially proud of or that makes it unique.

Some sample SOCKOs™ follow. The first series are a version of actual SOCKOs™ that we developed for oil-spill responders and oil-company spokespeople. You can also format them to show which bullet points you want volunteered to all and which are to be given out only if the spokesperson is pressed for more information.

Issue: Tanker Safety

SOCKO™ In our 100-year history of marine operations, we haven't suffered a major oil spill from a company-owned ship. Public Affairs can provide you with more background.

Background

- We manage marine operations in all major waterways and are engaged in shipping crude oil, refined petroleum products and, to a smaller extent, petrochemicals.
- We have a long and honourable record of environmental responsibility. We are committed to protecting the environment and to safeguarding the health and safety of both our employees and the general public.
- We fully accept our duty to ensure that the hazards associated with our operations are identified, assessed and appropriately managed to minimize risks and prevent accidents.
- When an accident does occur, we provide an effective and timely response in order to safeguard public health, our employees, wildlife and the environment.
- We maintain the capability to provide a rapid response to all spills, and we are prepared to speed up our response as appropriate.
- The vast majority of oil spills in our waters—in fact 99.7 per cent of them—are expected to involve less than 1,000 barrels.
- Over the next three years we will invest about $8–10 million to improve our initial response capability at our key marine terminals and spill cooperatives.
- We have taken initiatives to improve safety on our tankers by carrying two pilots, moderating speed and having a tug escort where appropriate.
- We have taken special preventative measures: ensuring that all foreign-flag tankers we use are well suited for their intended trade, are operated by responsible owners and have good safety and environmental records. On docking, they are attended by a contracted inspector who monitors, inspects and reports on the vessel's condition and performance.
- We are committed to working with industry and governments to develop a response plan for all spill scenarios, including contingency plans for large catastrophic spills that would utilize both national and international resources.

Issue: Gasoline Pricing

SOCKO™ Many studies, including major government inquiries, have shown that the oil industry is highly competitive. Gasoline prices are based on dynamic market forces.

Background

- The distribution distance from refinery to gas pump is shorter in the US than in Canada. In the US larger markets lead to greater economy of scale and so to lower gas prices.
- Station prices for full service in Canada are sometimes lower than in the US.
- The American preference for cash sales and self-service tends to lower pump prices.
- Over 40 percent of the current selling-price of gasoline in Canada is tax.
- In the United States, taxes on a litre of gasoline account for only about 10 cents of the pump price. Other factors that contribute to lower gasoline prices in the United States are lower refining, transport and distribution costs and a more efficient retail network.
- In Canada, federal and provincial taxes, on average, account for about 24 cents per litre of gasoline. In fact, one of the single biggest sources of gasoline price increase to Canadians in recent years has been higher taxes.
- The price of gasoline and other refined petroleum products is primarily determined by the market.
- Competition in the retail gasoline marketplace is intense. There has been a sharp rise in the number of regional refiners and marketers and small independent marketers or 'private-branders.' Today the regional and independent competitors evenly split about 40 percent of the market. In making their gasoline purchases motorists have more choices than ever before.
- In the long term, both the gasoline retailer—who is often an independent dealer—and the refiner and marketer must recover their costs and earn a return on their investments in order to stay in business.
- Retailers receive about four to five cents per litre of gasoline to cover their operating-costs and earn an income and return on their investment. The refiner and marketer receive about 15 to 16 cents per litre to cover operating, distribution and marketing-costs, pay income tax and provide a profit.
- According to the federal Petroleum Monitoring Agency, the profit margin for the refining/marketing sector of the Canadian petroleum industry has typically been about one cent per litre of petroleum product.
- The Petroleum Monitoring Agency reports that for a recent five-year period the industry's average return on capital was substantially less than an individual could earn with a risk-free bank investment.

Issue: Global Warming/Greenhouse Effect

SOCKO™ Our company has published a paper, done research into this field and taken several positive steps. You are welcome to a copy of our discussion paper.

Background

- We are responsible for about 2 percent of CO_2 emissions from fossil-fuel combustion and a lesser share of the other direct greenhouse-gas emissions.
- We have conducted a comprehensive examination of the potential for further improvement in energy efficiency to reduce CO_2 and other combustion-related greenhouse-gas emissions in our operations.
- We have completed an inventory of greenhouse-gas emissions resulting from our operations. It includes CO_2, methane (CH_4), nitrous oxide (N_2O) and chlorofluorocarbons (CFCs) and also the indirect greenhouse gases, namely nitrogen oxides (NO_x) and volatile organic compounds (VOCs). NO_x and VOCs are precursors of ozone (O_3), a greenhouse gas.
- Many industrialized countries have committed themselves to establishing national strategies to stabilize emissions and levels of CO_2 and greenhouse gas.
- We believe it is technically feasible to dispose of about 3.5 percent of our CO_2 emissions into subterranean formations at a cost of $15 to $50 per tonne.
- Alternative transport fuels offer a rather limited potential to reduce greenhouse-gas emissions and in some cases would actually increase them.
- We have been a consistent leader in developing more efficiently burning fuels and new combustion techniques.
- Improved refining-techniques and technology have dramatically reduced fuel contaminants. We have a vital stake in helping to develop environmental public policy and are committed to taking an active role.
- There is an urgent need to reduce uncertainties and to improve understanding and awareness of both the scientific and socio-economic dimensions of the threat of climate change.
- Steps can be taken now without weakening the country's ability to compete in a global trading-economy.

Issue: Long-term Recovery and Clean-up Strategy

SOCKO™ Government and industry recognize that responders can recover 5-25 percent of oil spilled on water in the first six days. This wide variation is due to weather, currents and remoteness. We recognize this and have plans to protect sensitive zones, consider the use of dispersants where feasible and direct the oil to non-sensitive zones for beach clean-up.

Background:

The key to achieving the best recovery rate on water is to have the response equipment and trained personnel available for fast mobilization. Our industry has established four major equipment centres with trained response contractors across the continent.

The equipment and trained personnel from these response centres, plus the Southampton Oil Spill Centre in England, can be used to respond immediately to a major incident. We also have international access to equipment and response personnel.

Our first priority is containment and recovery. If the situation allows, we will consider using dispersants as a response tactic. The dispersant that we would use is approved by the national government but would also require approval by the local government before use.

We will use a deflection boom to protect sensitive areas and to direct oil to non-sensitive zones for shoreline clean-up priorities and disposal.

Along with the government, we will establish a joint committee to assess sensitive zones, wildlife restoration, shoreline clean-up priorities and disposal needs.

Each of our regions maintains an on-call response team that is supported by our *National Emergency Team* and our *Crisis-Management Teams.* Our NET is a group of highly trained response experts who are on call 24 hours a day. Our CMTs support the local teams in procuring equipment, dealing with government policies etc.

Issue: Skimmers

SOCKO™ Skimmers are mechanical devices that recover oil on water. We have a large variety of skimmers that help us adapt to the size of a spill and the type of product we have to handle.

Background

- We have first-response capability everywhere we operate and are a key player in oil-spill co-ops across the country and around the world.
- Skimmers are strategically placed across the country, based on the size and type of potential spills.
- If a spill is too big for us to deal with using our own skimmers, we have access to other oil-spill co-ops' equipment, as well as the Southampton Oil Spill Centre in England.
- The types of skimmers we have available include belt skimmers, rope skimmers, disc skimmers, weir-boom skimmers and suction skimmers.

Belt, rope, and disc skimmers can pick up as much as 95 percent of spilt oil.

Belt, Band or Rope skimmers use an oleophilic belt mounted on the front of a small vessel. The belt pushes the floating oil below the waterline, and any oil that it does not absorb is collected in a holding-zone behind it. The oil that is carried up the belt is recovered at the top of the system by a squeeze belt or a scraper blade and then pumped into a storage container.

Disc skimmers rotate through water like water wheels. Oil adheres to the disc until it can be scraped off into a holding-tank.

Weir skimmers have a much greater capacity but also pick up water with the oil. Oil adheres to belt skimmers, which transfer it to a barge in a continuous motion like that of a conveyor belt. The water and oil are then separated for disposal. **Weir skimmers** use gravity to allow oil floating on water to drop into the collecting-system for transfer to holding-tanks.

Weir booms contain oil. Gravity makes the oil fall into a hole in the boom, where it is pushed out for disposal.

Suction skimmers or **vacuum units** suck water and oil off the surface. The oil is then separated and dispersed.

- Skimmers can also provide storage places for collected oil. The oil is herded to a collection point along a containment boom located close to shore but in water deep enough for the skimmer to operate.
- Skimmers are powered by gas, diesel, hydraulic or electric engines.

- Skimmers with brushes pick up heavy oil.
- Skimmers operate best in waves of less than one and a half feet.
- Each skimmer can capture up to 200 barrels per hour.
- Skimmers generally provide a higher recovery rate than sorbents, when enough oil is present to make it practical and worthwhile to operate them.

It won't take long for you and a few colleagues to brainstorm the issues you'll need to speak about in a crisis—health, safety, the environment, compliance, equipment, training and so on. Now that you have an understanding of how to structure your messages, let's look at the groups you will be interacting with.

Communication Matrix

The Communication Matrix that follows is one method of listing activities through which companies can interact with stakeholders. It also enables you to measure and quantify the desired result, budgets and responsibilities.

This is a generic draft to provoke your thoughts on the topic long before an event happens. For example, it may serve your best interests to keep open the lines of communication with the chair of a legislative or regulatory committee even if there is no current issue to warrant contact. Regular phone calls displaying openness and willingness to exchange information enhance relationships. You could do this when a minor issue arises, so that during times of controversy and crisis, the chair or his/her members have previously interacted with your organization.

> *"Seriously consider reporting your own bad news. While the pros and legal requirements must be weighed in each situation, it's rare that withholding information pays off in a crisis situation."*
>
> *— A. Stanton (1989)*

Government lists should be updated twice a year, as should a list of other officials with whom you come into contact (see "Public Affairs Room" in Chapter 3 above).

Hold meetings with newspaper editorial boards (see illustration below). It is dangerous and unacceptable to have editorial writers helping to shape community opinions about your organization if they have never met you or been briefed by you.

Communication Matrix

PERSON/GROUP	ACTIVITY	DESIRED RESULT	FREQUENCY	COST	RESPONSIBILITY
Senior elected officials	example: Sending out news letters	Public Support	Monthly	$1,500	Joe staff writer
Selected cabinet members					
Mayors					
Selected other city officials					
Selected elected officials					
Business					
Citizens groups					
Editorial boards					
Reporters/editors/interviewers					
Selected media managers					
Selected educators					
Selected other officials					
Other boards					
Industry associations					
Councilor					
Councilor					
Councilor					
Councilor					
Councilor					
Fire Chief					
Other Fire Chief					
Police Chief					
Other Police Chief					
Other Officials					

DVD

Customize on the Companion DVD

It is equally dangerous and unacceptable to be interviewed by a journalist if he or she is encountering you, your issues or your organization for the first time. You can't know and meet everyone, of course, but a system of regular contact with reporters, editors and interviewers is a good start. This interaction may be as simple as sending them a background briefing-paper, a public-service announcement, a pamphlet or another document twice a year. Be wary of relying on emails—they are too easy to delete. Augment them with old fashioned compliments cards, handwritten notes on executive stationery, formal letters and phone calls.

Once you decide that you should interact with the media and others, implementing this communications matrix will be an ongoing task. You should regularly add new people or groups to the matrix, since media, government and community contacts are highly mobile.

Communicating about Crises

Discussion Points:

1. Who are our stakeholders?
2. Who will fill in the Communication Matrix?
3. What questions will stakeholders have about the risks we pose?
4. What other crises can we learn from?
5. What can we learn from other organizations with similar activities or in similar climates, geography, political climates, clientele and so on?
6. What can we learn from other local or other organizations, even if they have different functions?
7. Who will research and write SOCKOs™?
8. Are our spokespeople well trained to deal with difficult media and stakeholder interaction?
9. Who will manage annual testing of SOCKOs™ and spokespeople?
10. What outsiders can we involve in our testing and drills?

Public Affairs

How the Public Affairs Room (see Chapter 3, "Resource Rooms") is set up and run can make a big difference to how stakeholders view your organization. All Public Affairs activities can affect whether inquiries are held and charges laid.

Public Affairs Personnel Shifts

TIPS

Beginning Shift

- ✓ Check all status boards for new information.
- ✓ Locate the person you are relieving and obtain note or briefing.
- ✓ Read into three ring binder and ask questions as needed.
- ✓ Identify deadlines or goals during your shift.
- ✓ Familiarize yourself with issue and media analysis.
- ✓ View, listen and read media reports.

End of Shift

- ✓ Leave "to do" or "heads up" list for incoming shift. Five minute briefs with morning shift.
- ✓ Ensure that three ring binder is up to date.
- ✓ Clean desk.
- ✓ Ensure contents of wastebasket are shredded.
- ✓ Check all status boards to ensure they are up to date with your data.
- ✓ Remove personal belongings.
- ✓ Log out with senior person.
- ✓ Leave premises as soon as possible.
- ✓ Do not reveal information while socializing off-site.
- ✓ View, listen and read media reports.
- ✓ Do not leave draft versions of material anywhere other than in shredder.

DVD

Available on the Companion DVD

Public Inquiry Action Sheet

YOUR NAME	LOCATION (EMERGENCY SITE, HEADQUARTERS, CRISIS CONTROL ROOM, TOUR LOCATION, ETC.)

DATE	TIME	SUBJECT OF INQUIRY	ORIGIN: NAME, ORGANIZATION ADDRESS, TELEPHONE, FAX	ACTION TAKEN

DVD

Customize on the Companion DVD

Public Affairs

Discussion Points:

1. What stakeholders need to be informed when a crisis occurs?
2. In what order of priority should stakeholders be informed?
3. Who in the organization should interact with which stakeholders?
4. Which stakeholders should be contacted by phone, email or letter, and which should be contacted in person?
5. Can all required assets be procured quickly?
6. Who checks stockpiles of assets regularly?
7. Who is likely to want to visit should a crisis arise?
8. What outside consultants will help Public Affairs?
9. Are there retired employees or others who can help in a crisis?
10. Do we have on- and off-site locations for Public Affairs rooms as well as portable equipment?

But I don't Know Anything

My wife, the national newscaster, interrupted my shower one morning with the following information:

"Some developer has lent somebody at city hall a lot of money, and it's on the news."

Since I was executive assistant to the world's longest-serving mayor, this was not idle conversation. I shouted back, "Which developer? Who got the loan? How much money?"

"I didn't catch any details," my wife said. National newscasters don't catch any more details in newscasts than anybody else who's busy getting dressed in the morning. I rinsed off and drove to work.

In the car I heard the details. A prominent developer had given a $250,000 no-interest loan to the commissioner of planning and development. When I arrived, twenty-five reporters were camped outside my office. I made it through the gauntlet and began getting a hold of the situation.

My phone rang. "Ian Harvey calling," said the familiar voice of the tabloid reporter.

"What can you tell me?" Ian asked.

"Ian," I responded, "I don't want to be quoted in any story you might do on this topic."

"That's OK," Ian responded. "But what do you know?"

"Ian," I went on, "I don't want to be quoted euphemistically as someone close to the mayor's office."

"OK," Ian said expectantly. "But what do you know?"

"Ian," I pressed on, "I don't even want to be quoted as someone who doesn't know anything about this."

"No problem," said Ian, no doubt with his pen at the ready. "But what do you know?"

"Ian," I said, "I don't know anything."

I was not quoted.

CHAPTER 5: MEDIA RELATIONS

Event: *The Space Shuttle Challenger Explosion, 19,000 feet up, Cape Canaveral, Florida*

Date: *28 January 1986*

Summary: *The problem with the flight became evident at seventy seconds after lift-off, right after the 'throttle-up' exchange between mission control in Houston and Commander Richard Scobee. NASA scheduled press briefings and then postponed them. One official said it had been a good weather day (despite the icicles seen on the spacecraft before launch), and NASA also said the crew had died instantly, when some days later it was evident some had lived partway down the freefall to the ocean. NASA impounded pictures shot by the media, creating a First Amendment fight.*

Result: *All seven crew died.*

Lessons Learned: *Some studies showed that the O-ring that served as a seal in the solid rocket boosters had been scorched up to four times before on previous flights. Some blamed the pressure to launch because media and families were all present. This has come to be known by some as "the* Challenger *phenomenon," in which if you had cancelled the launch, you'd never know for sure that you had prevented a disaster. Some also blame the fact that NASA lost its momentum and mission after the moon shots and should not have been in near space with shuttle technology. Avoid optimistic reports that have no basis in fact or science. In managing the media, be consistent and careful.*

Media Relations

The Media Kit

A good kit helps provide a solid foundation for relations with reporters. This is where you get to tell your story – the background, salient points and supporting facts – without being interrupted. You get to present yourself the way you want.

It's unlikely that this material will ever be used in its entirety. But it can be a useful resource for reporters when they are battling deadlines or looking for interesting snippets of information to flesh out stories.

Your kit should contain:

- A history of your organization
- A chronology of significant dates
- Photographs of significant features (e.g. head office, main plant, product or activity)
- Biographies and photographs of the principals
- Fact sheet(s) listing the organization's statistics—employees, number and weight of widgets produced annually, number of countries importing widgets, etc.
- Workforce statistics
- Selected clippings from media reports
- Feature stories or op-ed pieces you've written
- Video disc with relevant clips
- Audio disc with relevant clips

This kit can then be augmented with more specific information and background to meet different needs. Sound and video material will help meet the needs of broadcast journalists.

However, resist the temptation to stuff the kit full of any and all publicity material that you've generated in the past. Reporters trying to meet a deadline don't have time to read the speech the CEO gave to the board of trade last fall. If time is an important factor for reporters receiving the kit, make sure the material it contains is relevant.

These kits can be handed out at news conferences, briefings and one-on-one interviews or sent directly to news organizations and their reporters who are unable to be present at your media event. You may not need to send the material anywhere. Just direct the reporters to your organization's website, which should already contain much of the material outlined above.

Some organizations think they can remain more or less silent during a crisis and wait it out. This is not advisable, since it merely creates an information vacuum which something or someone will fill. An organization should be prepared to be the most accurate and reliable source of information during its own crisis. Spokespeople must be available, and the organization must be seen to be cooperative and active. Whether you deploy all your resources and how quickly you communicate is another matter. But it's important to be ready to do so.

The news media's major strength is that they disseminate information extremely rapidly. On the other hand, they are notoriously ineffective at separating fact from perception or weeding out inaccuracies. This is why organizations need to be able to communicate actively during a crisis.

Such communication normally begins with admitting that there is a problem and explaining what you are doing to make it right. Be prepared to apologize if necessary, but get legal advice first. Remember, there's a difference between saying you're sorry something happened and you're sorry you caused it to happen. You should view every contact with the stakeholders and the media as an opportunity to enhance trust and rapport.

During a crisis the news media will ask for, consume, collate and disseminate more information at a higher rate of speed and more widely than crisis managers anticipate. Your company must be able to feed this insatiable appetite. Your attitude should be that the media, and the public they serve, have proper reasons for asking about the status of the incident. It will be important to use charts, graphs, status boards, corkboards or other tools in news-conference rooms to keep reporters up to date on as many facts as possible. To help anticipate the questions you'll be asked, or to coach spokespeople, use the traditional six journalistic questions (who, when, what, where, why and how) and sample the question categories that follow in the Journalistic Questions Matrix (see "Managing Media" below in this chapter).

Some of these questions may present legal predicaments. No one in your organization should speculate about the exact cause of the incident unless it is completely obvious—as with an explosion, fire or destruction of a plant. There's no point in being coy about something that everyone can easily find out. Only senior management should address issues of liability and responsibility—and then very carefully. No one may know who is actually liable for months. Avoid over-optimistic statements.

"In a large-scale crisis, it is hard to underestimate the significance of the mass media for the course and outcome of the event, as well as the formation of post-event perceptions. … [I]f the press are not properly provided with information, they will go out looking for it themselves, and in a large-scale crisis situation there are always plenty of people ready to talk about the whole spectrum of events from a wide variety of angles and personal views."

—Uri Rosenthal (1994)

Pre-written SOCKOs™ will buy you some time while you prepare new SOCKOs™ to deal with the new or developing situation. SOCKOs™ will make it easier for you to write and issue written or oral statements to the news media and handle news conferences or public meetings where you may be exposed to tough and even hostile questions. You'll need plenty of pre-authorized information as raw material.

A pre-prepared statement can be made available offering compensation to affected parties for their out-of-pocket expenses without prejudicing your company's legal position. If people need to stay in hotels, take cabs, replace personal items and so on, there's little point in insulting and annoying them by delay or officious administration. You need to set limits, because it is human nature to take advantage, but your company should remember it's trying to take actions that fix the crisis, not further annoy victims. The phrase I often use is, "Cheques will be written." What harm can it do if you write some of them before you are required to by law, or even if some are be a little bigger than what you'd have to write if you dragged your heels? Delay in helping victims will make a negative news story, further harming your reputation.

No purpose will be served during a crisis by questioning or lamenting why the media require as much information as they do as quickly as they do, nor by wondering why reporters are attracted to negative information. These are human traits, not just journalistic traits.

Request immediate media monitoring from a supplier that provides this service locally and nationally. Electronic coverage, including statements by politicians and others, should be monitored and analyzed to allow for proper response. This monitoring should also look at all sources of information, including telephone calls from customers and the public, suppliers and bankers.

Recordable DVDs, radios, and TV sets are very cheap these days. I'd want relevant news stories recorded right away, not the next day or even the next hour. Media-monitoring companies can miss some items or might not be sure exactly how long some programs will last and so are not set to record the whole broadcast. I recommend having your own capability.

Media Liaison Plan

You'll need wide and general public understanding in a crisis. So, you'll need the news media to transmit information to the public. It will be your responsibility to be understood, not the public's or the news-writer's responsibility to understand.

The news media have been as hard hit by bad economic times as any industry. So, you may find fewer and fewer reporters in the average news organization. You may find no one is working weekends or nights any more. Technology and cross-ownership may mean that the reporter you do encounter may be working for several media outlets at once. Use this as an opportunity to reach more people through one journalist.

When your organization is grappling with a crisis, it is vital to get your side of the story out. It is not enough to send one press release to every newsroom in the community and assume that every reporter is aware of it. It is a mistake to assume that a press release sent to a wire service will be passed on to newspapers and electronic members of that network. If one editor doesn't think the press release is newsworthy, it won't get on the wire. But if a member media outlet also receives that press release independently, a local editor may well find it newsworthy.

If you send a press release to "The Editor" at a newspaper or a radio station, that's no guarantee it will be passed on to program hosts, interviewers, columnists, talk-show hosts, morning-show producers and others.

The most effective thing for your organization to do is to take responsibility for communicating with a wide range of journalists in the community. Build relationships with various media contacts before an event or crisis occurs. The Media Liaison Plan sets out one way to do this.

This draft offers some examples of how to communicate systematically with a variety of people in the print and electronic media. You may want to plan one event or interaction with reporters per month, for example.

Augment media lists with your own information about journalists in your markets and the websites of media outlets.

Media Liaison Plan

MONTH	ACTIVITY	ISSUE	TARGET/ AUDIENCE	DESIRED RESULT	COST	RESPONSIBILITY
January	example: Annual Report	Statutory responsibility	Business journalists	Positive public relations	$ 5, 000	Finance Department/Board of Directors
February	example: Speech by Chairman	Environmental sustainability	Local agriculture association	Decrease in rumours of environmental hazards	Free	R & D with public affairs
March	example: Charitable giving	Unemployed workers	Union and general public	Showing community responsibility	$100,000	Finance and Public Affairs
April						
May						
June						
July						
August						
September						
October						
November						DVD
December						Customize on the Companion DVD

Writing for the Media

Press releases are an effective way to deal quickly with a large number of reporters spread over a wide territory. They do not take the place of one-on-ones, availabilities, tours or other means of communication but rather supplement these.

Managers should be prepared for the possibility of both evacuations and having to stay at their offices and plants round the clock for a few days. Evacuation notices and news releases should be edited to suit local needs. You may need the media to announce to workers' families that they're staying in the plant and not coming home or that the workforce should not come in for the next shift because the plant is shut down. In a crisis, accurate releases or public service announcements (PSAs) should be issued as quickly as possible. Pre-written releases are a good start and can be modified when the time comes.

One helpful tool that spokespeople can use in advance of sending out a news release or statement is the matrix that follows entitled "Issue Analysis." News-release writers should follow much the same techniques as journalists use before writing news stories. You can gather facts using the traditional five journalistic questions (see "The Media Kit" above and also the Journalistic Questions Matrix in "Managing Media" below in this chapter). The matrix provides a way to filter the five questions through newsworthiness criteria such as timeliness, proximity or the number of people affected.

In a crisis, SOCKOs™ (see "Communicating during a Crisis" in Chapter 4 above) will also help you write and issue effective written statements to the news media.

Before beginning, ask:

- Who will benefit?
- What is being done?
- What is new?
- When will results show?
- Where will the greatest impact be?
- Why is this being done?

These facts and many others should then be filtered through a matrix of standard criteria for newsworthiness such as:

- timeliness
- proximity
- number of people affected
- lasting importance
- historical significance
- geographical dispersal

The "Tests" column can trigger some interesting games for issue-managers. What would be the counter-spin? Politicians, especially during elections, get outraged over government waste. The opposite would be bragging about government waste—and that just doesn't happen. So, a story about political outrage over waste is expected and not really newsworthy unless the waste is huge or the money was spent on unusual items.

Was enough empathy expressed, or were too many negatives used? Does this story piggyback on previous similar stories or industry events? What prism will people use to view this event? If it's a plane crash, perhaps it's human error, weather, technical failure, commercial considerations or skimping on maintenance to save money. What past events will be brought up to put this event in its historical context? Taking account of these and other factors will help a crisis manager or communicator write a great news release and stay on top of whatever reactions may follow.

Issue Analysis

	TIMELINESS	PROXIMITY	NO. OF PEOPLE EFFECTED	LASTING IMPORTANCE	TESTS
"WHO will benefit?"					Opposites
"WHAT is being done?"					Empathy
"WHEN will this happen?"					Negatives
"WHERE is the most impact?"					Piggyback
"WHY now?"					Prisms
"HOW will it work?"					History

DVD

Customize on the Companion DVD

Leads

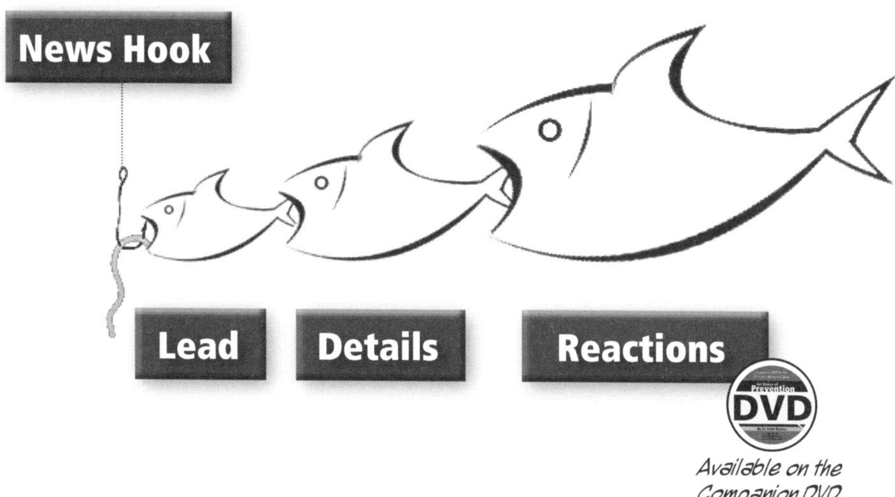

Once you have gathered all the information, you have to start writing. One of the most important writing-decisions is how to get into the story or how to write the lead. There are many ways to begin a press release. Unconventional beginnings include using a question, a quotation or humour. These, however, are normally not appropriate for crisis situations but rather for the launch of products or tours by entertainers. For crisis situations more serious types of leads will be appropriate:

1. An 'umbrella' lead is an all-encompassing overview of a situation. EXAMPLE: Consumers in thirteen states are worried about potato prices.
2. A 'rifle' lead focuses on one small emblematic aspect of a situation. EXAMPLE: Nobody likes French fries more than 12-year-old Amy Bloggins.
3. An 'historical' lead would begin with past events and lead up to the present.
   EXAMPLE: Ever since scientists developed a hearty strain of potatoes, French fries have been popular here.
4. A 'geographical' lead would describe the effect on a large territory or several political jurisdictions.
   EXAMPLE: The whole eastern seaboard is concerned about potato blight.

The type of lead chosen will dictate the tone and method for the rest of the release. For example, an historical lead should begin a press release that continues to set out facts in chronological order. Whichever method you use, some general rules always apply:

- One thought per sentence
- Present tense
- Active voice ("We fixed the problem," not "The problem was fixed by us")
- Use word pictures
- Short sentences (fewer than 18 words)
- Tell a story simply and clearly

Hooks

News hooks are a journalist's reasons for doing a story today and in this way. Unusual features, human interest and striking photographs are special cases where the story itself may be the hook. Generally, though, a news release must carry a reason for the news outlet to use it. Obvious hooks include the national implications of local stories, local angles to international stories, notable developments in continuing stories and the organization's reaction to continuing stories. The news release should be written so that an editor will not put it away for review or possible use another day or another week. It should carry compelling reasons for immediate use.

Tips for Press Release Format

TIPS

- ✓ Leave generous margins all around.
- ✓ Use your organization's stationery.
- ✓ Remove mundane, procedural data and get quickly into the headline and body.
- ✓ Type "for immediate release" or "not for release before 2 p.m." and the date in the upper right hand corner.
- ✓ Use a short, grabby headline typed in capitals.
- ✓ Write in a conversational, journalistic style (use a style book).
- ✓ Avoid boring details—start with a quote, list dates, places and other details further down.
- ✓ Double or triple space.
- ✓ Tell the complete story, even if it takes two or three pages.
- ✓ End with the traditional marks, -30- , which signify the end of a story.
- ✓ Name a contact person and provide a phone number at the end.
- ✓ Attach something, prepare a kit.
- ✓ Edit your kit—don't waste journalists' time.
- ✓ Re-read to see if you have "buried the lead" part way through—the most common error.

DVD

Available on the Companion DVD

Sample Press Release **Date:**

For immediate release

(In the case of a fire, explosion, or spill with no loss of life:)

A (serious) fire/explosion/spill has occurred at the (name of organization) plant in (location).

So far there are no confirmed injuries, and the company has a team of expert fire-fighters on the scene.

The fire/explosion/spill started at about (time) in (location); the cause is so far unknown. (Number) fire-fighters and (number) emergency responders immediately began to put out (deal with) the fire/the consequences/the spill.

Environment officials, local residents and other appropriate groups are being notified.

(Organization) spokesperson (name) says (organization) will do everything it can to protect the environment and lessen the impact on local residents.

Tomorrow morning, (person) of (organization) will begin meeting with governments, local residents and officials to help ensure this incident is handled in the most efficient way possible. (A spokesperson will be available at (location) at 6:00 am).

(Name of organization), a division of (name of parent organization) of (city, province/state), is a supplier of (list the products, services) to the (name type of organization). (Organization) employs (number) persons at its (number) locations.

For more information contact: (name of Public Affairs contact)
Phone: (number)

-30 –

Customize on the Companion DVD

Sample Press Release **Date:**

For immediate release

(In the case of fire, explosion or spill with loss of life:)

(Name of organization) has now confirmed that (number) person(s) were (was) killed as a result of a serious fire/explosion that occurred at its (product) plant located in (city, province/state). Names will not be released until families have been notified. President and C.E.O. (or other title) (name) has expressed his/her deepest regret and sympathy to the family(ies) and friends of those affected.

The fire/explosion started/occurred about (time) in (location) ; the exact cause is so far unknown. (number) fire-fighters and (number) emergency responders immediately began to extinguish the fire (deal with the consequences/spill).

Environment officials, local residents and other appropriate groups are being notified.

(organization) spokesperson (name) says the (organization) will do everything it can to protect the environment and lessen the impact.

Tomorrow morning (person, organization) will begin meeting with governments, local residents and officials to help ensure this incident is handled in the most efficient way possible. (A company spokesperson will be available at (location) at 6:00 am.)

(Name of organization) , a division of ____________ Corporation of (city), (province/state) is a supplier of (list the products) to the (name type of industry). (organization) employs (number) persons at its (number) locations.

For more information contact: (Name of Public Affairs contact)
Phone: (Number)

-30-

DVD

Customize on the Companion DVD

General Evacuation and Hazardous Material Release Notification

For Radio, Television, P.S.A. and Phone Message Machines

(Sample)

This is (spokesperson's name) at the (organization or division name).

A (large/small) ____ amount of (name of chemical), a highly hazardous substance, has been (spilled/released) at (location). Authorities are asking all residents within (number) kilometres/miles/blocks of the location to evacuate. If you are within the (give evacuation zone boundaries), you and your family must/should leave (now/as soon as possible). Go at once to the home of a friend or relative outside the evacuation zone or to (indicate shelter). If you can drive a neighbour who has no transport, please do so. If you need transport, call (telephone number). Children attending the following schools: (list schools) ____

____

will be evacuated to (list locations and addresses) ______________

____

Do not drive to your child's school. Pick up your child from the school authorities at the evacuation centre.

For more information, call this number: (telephone number).

For instructions listen to this radio station (station name and call number) and television station (station name and call number).

The material is highly toxic to humans and can cause the following symptoms: (list the symptoms). ______________________

If you are experiencing any of these symptoms, seek help at a hospital outside the evacuation zone or at the evacuation centre (give address).

To repeat, if you are within the area of (give evacuation zone boundaries), you must/should leave for your own safety. Please do not use your telephone unless you need emergency assistance.

-30-

DVD

Customize on the Companion DVD

Speaking with the Media

When a Reporter Calls . . .

You need an organizational protocol for dealing with reporters. You certainly need to keep track of who called, what they asked and what you said (see "Record of Contact Made by Media" later in this section). Reporters can be a distant-early-warning system to alert you to what they've found out from their sources. You might not have as many contacts in government and response organizations as they do, and you just may gain valuable information.

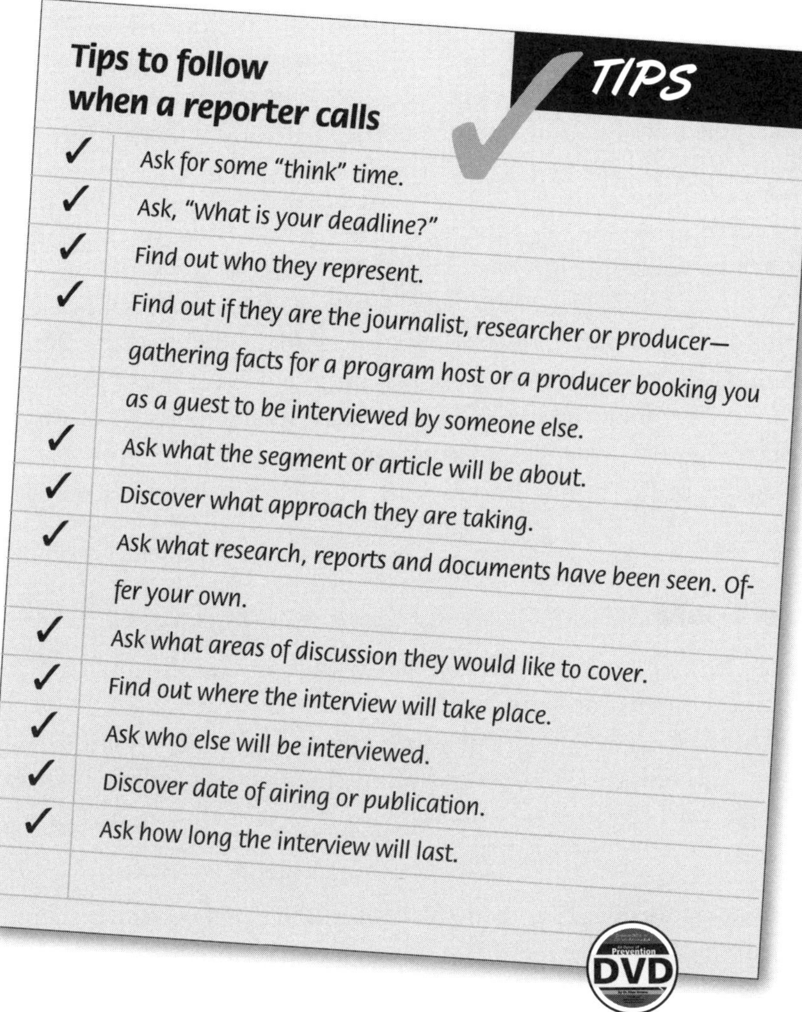

Reporters may not know the answers to all these questions. An editor may have assigned the reporter to speak with you, and he or she may not know all the other ways that media outlet is covering the story. But if you don't ask, you certainly won't find out anything of interest.

Consider the outcomes of not cooperating.

For contentious stories, record the call with the reporter. Depending on your organization's policy, tell the reporter you are doing so in a non-combative way. Explain that you're making the recording so you can review it and tell your boss exactly what you said.

When the interview is over, you'll breathe a sigh of relief and want to get back to managing your crisis. Don't. Take a moment to analyze how you did. Did the reporter persist in certain questions or with a particular story line? Write a note for your organization's chief communicator, so others will know what this particular reporter found interesting.

Better yet, keep communicating with the reporter. After you've taken stock, send a courtesy email thanking the reporter (if appropriate) and confirming what you had to say. Do this in a nice way, but put the reporter on notice that you know what was said and will be expecting accurate coverage. You can also use this note to correct misimpressions. You can write something like, "What I meant by the phrase '….' was the following: '….'" You should not change your story, but you have a great chance of shortening it, removing a quote or making it a little less controversial.

Media Contacts

You need to keep records of all contacts with reporters. Record data gathered at local bureaus and site locations (hotel, rental office, etc.) as well as head office (network, regional, local). There's not much point in only knowing the New York address and phone number of a radio network when their local reporter is hounding you at the site of your crisis in California.

The following forms will provide places for notes on both the questions asked and the answers given. Even in non-crisis times, media interest in a topic should still be tracked and categorized by season of the year, type of media outlet (radio, TV, print) and other criteria.

How to Be a Good News Source

TIPS

- ✓ Help build the story.
- ✓ Prepare, rehearse out loud, with a buddy at least three times.
- ✓ Be convincing, not combative.
- ✓ Have the audience think well of you.
- ✓ Grab the good words, good concepts and moral high ground for yourself.
- ✓ Never forget you're talking to a journalist—it's not a conversation.
- ✓ Stay cool and firm.
- ✓ Show caring, knowledge and action.
- ✓ Don't make the journalist work too hard for the story.

DVD

Available on the Companion DVD

Another useful purpose the forms serve is to guide staff who are not designated spokespeople but may speak to reporters in chance encounters over the phone. Your organization should have a written policy on dealing with the press and circulate it widely among staff. Potential spokespeople can be asked to distinguish between information about the company that is factual and readily available and information that breaks new ground or announces new policy or about which there may be controversy. There is little risk in giving out the first type of information but plenty in giving out the second.

Radio

REPORTER	STATION DIAL AM/FM	ADDRESS	CONTACT INFO	NEWS DIRECTOR	NEWS BROADCAST TIMES	STATION FORMAT / COVERAGE AREA	INTERNET PRESENCE	SOCIAL NETWORKING SITES	NOTES
		Street: City: Prov/State: Postal/Zip:	Email: Tel: Fax:						

DVD

Customize on the Companion DVD

Print

REPORTER	PAPER/ MAGAZINE	ADDRESS	CONTACT INFO	EDITOR	DEADLINES	CIRCULATION / COVERAGE AREA	INTERNET PRESENCE	SOCIAL NETWORKING SITES	NOTES
		Street: City: Prov/State: Postal/Zip:	Email: Tel: Fax:						

DVD

Customize on the Companion DVD

Television

REPORTER	STATION CHANNEL (CALL LETTERS)	ADDRESS	CONTACT INFO	NEWS DIRECTOR	NEWS BROADCAST TIMES	STATION FORMAT	INTERNET PRESENCE	SOCIAL NETWORKING SITES	NOTES
		Street: City: Prov/State: Postal/Zip:	Email: Tel: Fax:			Live Coverage Capability: Yes No Coverage Area:			

Customize on the Companion DVD

New Media

REPORTER	TYPE OF MEDIA	NAME OF OUTLET	ADDRESS	CONTACT INFO	EDITOR	FORMAT	INTERNET PRESENCE	SOCIAL NETWORKING SITES	NOTES
			Street: City: Prov/State: Postal/Zip:	Email: Tel: Fax:					

Customize on the Companion DVD

Media Relations

Discussion Points:

1. What is our historical relationship with the news media?
2. What is our current relationship with the news media?
3. Are there potential events we can write a generic press release for?
4. What work do we need to do to create or further cultivate relationships with media?
5. Who will make media kits?
6. What can we write PSAs about in non-crisis times?
7. Have all spokespeople recently visited radio and TV stations and newspapers?
8. Have all spokespeople recently read relevant blogs and websites?
9. Have all spokespeople recently watched news programs from the major networks and local stations for their own professional development?
10. Have all spokespeople recently listened to radio programs from the major networks and local stations for their own professional development?

Managing Media

Organizations are so close to their own operations that they often fail to see how newsworthy and interesting their daily activities are to an outside audience. This will be especially true in a crisis when you have the undivided attention (albeit unwanted) of the media. Besides the SOCKOs™ described above in Chapter 4 in "Communicating during a Crisis," you may need more technical information. How do you do what you do? How do you make what you make? Where does the raw material come from? How do you ship your finished goods? How do you put out a fire or investigate an incident? All this will make a great story and could put you in a good light. At the very least you will take up some of the space that might otherwise be given over to your critics or negative speculation about you.

General Media Management Checklist

ACTIVITY	RESPONSIBILITY	COMPLETED
Contact Public Affairs department for assistance on media and community liaison.		
Acquire up to date lists of government departments and contacts as well as media lists and augment them.		
Meet counterparts in industry and governments so you can refer reporters to friendly sources.		
Plan and execute regular media and other stakeholder interactions.		
Hold open houses.		
Train key spokespeople and support staff.		

Customize on the Companion DVD

Open House

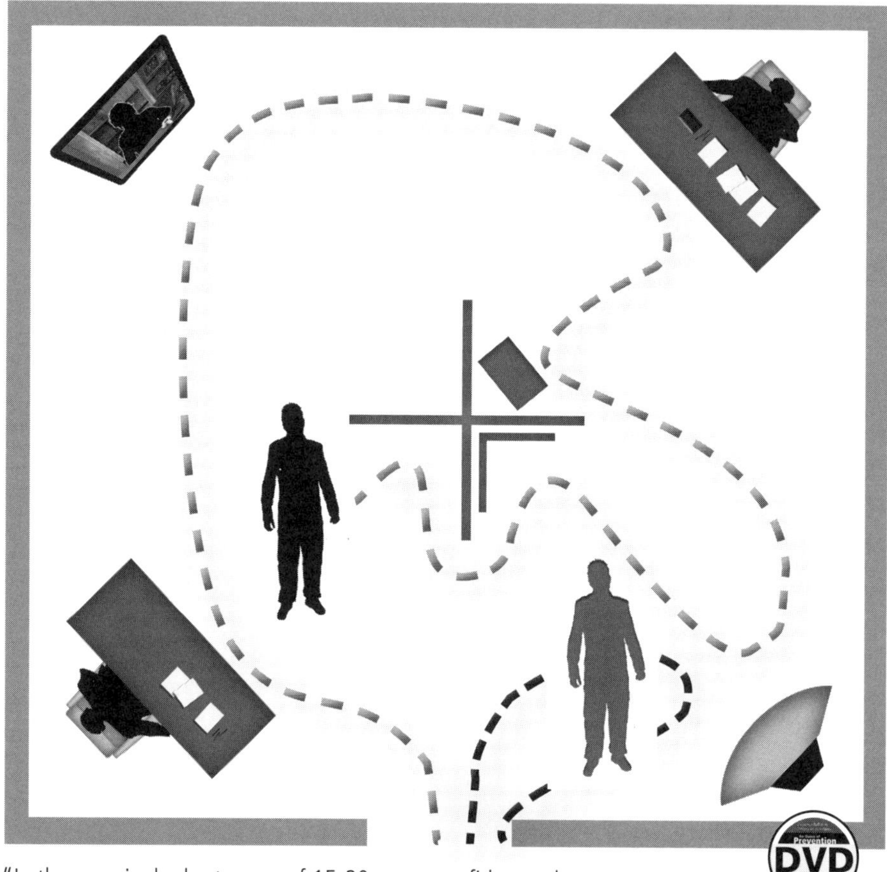

Available on the Companion DVD

"In the amazingly short space of 15-20 years, confidence about the physical world has turned to doubt." (**Douglas, M. and Wildavsky, A.,** 1982)

Officials/Technical Experts/Spokespeople

In a prolonged crisis, an organization cannot have just one spokesperson. Responders have to eat, sleep and be briefed, and some may even get sick during a crisis. Having only one spokesperson is dangerous. So several people need to speak for the organization and should all transmit the same supportive message or messages. A system of overlapping shifts for both spokespeople and staff at the Media Briefing Centre should allow for rotating spokespeople to be briefed by their predecessors (see "Public Affairs Room" in Chapter 3 above).

The on-site crisis manager needs special skills. S/he may not necessarily be the most senior person in the company. Spokespeople require equally special skills and may be drawn from a variety of job descriptions. The ability to collate and analyze large amounts of data quickly is a primary skill. Fast thinking, an ability to deal with pressure, an ability to embody corporate culture convincingly and superior presentation skills are required.

The news media will respect and return to a source that is honest, knows and honours deadlines and provides useful information. Most crises begin by being local and are covered by general reporters. An effective news source helps reporters distinguish what is known from what is not known and continually tries to raise their knowledge to the appropriate level.

Good information, delivered in a timely way by technical experts, can help defuse a crisis. Technical experts have specific challenges in translating complex information into the usable sound bites that reporters need and the public will understand. Some spokespeople have professional codes of conduct they must follow, as in law, accounting, engineering and other fields. Regardless, it is possible and imperative for spokespeople to communicate in ways that meet the needs of both the media and their organizations.

Normally technical experts are not general spokespeople for an organization. Being an expert is both a strength and a weakness. Experts can rightly tell reporters that they are only able to provide information on their particular fields and cannot give the general response or broad information about the organization, but they can easily find themselves drawn into a broader discussion. Loyal employees may want to defend their organization, while their own excellent technical knowledge may lead experts to believe they know more about the organization than they actually do. All spokespeople need to be cautious.

TIPS

Dos and Don'ts Before and During a Press Conference

DO

- ✓ Practise statements out loud.
- ✓ Field rehearsal questions from Public Affairs or other colleagues.
- ✓ List three or four simple messages or themes to which you wish to return regardless of the questions asked (SOCKOs™).
- ✓ Use quiet room for 10 minutes before and after conference.
- ✓ If you're not the right person to field a question, say so and refer the reporter to others in the organization.
- ✓ Keep your answers short and to the point.
- ✓ Be professional.

DON'T

- ✓ Don't try to run the news conference—defer to the moderator.
- ✓ Don't argue with reporters.
- ✓ Don't stray from your areas of expertise! If you don't know, say so. Offer to find out and get back to the reporter as soon as possible. Then be sure you do!
- ✓ Don't say it if you don't want to read about it in the paper.

DVD

Customize on the Companion DVD

Reporters arrive on the scene of an event to find a mess—fire, explosion, spill, bankruptcy. They ask the questions "who, what, when, where, why and how." But in a breaking story, the available spokespeople usually don't know the answers to all these questions. Imagine you're the spokesperson for a factory that has just blown up. You are unlikely to know whether the explosion was caused by bomb or an accident. If it was bomb, you wouldn't know what kind. If you did know some of these details, the police and other agencies might not want you to release this information. If there were deaths, you wouldn't know the cause. With injuries, you couldn't speculate on recovery. You also wouldn't want to speculate on insurance or when you'd be up and running again.

Naturally no one could know the answers to most of these questions in the first few minutes or even hours of an event. But that doesn't mean reporters won't need to file stories. They will turn to other news sources—eyewitnesses, professors who study related issues, employees, former employees or anyone who can speak with some authority. Reporters will also resort to writing sidebar or feature stories. These will focus on the history of the problem, the last time this happened, the physics of the matter and so on. Who better to provide this kind of technical information than your experts?

Reporter Pools

One of the first things a group of reporters will ask for when covering an event will be a visit to the site, conference room, ceremony or other newsworthy venue. Within reason, you should agree to these requests. In fact, it is beneficial to be able to offer the press tours of such venues before they ask you to. Reporters will do everything in their power to gain access to your crisis site, so why not try to influence and control their access? Information opportunities should be regularly scheduled and publicized.

Reporter pools are a vital tool at hard-to-access sites. A pool is a small group of reporters who visit a site on behalf of their colleagues who are too numerous to attend. This system provides many advantages to those managing a crisis. Security is easier, there's less misinformation and less competition among the journalists, and you get to demonstrate that you are managing the event professionally.

The reporters present need to select a small group to visit the venue(s) in question. This group may comprise a newspaper reporter, a wire-service reporter, radio and television reporters, a social-media reporter, a camera crew, a still photographer and reporters from other linguistic groups. It should also include foreign journalists if they are present. The choice will emerge from a negotiation among the journalists and your public-affairs person.

Pools present security and legal challenges. You need to provide accreditation checks and safety briefings, notify news management not on site, and ensure that all pool members sign indemnification agreements and use safety equipment (glasses, shoes and hard hats) as warranted.

You will see from the following diagram, "A Reporter's Building-Blocks," voice-overs and visuals are an integral part of any news story. If your

A Reporter's Building Blocks

Time: 1:40

Available on the Companion DVD

organization refuses to allow access to the newsworthy visuals, however disturbing or negative, reporters will simply expand their own commentary at the beginning and end or the time they allot to third-party experts and/or angry public reaction. The only result will be to present the newsmaker with a much tougher challenge after the story has run.

Pools and photo opportunities may also become briefings or quasi-news conferences. You can adapt the relevant sections and checklists in this book to suit field conditions.

Organizing and Managing a News Conference during a Crisis

A news conference is not a preferred method of dealing with reporters, but it is the right tool when there are too many requests and too short a time to schedule individual interviews. Most reporters prefer one-on-one interviews but will take clips from a news conference if that's all that's available.

By definition this event involves added pressure, friction and a unique group dynamic. There is more of a chance that reporters will be probing, challenging and competitive.

Effectively managing a news conference involves four steps:

1) Planning
2) Preparing
3) Managing
4) Mingling (follow-up)

Planning

You can do much of the planning long before a crisis hits. Completing the following tables and allowing a few minutes for thought and rehearsal can start you off on the right foot.

Timing is vital for success. A news conference held just after a newspaper's daily deadline is of little use to that paper. Ten minutes past the deadline is almost as bad as 23 hours past. So your crisis-planning documents must include the deadlines of the media you will be interacting with.

You also need to allow enough time between the end of the news conference and the reporters' deadlines to allow for writing, editing, production (TV) and so on. Remote locations dictate longer time for such activities.

Increasingly all media, especially social media, can file stories immediately, but even traditional radio, TV and print are working to ever shorter deadlines, and you may find yourself reacting to a story filed during your news conference before that news conference is over.

Historically television required the greatest lead time before broadcast, followed by print media, then radio. Typically PR people planned to end their news conferences before 4:30 p.m. to allow for cumbersome editing back in the TV station. But with cable news and wire services having deadlines all day long and portable satellite equipment, your event is likely to be broadcast live somewhere. Multiple and continuous deadlines mean you need to check even more carefully about media deadlines to be effective. You also have to meet in multiple media venues. Some programs would never attend a news conference—talk shows for example. Some cover all items from the field and others never leave the studio. Some radio programs only use the telephone for interviews and others always have live guests. Some TV shows only use remote, double-ender interviews and others insist on studio interviews. You'll need a media tour in addition to a news conference to reach all interested reporters and interviewers.

Preparing

The physical set-up of the room was dealt with in "News Conference Room" above in Chapter 3. You must appoint responders to carry out this task as soon as you hear of the crisis. Preferably some work will have been done long before an event to procure assets and ensure quick set-up (see checklists in "News Conference Room").

The presentation should be enhanced with maps, aerial photographs or graphs. This support material must be designed for use on television. Avoid too much detail, and do not cover it with plastic, because that will reflect the TV lights. The person referring to this support material must use a 'lavaliere' microphone (or clip-on mike) linked to the audio pool feed system. Otherwise the media will be unable to record the comments.

Rehearsal

All spokespeople must rehearse out loud. Taping rehearsal and playing it back is optimal. The rehearsal questions must be tough and realistic, or the spokespeople will be lulled into a false sense of security. They must also be thoroughly briefed on the sequence of events planned for the news conference.

Spokespeople must be trained with the organization's SOCKOs™ and provided with a short analysis of the issues they may face and information on the political district, the history of media and public interest in their organization and the type of event they are facing. Someone from the organization must circulate among reporters before the conference and identify their fields of interest. This person can then use the Journalistic Questions Matrix that follows in this section to help prepare the spokesperson.

Dress

Spokespeople must avoid seersucker, chequered suits, stripes or other fabrics with small repetitive patterns. In close-up shots these will create a distracting rainbow effect on the screen. Bracelets and any more than two rings must be removed. Women must watch hemlines and necklines and remove obtrusive necklaces or dangling earrings. Men in business suits need to wear long executive socks.

Dressing-Rooms

A small room close to the news-conference location must be used as a holding-room for spokespeople. This is to get them away from their duties and to avoid last-minute rushes. Before the spokespeople leave for the news conference, examine them to ensure they are presentable. They should be in this room ten minutes before and ten minutes after each news conference for rehearsal and composure.

In non-crisis situations, you may give reporters a few days' notice of an upcoming 'good news' event such as a press conference launching a new product. You can use the mail, email, faxes, couriers and phone to spark interest among reporters, editors, talk-show hosts and others.

In a crisis, the roles are virtually reversed, with the reporters set up on site and demanding access to a spokesperson.

When planning a news conference during a crisis, you may have only five minutes to 'round up' all reporters on site. It is your responsibility to herd them into the conference room—not theirs to know you have called one. Depending on the site, you may find reporters using a phone, eating, shooting video outside or talking to workers. Find them!

News-Conference Checklist

Before any news conference an individual or select group should be appointed to complete or assign each of these tasks and roles.

ACTIVITY	RESPONSIBILITY	COMPLETED
Contact Public Affairs/ Communications to discuss local approaches and needs.		
Ask for legal advice on proprietary or other matters that may be discussed.		
Procure training for potential moderators and technical experts.		
Prepare and update background material to brief spokespeople.		
Prepare material for handing out to reporters.		
Designate on and off-site rooms to be used for news conferences.		
Inspect conference locations on and off site.		
Acquire quiet and secure rooms for before and after.		
Identify assets required on and/or off-site and maintain an inventory.		
Identify outside resources and update list and phone numbers every six months.		
Review news stories to date.		
Circulate among reporters to determine interest level and/or questions.		
Prepare local issues brief.		
Alert and brief technical experts/spokespeople.		
Develop anticipated questions for speaker/expert.		
Prepare written statement/notes for speaker/expert.		
Give advance copies of all materials to Crisis Management Team, PR Representative, Security Liaison, Information Center Coordinator, other officials, submit copies to the record file.		
Rehearse, train and practise.		

DVD

Customize on the Companion DVD

News Conference Set-up Checklist

ACTIVITY	RESPONSIBILITY	COMPLETED
Obtain assets and outside resources (see Materials & Services List for News Conference)		
Compile list of media attending		
Notify absent press who should attend		
Compile information for reporters		
Invite outside officials		
Acquire and set up room		
Alert reporters on-site		
Update Status Boards		
Check media deadline times		
Refreshments		
Set out background material		
Check equipment		
Operate fax, email and photocopier		
Staff room - greet reporters		
FOR MODERATOR		
Activity/Asset		
Accompany spokespeople/experts to "quiet room"		
Brief spokespeople on local issues.		
Ask rehearsal questions with other public affairs staff.		
Go over each spokesperson's checklist (See Journalistic Questions Matrix for guidance).		
Check each spokesperson's attire and grooming.		
Provide pens, paper, water or other necessities to spokespeople.		
Insist on a minimum of ten minutes of quiet time before and after news conference.		
Check each spokesperson's attire and grooming.		
Provide pens, paper, water or other necessities to spokespeople.		
Insist on a minimum of ten minutes of quiet time before and after news conference.		

DVD

Customize on the Companion DVD

Managing the News Conference

In many capital cities, a member of the press gallery chairs news conferences. In other locations, such as the scene of an emergency, an organization's Public Affairs representative may be assigned to moderate. Travelling delegations should be mindful of local customs, and local officials should discuss needs with visiting officials. Many times an 'availability,' where the visitor agrees to linger after an event or join the press table for a few questions, will be welcome.

Before a formal news conference starts, the person chairing or acting as moderator should come to the lectern, introduce him/herself and lay out the ground rules. The key for all participants is to be polite but firm and maintain the agenda.

Ground Rules for Moderators

- Thank the media for showing up and introduce yourself.
- Announce any changes to previously arranged schedules, timings or facts.
- Both the moderator and officials should expect tough, even abrasive-sounding questions. Participants should focus on their answers and messages and not get flustered. SOCKOs™ will make this easier and more effective.
- Announce if there is going to be an opening statement and explain any other procedural matters.
- Identify the corporate officers making statements by name and title. Offer their bios.
- Say there will be 10 minutes for questions and stick to it.
- Identify the technical experts who will be available for individual interviews after the news conference.
- Remind the media that background material has been prepared for them and is available at the back of the room.
- Call for the spokespeople/experts to walk in and take their seats at their name cards.
- Call for the opening statement.
- After the opening statement, call for questions.

- Announce that you will take one question and one follow-up per reporter until everyone has had an opportunity to ask a question (time permitting).

During the News Conference

- After statements have been made, the moderator (if there is one) takes over again. Remind the media how long the question period is and choose the first reporter. (Some formats have reporters direct their questions through the moderator for greater control.)
- If tension begins to build between the media and the spokesperson, the moderator must diffuse it by clarifying the point being made, offering to provide background material later, calling for other questions or by some other means.
- About two minutes before the question period ends, the moderator should announce that there is time for two more questions.
- After the time for questions has expired, the moderator will end the news conference by thanking the media for coming out. If it is part of the plan to offer technical spokespeople for individual interviews (a good idea), the moderator will introduce them at this point. This will give time for the previous spokespeople to leave gracefully if they cannot remain.

Tough Questions/Situations

Expect repetitive questions or lines of questioning that return to a controversial theme. Arguing with reporters or walking out are not options. Only the moderator should cut short a line of questioning or cut off one reporter and recognize another. If the moderator has to step in, the spokesperson should sit quietly and act pleasantly. The moderator should intervene only after at least three similar tough questions by the same reporter or five by two or more reporters (this is only a guideline).

Then the moderator may:

- note that the question has been answered x times to the best of the organization's ability given the facts at hand;
- say technical experts are available after the conference;
- say fairness dictates moving on to other reporters but the reporter being cut off may obtain further information after the conference;

- commit to obtaining written background material for the questioner; or
- cut the question period short, but only in extraordinary circumstances involving danger to participants.

If the public or third-party interest groups try to intervene, be polite and receptive (see "Public Meetings" below in Chapter 6). Say a public meeting has been or will be scheduled, offer to meet the questioner after the news conference and state that this is the media's event and if they wish their time to be given over to public questions, you will cooperate. Let the reporters decide—it's their news conference.

Mingling—Follow-up

The end of a news conference is often a time for reporters to mingle with news-makers and obtain rudimentary and mundane information. Unless the speaker is an extremely senior person or has pressing business known to reporters, all organization officials should be encouraged to mingle after news conferences.

Be prepared to offer reporters clarification, such as correct spelling of names and titles as well as technical terms and their definitions. Reporters may wish to take still photographs, conduct one-on-one interviews and get reaction shots or cover footage with spokespeople.

The moderator and other public-affairs representatives should introduce themselves and ask whether the reporter has what s/he needs to do a complete story. Earlier questions or comments can be followed up, and the corporate message can be reinforced. The moderator and public-affairs representatives should try to assess the level and nature of media interest and begin to assess whether remedial action is needed. The feedback gathered during mingling will be a first indication of how your corporate message has been received. This is an opportunity to influence how your story is covered and is among the most important work in a news conference.

Journalistic Questions Matrix (to rehearse spokespeople)

INFORMATION	WHO	WHEN	WHERE	WHAT / HOW MANY	WHY	HOW
Injured						
Dead						
Responders						
Victim						
Hero						
Experts						
Knows more about this						
Called responders: fire, EMO, police						
Others (coroner, governments)						
Estimate of damage						
Cause of incident						
Related incidents						
What happened						
Witness opinion						
Responder's opinion						
Equipment being used						
Saved or destroyed						
Arrival of responders						
Evacuation of people						
Organization notification						

INFORMATION	WHO	WHEN	WHERE	WHAT / HOW MANY	WHY	HOW
Last similar incident						
Fire - who discovered?						
Senior management						
Briefings						
Status of response						
Information						
Legal implications						
Financial implications						
Future actions						
Prevention						
Responsibility						
Investigation						
Clean up						
Primary contact						
Environmental impact, long/short						
Air, ground, water						
Benefits						
History of relationship						
Trade figures						
Cultural ties						
Issues						

Customize on the Companion DVD

Photo Opportunities

Photo opportunities disseminate visual information to TV and print journalists. Radio reporters may also wish to attend for background. Reporters for social media, wire services and even radio may also need pictures for their websites.

Photo opportunities are usually neutral or positive for an organization. They lack the confrontational elements of news conferences, interviews or availabilities. Much of what reporters shoot will appear mundane to you (logos, building exteriors, equipment and people). Reporters will always look for movement, colour and the unusual. A confrontation will make the most exciting visual possible and should be avoided at all costs.

Even if reporters do not ask for a photo opportunity, you should still schedule several. Pick venues that do not interfere with normal operations or response. If reporters are using easily accessed material direct from your organization, they are less likely to use questionable materials from a third party.

If logistics permit, a security person who is sensitive to media needs should accompany public affairs/communications and media on photo opportunities.

Photo opportunities can also feature statements by officials, briefings by technical experts, availabilities, demonstrations of equipment or procedures, and handouts of background materials.

You should try to follow the procedures that your organization outlined ahead of time for preparing spokespeople and conducting briefings as the physical surroundings permit. However, you must take care to keep the event more informal and less self-serving than a news conference. The main objective is to show media people something visual that they can use in their reports.

Photo Opportunity Checklist

ACTIVITY	RESPONSIBILITY	COMPLETED
Contact public affairs/communications for guidance.		
Contact security and senior management for local needs including safety & propriety.		
Identify interesting and camera-friendly locations and assets.		
Scout location of photo-op for safety and security concerns.		
Plan itinerary.		
Compile list of media attending.		
Post photo-op times in media work centre, press briefing room, other public locations (see information opportunity chart).		
Notify media in person or by phone at least 15 minutes before event.		
Preparation of materials, and/or equipment.		
Obtain all needed safety gear and distribute to media as needed.		
Conduct safety briefing of reporters.		
Have all media sign indemnification agreement when needed.		
Notify security.		
Preparation of potential spokespeople or experts.		
Notify those at site of photo opportunity.		

DVD

Customize on the Companion DVD

Video News Releases

You may want to give out your own visuals to news organizations. The site of an event may be inaccessible or dangerous. It may be prohibitively expensive to take reporters to a remote location, or it may just take too long. Regardless, your own video, audio and still pictures may be invaluable to reporters.

All media now use information in all formats. Newspapers have websites that use video. TV and radio reporters have blogs that use pictures and text. Every reporter and every outlet is likely to use sound, pictures and text.

What few reporters or news outlets will use is much, if any, of your editorial or artistic input. Music is the chief offender. Many news organizations don't allow music in news stories, and those that do would rather pick their own. Shooting video for TV news is a special skill that features static shots establishing the scene and context followed by close-ups of relevant details. Too much panning, zooming, soft focus and so on will make editors reluctant to use your footage. What works best is raw footage, wild footage or so called 'B roll' (general visuals that help the story and are used in editing) that reporters can edit as they see fit. The same is true of clips of your technical experts. Their statements should be short and to the point. News organizations will seldom want to use a long interview featuring a non-journalist as questioner.

Scrums

The term 'scrum' comes from British rugby. A scrum involves several players locked together trying to get at the ball or the player holding it. In media terms, you're the ball and the reporters are the rugby-players. A scrum occurs when two or more people want to interview the same spokesperson simultaneously. Reporters approach the spokesperson (often in a hall or parking-lot or when entering or exiting a building), thrust microphones and cameras in the subject's face and begin peppering him or her with questions. A scrum can be an ambush interview by more than one reporter, or you may know in advance that reporters are waiting in the parking-lot or hallway.

Scrums are intimidating and dangerous for news-makers. They should be avoided and treated as the least preferred means of interacting with reporters (well behind one-on-ones, news conferences and availabilities). This is seldom hard to achieve, because reporters don't like the format either. They only resort to it if other forums are not on offer or not satisfactory (i.e. too short).

Occasionally, though, when an interview or news conference is inadvisable, you can use a scrum to your advantage. You can stop, look one reporter in the eyes, take a few questions from several reporters in turn, deliver your message and say that's all the time you have. A public-affairs assistant can also say "Thank you" in a loud voice to signal the end of the scrum. I've worked for international diplomats and trade negotiators whose political bosses would be upset if they gave media interviews. Some of them just field a few questions in a hallway scrum and tell their bosses they had no choice. That gets a message out without having to participate in a formal media interview.

If you suspect a scrum will occur, go over the following points with your spokesperson:

- Have three or four messages or themes to deliver and repeat.
- Identify questions and SOCKOs™ and rehearse the spokesperson.
- If there is little to be gained from interaction with reporters, keep walking slowly, be pleasant but serious, and keep repeating your message.
- If there is much to be gained—new information to get out, the record to correct and several positive messages to be embedded in people's minds—walk out to meet the reporters, then stop and deliver your messages. Ensure your message gets out regardless of the questions.
- The moderator or Public Affairs representative will touch the spokesperson on the arm or back, say "Thank you" in a clear, loud voice and begin moving to end the scrum after about three exchanges. Once you are moving, don't stop.
- Remind your spokesperson to look the reporter in the eyes to acknowledge the question, answer the reporter while maintaining eye contact, then acknowledge another reporter in turn (see diagram).
- Treat hecklers and other non-reporters like any other stimulus. Address the hecklers' questions if reporters want you to. Tell hecklers there will be a public meeting to address their concerns, if that's true.
- Stay cool. Don't get as excited as the reporters seem to be. Take a deep breath, think, then answer.

What follows are a series of illustrations to assist you in successfully encountering media in a variety of circumstances.

Scrums

If several reporters walk up and start asking you questions at once, you're in a scrum. The Canadian term is a rugby metaphor and you're the ball! If you sweep the scrum with your eyes you will generate multiple questions because all reporters will think you are acknowledging them. The antidote is to look at one and if s/he doesn't ask a question, look at another. But engage with one at a time. When one has asked a question, move your physical attention and eye contact to another and address each in turn this way. Let the cameras eavesdrop on the conversation. Don't address them because camera operators may want to get a profile shot of you. Moreover, you won't know which reporter is with which camera operator. When you're done, perhaps after half a dozen questions, say "Thank you" and walk away purposefully. You can also have a staffer do the same.

TV Panel discussion

If there are three guests on a TV talk show, being in the middle can be difficult. You will have a tendency to move your head back and forth when others are speaking and you can look nervous. Try to sit on one end. If you are next to the host, focus on that person and just turn slowly to look at other guests when they are speaking. If you are on the opposite end to the host, you can look in the same direction at all times. A camera shot can't normally show whether you are looking directly at another guest or just in that general direction, so you don't have to turn around fully when someone else is speaking, just look attentive and in that direction. You will be able to interrupt or extend your speaking-time with body language more than by verbally asking to speak. Use a bright look on your face, a raised hand or finger as if you have an idea.

TV Phone in Show

Where to look when there's no one there? Naturally you can look at the host on a TV call-in show. You can take notes as the caller is speaking. You will see many hosts reacting non-verbally to what the caller is saying and you can join in with slow and gentle nodding or a brightening of the expression on your face. You should check with the floor director or producer about production preferences, but when callers are speaking, you can also look in the lens of the camera that's on as a metaphor for looking at the caller. It's best to watch the show a couple of times before you are on to see how it's produced.

Stand up Interview

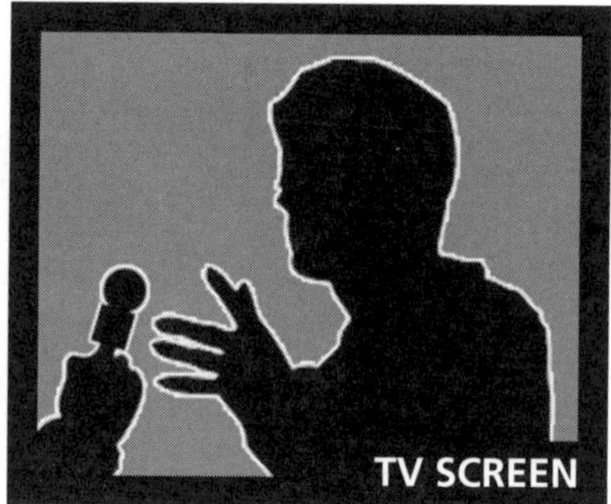

Among the most common TV interviews you'll encounter is the one-on-one interview with a journalist and camera operator. Unless asked to do otherwise, look at the journalist as if s/he has asked you the most fascinating question you've ever been asked and answering it is the most important thing you could be doing at the time. The journalist and microphone will feel very close to you. That's not to intimidate, but just to produce a good shot and get clear sound.

Eye Contact

Note that there is no peripheral vision on TV. If people are looking at you speaking at a social gathering and your eyes wander to look at other people or things you might be looking through 10 per cent of their field of vision. On a TV screen however, the same act of looking away would have your eyes sweep through 30% of the field of vision on the TV screen.

Double-Ender

Double-enders have two ends to them—yours in your office, a TV booth or studio, or at the site of an event, and the journalist's back in the TV studio. You could be standing or sitting. You will have an earphone in your ear to hear the questions and you might have a monitor in the corner of your eye. Ignore your picture in the monitor and concentrate on the lens of the camera. Practise with a home camera and see how looking away looks untrustworthy.

All is magnified on TV. Use the positive body language described for other venues and keep looking at the lens. If you are very accomplished, you can try a 'refocus,' which involves looking up or down to gather thoughts and then right back to the camera lens. It's tricky, so be sure you have it mastered before trying it in real life.

Videographer

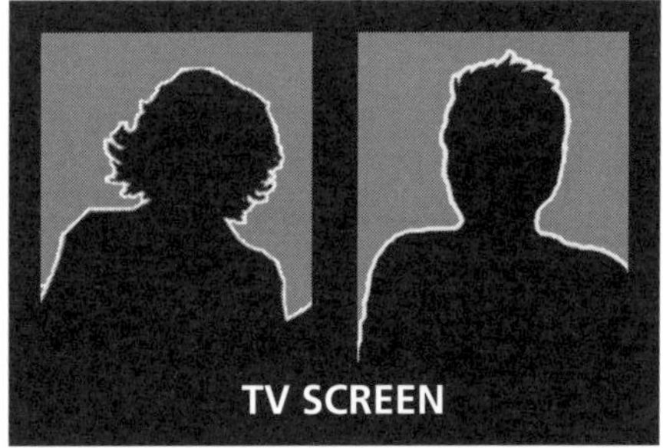

A videographer is a combination camera operator and interviewer. You may be asked to look off at a 45 degree angle and speak to a spot on the wall. This is so when they put you on a split screen (see diagram) with the host, the two of you will look as if you are speaking to each other and not incongruously looking away from each other. You might get the direction to speak to a spot on the wall right beside the camera lens as if an interviewer were sitting there with you. That's how it will look when your clip is used in a news report. If the videographer is also interviewing you, it would be best to look right in his or her eyes beside the camera lens. If you can't see the videographer because one eye is shut and the other behind the lens, then look at the camera lens. If there is movement, follow the movement of the videographer or the lens.

Side by side TV Interview

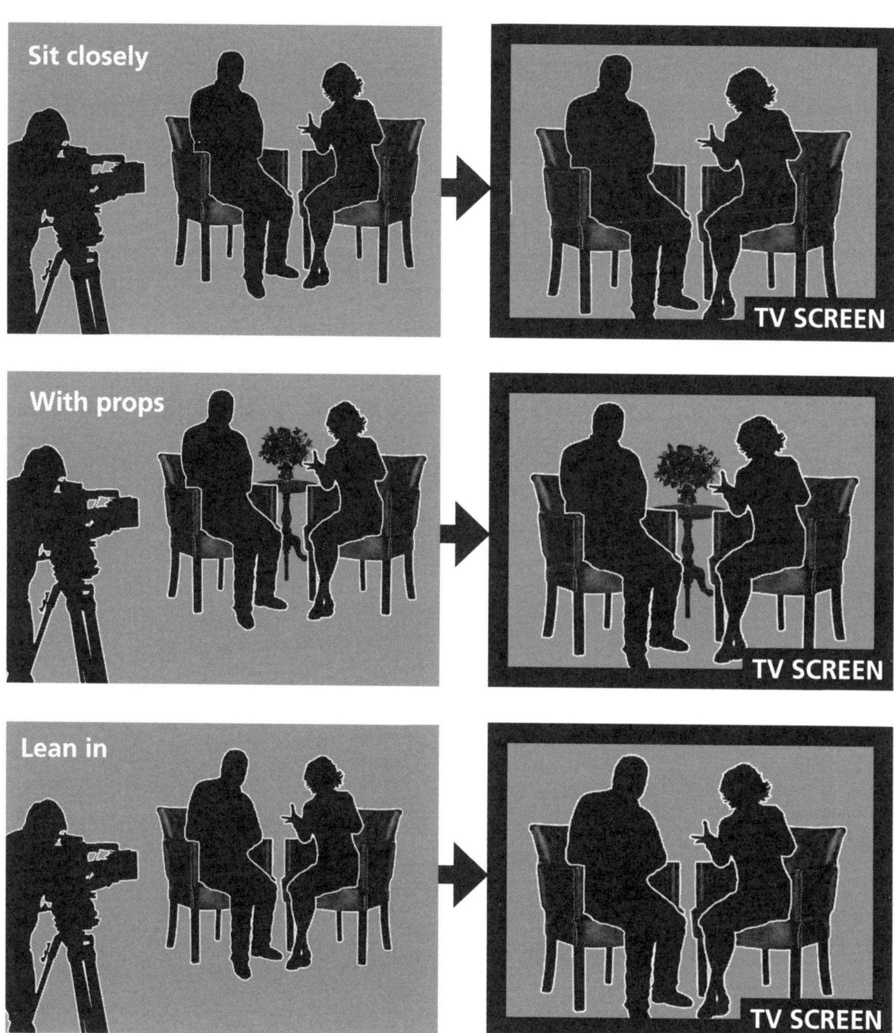

There is an optical illusion on television. You will appear to be sitting much farther away from the host than you actually are. Your knees might be touching, yet you will look a comfortable distance apart. This is because of the proportional distancing involved. Your heads and torsos will be far enough apart, and you will be framed by a narrow border on the TV screen. A net result is that the distance between your heads and torsos will look greater than it actually is. Set designers deal with this by putting the host and guest close together, or by putting a table, vase of flowers, pitcher of water or other props in between you to take up room. You will need to lean in from the waist, gesture with open, double hands and engage the host. Fill up the space between the two of you with your positive gestures.

Editorial Board

Eye contact and body language is important in newspaper and magazine editorial boards. Leaning in a little, open, double hand gestures and eye contact all show that you are engaged and committed to what you are speaking about. Look at each person in turn and linger on that person for a sentence or two. Include all with your body language.

Managing the Media

Discussion Points:

1. Where can you hold an off-site news conference on 20 minutes' notice?
2. Are your facilities appropriate for a news conference?
3. Who will schedule unannounced mock news conferences to test response capability?
4. Where will you hold your photo opportunity?
5. What stills and video will you shoot?
6. What technical experts will you record for clips?
7. Do you need a dark website?
8. What audio, video and stills can you put on your website?
9. What transport might you need for reporter pools, and where can you obtain it?
10. Who will research the legal implications of pools and photo opportunities?

WE/THEY

State legislation required public meetings and a community liaison committee to share information from local government and field questions from affected residents. Problem was, the community liaison committee was using state funds to oppose the new water and sewage-treatment plant, not to find out more about it. The committee had been influenced, and partly taken over, by:

1) A popular reform governor from the 1990s;

2) A best-selling author with a new book coming out on the environment; and

3) Ralph Nader, who made several brief appearances.

Scientific matters are always debatable. But some points that don't seem to be debatable are that waste has to go somewhere, using less water is best, more treatment helps and putting pipes that take in drinking-water near other pipes that discharge sewage effluent is obviously dangerous.

This new plant would have addressed many of these issues. It also had the potential to replace or help clean up older plants that were still in use but were less modern and safe.

Then came time for the public information session. This was many years after lots of public outrage over the facility and just hours before a legislature vote on a moratorium, which would cost millions of dollars in contract penalties because the plant was already under construction.

The state was set for confrontation—literally.

The state had hired the same company that ran political conventions for the party in power. As interested parties drove up to the legislature, they saw signs pointing them to "VIP Parking." There were uniformed state troopers, lots of plain-clothes police with holstered guns and badges on their belts, and lots of older building security officers in well marked T-shirts and windbreakers.

The average age of interested citizens appeared to be about 66.

The meeting was scheduled for noon. At just a few minutes after the hour, there was still a long line of people, because the door hadn't been opened. The room that had been booked held about 80 people, and more than 100 were turned away. They had to listen to the event on loudspeakers in the parking-lot.

Inside, the political-event company had brought in a stage, with a blue curtain behind it for better TV shots. There were signs warning that everyone was being recorded on video to protect state workers.

The plan was for the experts to go up to a podium, speak into a mike and talk through a bullet-point presentation. This didn't happen, because about halfway through the first presentation, citizens got up and rightly said they knew all this information and what they wanted to do was express their views. The moderator tried to follow the agenda but had to bow to the will of the group. Questions became speeches and accusations.

One consulting engineer was asked why he wouldn't reveal his proprietary computer modelling-techniques that showed the plant would improve water quality. He spoke for about two minutes about a pending lawsuit and how his lawyers had said he shouldn't say any more than he had and then finally gave a technical answer no one remembered. A better answer might have been that when the state bought the report, it didn't also buy the computer it was made on or the software.

One questioner asked the engineer why certain components of the plant were only guaranteed for 3 years. He spent two minutes talking about normal industry standards before pointing out that the life expectancy of the material was about 150 years—as state regulations required. He could have noted that our cars and appliances usually last much longer than the manufacturer's warranty, especially if well maintained. He could also have pointed out that the material in question was not required by state regulations but was a redundant system to reassure citizens.

When audience members' eyes wandered, they landed on one more symbol of the confrontational atmosphere. The first two rows of seats were roped off for VIPs. The names of the prominent activists were printed in large letters for all to see and the TV crews to shoot. The prominent people hadn't shown up—but their presence and opposition was felt, courtesy of the state office of information.

One final touch—Ralph Nader's name was spelled incorrectly.

CHAPTER 6: MAKING PUBLIC REMARKS

Event: *Flixborough Explosion*

Date: *1 June 1974*

Summary: *Chemical engineers predominated in a facility that occasionally needed mechanical-engineering expertise. Some repairs had been made, including using 'dog-leg' pipe and substituting pipe with a smaller diameter, which had caused increased pressure. The manufacturing-process included heating gasoline. A vapour cloud ignited, causing an explosion—one of the largest petrochemical-plant explosions in history. Debris fell up to 12 miles away. The explosion occurred on a Saturday. Had it occurred during the work week, many more people could have been killed and injured. Half the people on site didn't hear the warning bell, and 80 percent did not hear the public-address warning—40 percent heard neither. Some even ran towards the alarm rather than away from it. Local response was hindered by a lack of communication, expertise and coordination. The explosion triggered many local burglar alarms, adding to the confusion.*

Result: *28 workers killed, 36 injured. Outside the plant there were 53 casualties and hundreds of minor injuries. Damage was about $60 million dollars.*

Lessons Learned: *The need for special expertise, including metallurgical and mechanical, in a chemical facility. The need to coordinate outside response agencies—a lesson learned far too often during 9/11 and in the years after. How human behaviour is unpredictable—including walking towards, rather than away from, an evacuation alarm.*

Making Public Remarks

Most people find speaking in public a great challenge in the best of times. Speaking during a crisis or controversy is not only a great challenge for the individual but also a pivotal point for that person's organization.

Your public communication may go to victims, family members or outraged citizens. You will need stamina to keep responding to their concerns. You will need facts and empathy. Rehearsal and practise will help, and so will the tips that follow.

Alarming Phrases to Avoid

- "You don't understand …"
- "Obviously ..."
- "In simple terms ..."
- "Let me explain something to you …"
- "With respect …"

Effective speakers must also be good listeners.

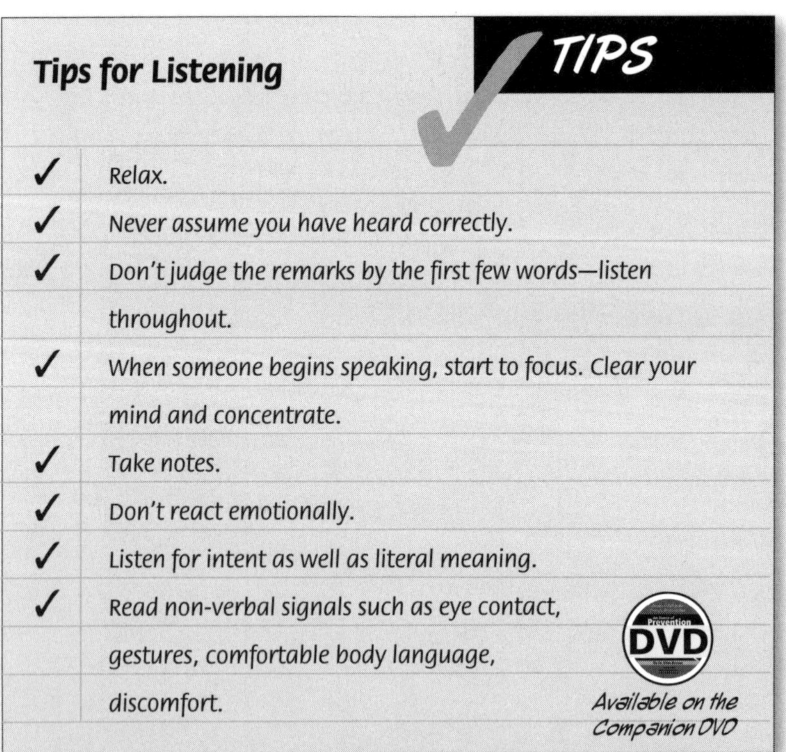

Tips for Listening

- ✓ Relax.
- ✓ Never assume you have heard correctly.
- ✓ Don't judge the remarks by the first few words—listen throughout.
- ✓ When someone begins speaking, start to focus. Clear your mind and concentrate.
- ✓ Take notes.
- ✓ Don't react emotionally.
- ✓ Listen for intent as well as literal meaning.
- ✓ Read non-verbal signals such as eye contact, gestures, comfortable body language, discomfort.

Ten Common Reasons for Poor Communication

Top 10

1. Lack of rapport with the audience
2. Stiff or wooden body language
3. A dry intellectual presentation with no audience involvement
4. A frightened speaker
5. Poor eye contact
6. Unclear intent
7. Inadequate preparation
8. No use of silence for impact
9. Lack of energy
10. A boring and uninteresting presentation

Visual Aids

TIPS

Visual aids can be a valuable addition to a presentation/meeting but should be used with caution. Consider the following:

- ✓ Are they needed?
- ✓ Are they a support or a replacement?
- ✓ Can they be seen properly?
- ✓ Are your graphs and charts too complex? Keep items to 4 across and 4 down.
- ✓ Talk to the audience; don't face your aids.
- ✓ Vary your visuals.
- ✓ Keep the lights on.

Available on the Companion DVD

Public Meetings

Public officials and corporations may have legal and regulatory obligations to release information to stakeholders and the general public. Sometimes the law dictates disclosure, and at others the organization's membership in associations mandates compliance with codes of conduct. During a crisis your organization needs to meet with people whose lives, property and businesses are affected as regularly as they require, to deal with their concerns and allay their fears. You need to set up information centres and hold public meetings to keep those not directly affected up to date. You're often better off telling stakeholders that there's nothing new to tell them, rather than letting them build up a head of steam and anger before calling you for information.

Public meetings are often held at the discretion of third parties. You and your colleagues may be the invited guests at a meeting called by a citizens' group, politicians, advocacy group or others. Since reporters are also members of the public, it will be hard to prevent them from attending a public meeting, so you usually shouldn't try.

All speakers and organization officials attending a public meeting must review the appropriate checklists in this manual. They should also be told to expect to be confronted with some concrete symbol of the event (a dead bird, a story from an affected citizen, a visual aid, sand from a beach covered in oil, etc.). In fact the spokesperson may wish to bring his/her own such visual aid *and* the equipment and/or data that will address the problem.

Seek the audience's approval for audio- or videotaping before the meeting to keep a record of their concerns and your commitments.

Rehearsal

Rehearsal for public meetings is just as important as it is for appearances before the courts, regulatory bodies and the media. Mock questions must be tough and realistic. Spokespeople must be thoroughly briefed on the issues and the agenda. Officials should phone or circulate among members of the public, interest groups and community leaders before the meeting to identify topics of interest.

Dress

Normal business dress is generally appropriate, and attempts to 'dress down' for a rural or remote venue will often ring false. However, if your organization's spokespeople normally wear suits and ties to work, a blazer and open-necked shirt might be an appropriate compromise. In rural or remote locations women may choose pants instead of skirts.

Quiet Rooms

A small room close to the scene of the public meeting must be used as a holding-room for spokespeople. They should take ten minutes before and after public meetings to rehearse and regain composure.

If you are calling the meeting or can influence the timing, set-up and agenda, you have some decisions to make. There are always trade-offs between control and audience participation, between authenticity and security and so on. One good approach is to set up the room so that audience members can interact with displays to help them understand the situation. This makes the audience feel empowered. It also avoids the confrontational atmosphere that naturally can develop if speakers are up on a stage or standing behind lecterns. Displays can be interactive, allowing visitors to glean information from paper pamphlets, interactive computers, experts, DVDs, CDs and so on. Members of the public can mill around the displays all night, come and go as they please and attend round-table discussions if they wish (See Town Hall diagram).

The second best scenario is to set up a room much like the diagram that follows. This is the set-up you will probably encounter if others are responsible for the meeting-room. You can still have some influence if you arrive early. Audiences feel greater comfort sitting near aisles, so have as many as possible. Each participant should have the opportunity to take away some material and to sign a document requesting more information. Security should be in place, but it should be unobtrusive. The more hostile the audience, the better it may feel for the speakers to separate themselves from the public. Stages, lecterns and tables achieve this purpose. But spokespeople need to know that by using these barriers they may only intensify the friction between themselves and members of the public.

Public Meeting Checklist

ACTIVITY	RESPONSIBILITY	COMPLETED
Contact Public Affairs/Communications and Security for guidance and local conditions.		
Survey on and off-site venues (schools, movie theatres, union/service club halls, religious institutions) with security for special challenges (wheelchair access.etc.).		
Identify physical assets which may be needed (p.a. system, visual aids, chairs etc.).		
Prepare visual aids.		
Compile and maintain a list of outside services that may be required (signing for the hearing impaired, etc.).		
Select potential speakers at public meetings and obtain training as needed.		
Ensure all literature, visual aids and statements can be provided in other languages as necessary.		
Determine if other language capabilities are required.		
Circulate among third party groups to determine concerns and prepare organization's positions.		
Prepare and rehearse spokespeople/technical experts.		
Contact all community leaders to inform them of meetings; determine concerns and prepare organization's positions (mayor, notary, fire, police, service clubs, school officials etc.).		
Review checklists (moderator, spokesperson, expert, VIP) and perform tasks (rehearsal, quiet room, assets etc.).		
Write down all concerns/questions from public on flip chart during meeting.		
Prepare follow up list with tasks and names of citizens needing information or action.		

DVD

Customize on the Companion DVD

Public Meeting Room

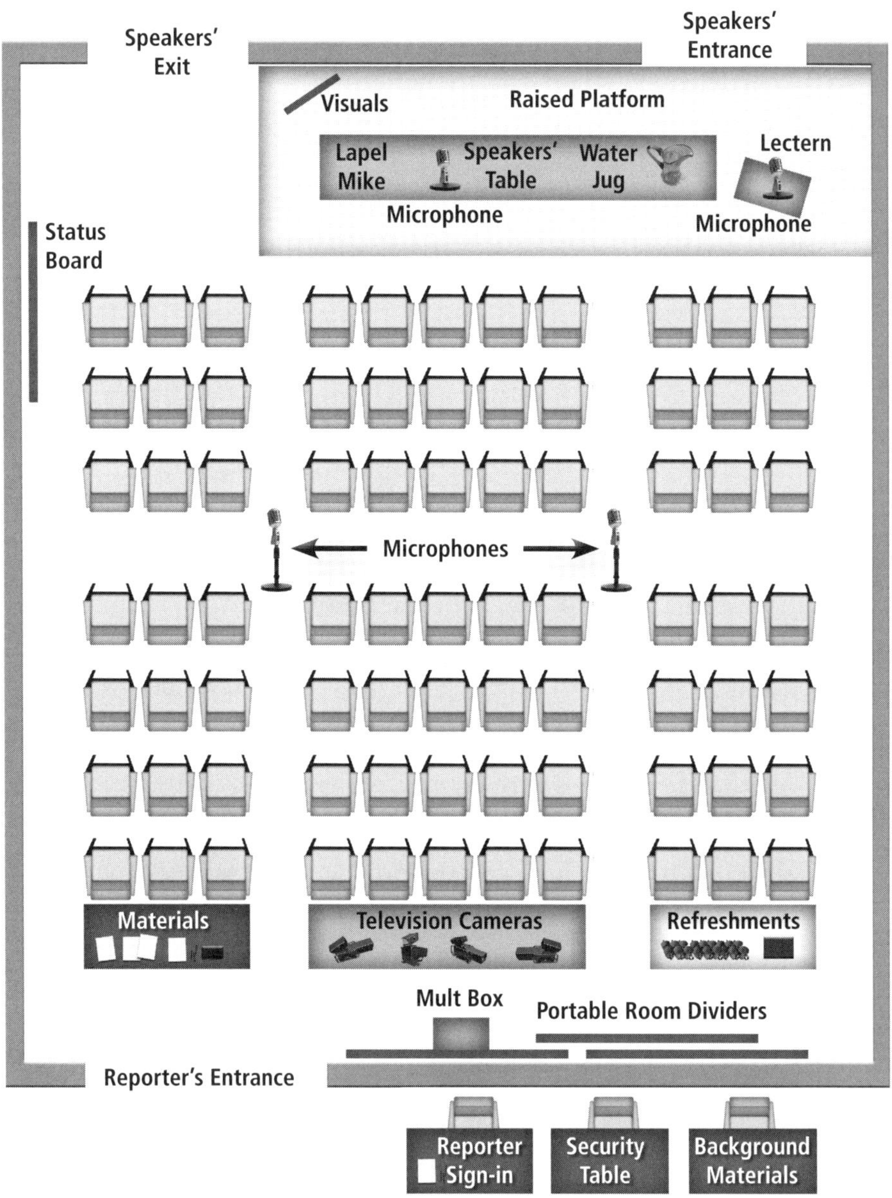

Speakers' Exit

Speakers' Entrance

Visuals

Raised Platform

Lapel Mike

Speakers' Table

Water Jug

Lectern

Microphone

Microphone

Status Board

Microphones

Materials

Television Cameras

Refreshments

Mult Box

Portable Room Dividers

Reporter's Entrance

Reporter Sign-in

Security Table

Background Materials

See also p. 123

Available on the Companion DVD

Managing the Public Meeting

Many public meetings will be held under the auspices of an outside group that will also take responsibility for the agenda and managing the event. But if you're in charge, your moderators and spokespeople must show concern and empathy. All officials should be prepared to stay until the end, regardless of the hour, except in extraordinary circumstances where they feel their safety is in danger.

General Presentation Skills

Ground Rules for Moderator/Spokesperson at a Public Meeting

- Thank the public for showing up and introduce yourself and other spokespeople.
- Apologize for the event, inconvenience, and any damage to wildlife, property, the environment or people in a sincere way, several times, in different language.
- Make logistical announcements regarding future public meetings, telephone numbers, access to officials or information, claims offices and so on.
- Explain that there will be opening statements followed by time for questions and answers.
- Note that there is background material available in the room for members of the public.
- If the public don't want a presentation, let them talk.

Note: All officials should focus on their answers and messages and not get flustered (see "Communicating during a Crisis" in Chapter 4 above). What they say will be reported by the news media.

Audience Eye Contact

Don't sweep a room with your eyes in a 'windshield-wiper' move. Look at one person at a time. Linger on that one person for a sentence or two and then move to another person in a different quadrant of the room. Even in a very large auditorium, most people will think you looked directly at them for a time. If there are bright lights and you can't see your audience, you must still look at one spot for a sentence or two in all four quadrants of the room. If you are asked a question, look right at that person. If you can't see the person, look at the spot the sound is coming from.

Focus and Include

In the two figures above, a person at a social gathering is looking over the heads of the small group of people he is speaking with. This is rude. Eye contact should be with the people you are speaking with at all times. If you are speaking with more than one person in a small group, establish eye contact with each in turn and linger on each for a sentence or two.

Note how unforgiving body language can be. In the illustration on the left a speaker is including just one or two of the figures on the right-hand side of the grouping (his left). In the illustration on the right, the speaker has turned his body, opened his arm and hand gestures and is including all five people in the group. Eye contact should be with each in turn and linger for a sentence or two.

Directing your gaze in a large room

Confronting a sea of faces and not knowing where to focus, speakers will often look up from their notes and let their eyes dart from side to side across the room. This leads to an odd delivery that I call the 'windshield-wiper' effect. The solution is to picture the room divided into four equal quadrants. Pick one of the quadrants and deliver several sentences to a person in that quadrant. Then pick the next quadrant and deliver another few sentences, and so on.

When a speaker is on a riser, audience members are looking up at the speaker. A podium obscures part of the speaker's body at any angle, but when combined with the use of a riser, often all audience members can see is from the top of the speaker's head to about chest level. Speakers can use lapel mikes to be mobile and move out beside and in front of their podiums. If there are head table guests or other obstructions, speakers can reach out with body language and gestures to connect with the audience.

General Presentation Tips

TIPS

- ✓ Be convincing, not combative.
- ✓ Grab the good words, good concepts and moral high ground for yourself.
- ✓ Show caring, knowledge and action.
- ✓ Be flexible with time, firm with key messages.
- ✓ Act professionally.
- ✓ Respect the formality of the event.
- ✓ Address issues, not personalities.
- ✓ Enunciate.
- ✓ Speak a little more slowly to ensure clarity and comprehension.
- ✓ Use visual aids sparingly.
- ✓ Don't read directly off your notes.
- ✓ Being nervous is natural.
- ✓ Nervousness is rarely as obvious as you think.
- ✓ Don't pace or wave your arms.
- ✓ Use larger but slower gestures.
- ✓ Stand tall. Avoid swaying.
- ✓ Use both hands for gesturing.
- ✓ Gesture bigger, but slower than normal.
- ✓ Use personal stories and anecdotes.
- ✓ Eye contact - include everyone, one person at a time—slowly.
- ✓ Explain the benefit, feature and advantage of your position or actions.

DVD

Available on the Companion DVD

Presentations

Checklist

Note: These tasks should be performed with Public Affairs or with trusted colleagues or advisors.

Pre-Speech Audience Analysis

The following questions, which analyze your intended audience, will help you to tailor your speech to their needs. The composition of your audience will always be different, so you need to ask yourself the following questions every time.

Title of Speech:			
Theme:			
Length:	Name of Group:	Size:	Age Group:
Audience Relationship:	Customer:	Manager:	Peer:
	Subordinate:	Public:	Other:
Audience Salary Level:			
Audience knowledge of speech subject/your organization: Level: High______ General______ Limited______ None______ Unknown______			
Audience vocabulary knowledge of the subject/your organization: Level: Technical / Non-technical High______ Low______ Unknown______			
Audience opinion of the subject/your organization: Level: Very Favourable______ Favourable______ Unknown______ Neutral______ Slightly hostile______ Very hostile______			
Audience motivation for coming: What will they gain from you? Open-mindedness: Eager_____ Open_____ Neutral_____ Resistant_____ Unknown_____			
Information and techniques likely to succeed with them Type: Technical Data______ Statistics______ Cost______ Figures______ Stories______ Diagrams______ Demonstrations______ Lectures______ Discussion______ Other:			

DVD

Customize on the Companion DVD

With the audience information you have gathered, reflect on the objectives you have set for your presentation.

Techniques to Handle a Difficult Audience

It's normal to come up against an intrusive audience member in a crisis. Although no two situations are alike, there are some key actions you can take to lessen the impact on your speech.

- Always be polite with the heckler, but remember that the rest of the audience came to listen to what you have to say.
- If the interruption comes early in your remarks, try to cope with it, unless the hecklers are persistent. If they are, say you will be happy to deal with them after you have finished your speech.

- Ask hecklers to hear all your material, and promise to return to their complaint afterwards if they still have issues.
- Stop speaking momentarily. The audience will realize you are aware of the heckler, and they will have time to make their own judgment about the interruption.
- Address the heckler. Dignify questions and bridge to your SOCKO™ message (see "Communicating during a Crisis"). Responses that acknowledge the heckler's point and are polite are the best approach. Statements such as "Another approach is ..." or "Here are some other considerations ..." dignify the question. (But be careful not to concede a point or agree to something unwittingly.)
- Suggest talking about the subject after the presentation.
- Try addressing the whole audience. Ask if others have comments or even solutions to offer.
- Keep your cool.
- Say you have answered the question x times to the best of your ability, given the facts at hand.
- Assure the heckler that technical experts will be available after the meeting, if this is true.
- With a repetitive questioner, say that fairness dictates moving on to other questioners but s/he may obtain further information after the meeting.
- If the situation seems completely unsalvageable, wrap up your remarks. Make that appear to be the natural ending. Thank the audience for sharing their views and leave the stage. But you should do this only as the very last resort.

Community Consultation

Special-interest and community groups have always had powerful skills. The power to mobilize public opinion and generate news reports has traditionally frustrated many organizations. Now that power is augmented by legislation. Many statutes require open community consultation as a condition for approvals.

Diversity in the Community

In a town-hall public meeting or negotiating-table, you can expect interest groups to have a distinct set of needs, a unique knowledge base, their own language and their own motives for attending. Usually these groups can be divided into categories. Here's a dozen for your consideration:

1) Scientists

Scientific information should treated carefully. Evidence is not fact, correlation is not proof, a statistical relationship is not necessarily a causal relationship and one set of results does not necessarily represent the consensus of the scientific community. One scientist's data are not necessarily reproducible by another and may not be the same as others have obtained.

There is danger in communicating complicated concepts. A little knowledge is a dangerous thing, and basing decisions on evidence that is not completely understood is especially dangerous.

Scientific information does not negate information from lay people. There may also be something new in this particular situation that scientists haven't yet thought about. Lay people express themselves in their own terms, and understanding them can pose a challenge.

2) The Private Sector

Since one of the natural objectives of private industry is profit, some may assume that that's the only objective. Private-sector representatives will want to know how your actions will affect economic conditions.

3) Politicians

To try to satisfy as many interests as possible, politicians will want large amounts of clear, concise information from all participants. While this can slow down proceedings, the advantages are that all issues stand a better chance of getting addressed and your goals gain the legitimacy of political approval.

4) The Public Sector

The public sector has procedures and policies to follow. Its representatives will likely focus on practicality—working within existing laws and regulations. They are usually averse to risk.

5) Non-Governmental Groups (NGOs) or Interest Groups

These groups exist to fight for a cause. They have clear and narrow agendas and will be the least willing to be conciliatory. Interest groups are used to manipulating events and speaking in absolute terms. They will be challenging and will ask detailed questions. The challenge is to avoid confrontation and find mutually acceptable ground on which to negotiate.

6) The General Public

Members of the general public may simply be looking for more information. They may want to protect the status quo. Resistance to change or to confusing information is normal.

7) Senior Management

Senior mangers will not have the credibility outside your organization that they do inside. You can't 'take your stripes' with you outside the boardroom. The general public will not show the deference that your chain of command shows.

8) Hourly Workers

Workers who metaphorically carry a lunch pail to work may have far greater credibility than you might think. They are in the enviable position of being able to tell a general audience that they work with the materials, safety systems and processes daily and are assured of appropriate safety.

9) Retired Workers

The credibility of these workers can work both for and against you. If you harness them, they can speak with the authority of someone who has worked behind the plant gates (literal or metaphorical) and is assured of the integrity of your processes. If interest groups co-opt these workers, they can position themselves as highly credible whistle-blowers.

10) Academics

Academics may not be scientists, and their academic field may have nothing to do with your issue. However, these people may have great credibility in the community. You may also find that even high-school teachers, Boy Scout troop leaders and others have the respect of their neighbours and friends. Try to harness support where you can.

TIPS

Tips for Community Consultation

(Please also see "Dos and Don'ts of Negotiation" and "A Negotiator's Reminders" for more tips that will enhance your community consultations.)

- ✓ Arrive early and stay late.
- ✓ Listen and respect.
- ✓ Acknowledge good points.
- ✓ "Expand the pie" of available benefits to all.
- ✓ Develop strategies which allow for complicating factors.
- ✓ Give all who want to participate the chance to be heard.
- ✓ Work towards the possible.
- ✓ How legitimate is your agreement?
- ✓ Can the proposed agreement be enforced?
- ✓ Explain any circumstances of non-cooperation.
- ✓ Ask questions.
- ✓ Never threaten.
- ✓ Try to reduce the list of grievances.
- ✓ Involve everyone from the start—especially your biggest critics.

DVD

Available on the Companion DVD

11) Community Elders/Leaders

Aboriginal/First Nation groups have literal Elders who are most often more important than elected band councils. Many Elders are women. Other cultural groups and societies also have both formal and informal Elders. Some Elders earn their stripes in interest groups or through long-standing public service. Others have life experiences that are respected. Be sure to single out these leaders for special and respectful treatment.

12) Groups with Special Credentials

Aboriginal/First Nation groups have special status in many jurisdictions. In some, Supreme Court rulings mandate a 'duty to consult' which you must respect. In others there are parallel justice systems, and in most there is deference to the First Nation attitudes toward the land and environmental matters. These groups can easily trump others' input and become the deciding factors in public consultations.

Other groups to watch are affected citizens, especially mothers of children with ailments linked to your operations. During the Cold War and in the environmental movement, mothers and grandmothers played decisive roles.

You should not view community consultation as a necessary evil. In fact, it can offer many opportunities for a positive outcome for your organization. Being available, listening and being open-minded will reflect positively on you. Consultations may be required by law and may figure in a 'due-diligence' defence against future damages. Community consultations may alert you to trends or public opinion even more effectively than research or polling. You may even discover unexpccted allies.

Making Public Remarks

Discussion Points:

1. Have you identified relevant community groups interested in your activities?
2. Is there anything you can do to enhance relationships?
3. Who will identify how others benefit from your project?
4. What is the science from various jurisdictions?
5. Have you researched your critics' positions?
6. Who will regularly search for your critics' positions?
7. Are there data that will counter your critics' positions?
8. Is there new technology that will mitigate?
9. What will happen if your project doesn't go forward?
10. How can you exceed legislation and regulations?

Your Negotiation IQ

To be a good negotiator, you first have to know your IQ—but that doesn't mean your intelligence. Your negotiation IQ is the "I Quit" position you are prepared to take, or must take, in a negotiation.

At work, you have an "I Quit" position. There are certain circumstances under which you will quit and look for another job. The new job may have lower pay but a shorter commute. It may have more status but a tougher boss. Most of us occasionally think about our "I Quit" positions and modify them after a blow-up with a co-worker.

We develop informal "I Quit" positions with neighbours who borrow tools and trample on our flower beds. After a certain number of broken tools, we decide to quit the friendship.

With teenage children or spouses, however, we are unlikely to have a stringent "I Quit" position over lending the car. Sure, it gets the odd dent, the gas tank is empty and it needs washing, but that's no reason to stop lending the car, let alone ending the family relationship. Beer bottles in the back seat might be a reason to stop lending the car to a teenager but not reason enough to cut off all contact. Lines are drawn even in families.

With a stranger, when buying a used car, it's best to do plenty of research to establish your IQ. Web searches, visits to used-car lots and asking friends who have owned similar cars can help you set a figure at which you're content to buy the vehicle. One dollar more and you'll quit the negotiation.

Let's say a car is advertised for $3000. If, as a buyer, you've set an "I Quit" position of $2800, you have pre-decided to leave the negotiations when the price gets to $2801. You may start lower and work your way up or let the seller start at full price and try bargaining down to your figure. If you base your position on sound, objective research that you can present to the seller, you will be a principled and ethical negotiator, destined to make better deals.

The big problem occurs if the seller has set an "I Quit" position of $2900. As negotiations progress and you start driving the price down below $3000, everything stops at $2900, when the seller quits the process. Or if you start low—say at $2600—all negotiations cease when you are driven up to $2801.

The only way this deal can be done without violating "I Quit" positions is if some factor other than overall price makes the value different from what it appears to be. A seller's sudden announcement that there are four relatively new tires in the garage that go with the car can play this role. So can a stereo, a car cover, a parking-spot and so on. The seller might also announce that you can make phased-in payments.

Calculations might show that an overall price above the "I Quit" position, when phased in over many months, is actually below the "I Quit" position (on a net basis). Any of these items may cause the buyer to pay a little more than his "I Quit" position, since he is getting more for his money.

Similarly, the purchaser may persuade the seller that a price lower than the seller's "I Quit" position is fair if it is a cash payment on the spot and if the car is bought 'as is,' with the mechanical inspection and any repairs needed to certify it done at the buyer's risk.

Expanding the "I Quit" position is also be called increasing the range of settlement. If I am willing to pay a little more for the used car, say $2900, and the seller is willing to sell for a little lower, perhaps $2850, then we have a range of settlement of $50. A deal could easily be done. All the elements listed above, such as tires and payment terms, can increase that range or create one that didn't exist when negotiations began.

Sometimes the settlement range expands when their negotiating partners work together to discover what interests underlie their positions. The position of not wanting to spend more than a certain amount on a used car is affected by a strong interest in safe, reliable transport. It is only by probing interests that a negotiator can direct the conversation to more substantial matters, craft the best deal possible, set a fair "I Quit" position and expand the range of settlement.

CHAPTER 7: CRISIS NEGOTIATION

Event: *Siege of Iranian Embassy, London*

Date: *30 April 1980*

Summary: *Six armed men stormed the embassy, taking 29 hostages and making various demands on the new Khomeini government. Police responded to an alarm, they knocked on the door and the head terrorist told them to go away. Crowds of Iranians arrived and began chanting support for the hostage-takers. Police set up a command post in a nearby school. To mask the noise of their work, commercial airline flights were diverted to fly overhead and a crew operated jackhammers, pretending to fix a gas leak. The Strategic Air Service (SAS) counter-terrorist unit was about to go on an exercise, having been alerted to a fake terrorist incident in the North of England. A former SAS member who was working as a dog-handler alerted his former colleagues that they might be needed. Authorities began making a full-size replica of the embassy to practise ways of storming the building.*

By the sixth day, hostage-takers threw one dead body out the front door, and police feared others were dead. The SAS began their assault from three sides at 7:24 p.m. Two stun grenades malfunctioned, and a soldier kicked in a window by mistake, alerting hostage-takers. Another solider got caught up in his ropes, blocking the way for his colleagues. Another SAS team came in from balconies and through an adjoining embassy whose wall they'd quietly been taking down all week.

Result: *All but one hostage-taker were shot dead. One other dead body was found—that of a hostage. The surviving hostage-taker was tried and sentenced to life in prison.*

Lessons Learned: *The situation was made more difficult by language barriers and crowds of protesters. There was the unusual procedure of police knocking on the front door and the equally unusual response when the hostage-taker opened the door and told police to go away. The happenstance of a former SAS member alerting his colleagues may have helped immeasurably, as did the happenstance of an SAS* *simulation at the same time as a real incident. Bad luck with stun grenades and the broken window could have been tragic. The need to involve countless others, such as air-traffic control, the gas company and nearby building owners, is a lesson. The surprisingly low toll, with 24 hostages and one hostage-taker surviving is a pleasant surprise.*

If your Crisis Requires Negotiation

Goal based Negotiations

One cliché is that negotiators strike their final deals at 3 a.m. and aren't sure what they agreed to until they read it in the newspapers the next day. Another is that topics are so many and complex that even friendly parties are not sure what their agreement entails.

Many parties aren't sure of the laws and regulations under which they are negotiating. There are 'non-table participants' who must approve the eventual deal. Union membership must ratify agreements reached by negotiating committees. The full board must vote on committee work, and a majority of the residents in a condominium corporation must vote on bylaws submitted by the board. Regulators, legislators, the media and citizens' groups can scupper deals and may even act against their own best interests. You have many partners in your negotiation, even if there are only two people sitting at the table.

Here are some principles negotiators should know:

Research

Can you obtain money at that interest rate? Can you procure those assets to clean up the neighbourhood over the weekend? Can you find enough day labourers to get the job done?

By making a promise you can't keep, you'll just annoy the community more. Whatever the task, you have to know your capabilities and limitations.

Research involves knowing what stakeholders will accept, what's within the laws and regulations and what may change in the future and need renegotiating. Research also involves knowing what the other side may want, need and accept.

Reality Checks

People like talking. Negotiations are often fun. Letting off steam can be fun too. But many discussion topics and activities in negotiations are unproductive. An action that breaks a law is not worth discussing. Offering to get something done quicker than it can be done or through defying the laws of physics is a waste of time.

In some jurisdictions, management is forbidden to hold direct discussions with union members during a strike. Talks must go through the union negotiating committee. An offer or request to speak directly is unlawful and shouldn't be made, unless perhaps as a tactic for publicity purposes.

I once coached law students in mediation skills at small-claims court. Judges' skills differ, depending on which court they preside over. Being a judge in small-claims court is a low-paying and low-status job that some lawyers take to gain experience for higher court appointments or for other reasons. When people had extreme positions—wanting total compensation and no compromise—I would sometimes interrupt the mediation and give a reality check. I'd point out that the court is a 'dollars-and-cents' forum where feelings, anguish and insult were mostly irrelevant. You had to show a specific and tangible loss with documents, receipts and proof. I couldn't predict how the judge would view the documents provided. Were they conclusive or ambiguous? What if the judge had had a personal experience relating to the event, such as a bad experience with a travel agent or home renovator? What if the judge hadn't dealt much in contract law or home renovations?

I'd conclude my reality check by pointing out that a judge could rule in favour of either side—or against either side. The judge could award anywhere between zero and 100 percent of the damages to either side. About this time each side would get a little more interested in dealing with the other, rather than having the judge impose a settlement.

The Sword of Damocles

Most of us need a deadline, reward or reason for doing something to motivate us. We need something metaphorically hanging over our heads, about to fall and injure us, to focus our attention. In a crisis, the possibility of blowing up, going to jail, being publicly embarrassed, injuring people, going bankrupt and so on focuses the mind.

In negotiations the Sword of Damocles can be a time deadline. It could be that one of the principal negotiators won't be available past a certain date. It could be a contract to provide services for the Olympic Games, which are obviously going to be held on a specific date. Lead time may be needed to obtain people and raw materials to perform the service. Negotiations may involve a truckload of fruit that will start to rot in seventy-two hours.

A good negotiator takes advantage of these factors to create a sense of urgency. A great negotiator may create deadlines to add this urgency. A really great negotiator may remove deadlines created by opponents. Imagine making sure the fruit is packed in a certain type of gas in a refrigerated truck that adds weeks to the storage time. Imagine new technology that means fewer people are required to meet obligations, those needed can be trained more quickly and less raw material is needed. Imagine alternative and redundant supply routes that ensure a constant supply of raw material.

Harnessing, making or removing deadlines can be a key to successful negotiations.

The Zeal for the Deal

There is something satisfying about doing a deal. It's done. It's an accomplishment. There are bragging-rights. The deal-makers can move on to other things. But in reality most negotiators try to bring the negotiations to an end far too soon. 'Too soon' means before parties really know whether it's in their best interests to do a deal, what elements could go into a successful deal, what the other party will settle for and whether a deal is the best outcome anyway.

I urge caution and thought before doing any deal.

The Need for Informed Partners

Making the pie bigger, distributive bargaining and creating more value for both sides are all great goals. But negotiating-partners need to know whether bigger pie plates exist and where value can be found.

I'll use the example I used in a leading law school with students who were very keen on making pies bigger. I asked how many owned homes. Only one or two did. I pointed out that most people have a vague understanding of a traditional mortgage, where payments are a function of the formula I = PRT (Interest equals Principal times Rate times Time). This is a blended mortgage, usually amortized over 20 or 25 years. But there can be hundreds of types of mortgages—interest-only, floating, balloon with a large payment scheduled in the future, and so on. If inexperienced home-buyers start hearing about all the different types of mortgages, they may well think they're being conned. At best, they may just get confused and move on. What the negotiation literature doesn't deal with is the difficulty in educating your negotiating-partner on all the options available to add value.

Educational theory gives us some advice on how to handle this challenge. The term 'incidental learning' refers to unofficial or enriched curriculum that can be delivered best when the learner is ready to learn. Angry, frustrated or scared people are not usually ready to learn. Calm them down. Wait for the right moment. The companion phrase is, "Just because the teacher taught doesn't mean the learner learned." Blurting out the facts or the truth at the wrong time usually won't get the job done.

"Let us never negotiate out of fear. But, let us never fear to negotiate."

— President John F. Kennedy, inaugural address, Friday, January 20, 1961

There are different kinds of learners. An experiential learner might want to see, touch, smell and experience the matter at hand. Some people like facts or statistics. Most seem to prefer pictures or stories. These may be visual or auditory learners. Some studies suggest that people learn more when all their faculties are engaged—talking, listening, seeing, touching, smelling, writing and so on. This is called kinesthetic learning—using the whole body. There are spiritual learners, intuitive learners and those who learn based on their gender, race or ethnicity. Role models and change agents from the community can be helpful catalysts.

Then there are the impediments to learning. In many public meetings literacy and numeracy present significant challenges. By definition, half the population is below average IQ. Much of the population won't have your education, training or experiences.

With so many styles and impediments, you can't be sure what technique to use. You will do best to have a sampling of all available to you and then see which seem to resonate. Move among the techniques. Make it easy for audience members to sample information in the way that's best for them. Keep alert for the moment when more or different information can be fed into the mix. See if you can harness the change agents and leaders who understand your position. Above all—be patient.

Negotiations about the Negotiations

Get to know the parties of a negotiation if you are a mediator, get to know the other side if you are a negotiating-partner (not adversary), and get to know your client well if you're an advocate or coach. But this respectful 'intake' is all done on billable time. This presents two ethical dilemmas. First, how much skill and permission do you have to provide quasi-psychological counselling to a client? Second, your long and respectful initial sessions with a client, and your research and zealous advocacy, all entail urging your client to use more of your services. You are in an ethical bind.

Sometimes the most respectful and ethical thing to do is just to get on with it or end negotiations.

Complexity

Negotiation is a process of persuasion. To persuade, you need to identify, and understand as far as you can, the other party's needs and the context in which they are negotiating and taking positions. Each context is complex. What will persuade a negotiating partner? Is it logic, money, psychological benefit? How do you find out which is the trump card in this negotiation?

Negotiators need to know what body language works and how to change approaches if they are negotiating in different regions of the country, with different cultures, with men or women. Establishing a rapport can be the first step in establishing common ground.

What constitutes 'positive' body language? Many people mistakenly think that looking relaxed and leaning back in a chair with expansive gestures is collegial—most of the time it looks pompous. The old rules from grade school of sitting up straight, looking interested, maintaining eye contact with people you're speaking with, using controlled gestures and so on will give you a great start.

Cultural sensitivities can be mystifying, especially when clichés and stereotypes don't apply to the particular person or group you're

A Negotiator's Reminders

TIPS

- ✓ You may not win, but you don't have to lose.
- ✓ There can be more than one path to a solution.
- ✓ Are there scientific data or "hard numbers" to support one opinion?
- ✓ Are your spokespeople, witnesses and experts prepared as speakers?
- ✓ Have you clarified expectations and interests?
- ✓ Are there areas of common ground from which to start?
- ✓ Is there a history of relations and negotiation between the parties? Does either party have a reputation for negotiating in a certain way?
- ✓ What authority do the opposing negotiators have?
- ✓ Do both parties have needs which must be met?
- ✓ Are there radical differences in the styles of doing business?
- ✓ Is one party presenting a proposal and the other party reacting to it?
- ✓ Is there potential for hostility if demands are not met?
- ✓ Is conflict a goal?
- ✓ Patience, please.

DVD

Available on the Companion DVD

encountering. The degree of formality a particular culture, age group or gender may prefer is as varied as potential negotiating-partners. I've seen informality offend a person, and I've seen formality offend as well.

Perhaps only experience can improve success. Research and thought before negotiations can help, but ability to read a person or group, anger-abatement techniques and control of the flight-or-fight response may just take time to master.

Dos and Don'ts of Negotiation

TIPS

DO

- ✓ Accept responsibility; admit mistakes.
- ✓ Make fair offers.
- ✓ Recognize and contain escalation.
- ✓ Find mutually acceptable statistics and facts.
- ✓ Suggest future joint efforts.
- ✓ Set limits on the time and money you're willing to invest.
- ✓ Demonstrate advantages of the alternatives.
- ✓ Have flexible methods, firm objectives.
- ✓ Use external standards of fairness.
- ✓ Maintain contact and communication.

DON'T

- ✓ Don't try to convince people they're wrong.
- ✓ Don't presume your opponent's intelligence or determination.
- ✓ Avoid "we/they" stereotypes.
- ✓ Don't settle simply to justify the time and effort expended.
- ✓ Don't be exhausted into a stalemate.
- ✓ Don't assume that size intimidates.
- ✓ Don't procrastinate.
- ✓ Don't attempt trickery—cooperate.

DVD

Available on the Companion DVD

Negotiations

Discussion Points:

1. Whom will you have to negotiate with?
2. Do you have the required skill in house?
3. Do you have a list of outside resources that can help?
4. What facts and figures should you have handy?
5. Are you prepared to walk away?
6. What might your adversaries need to know?
7. Is there third-party opinion or information that both sides would respect?
8. What long-term interests underlie the parties' positions?
9. What psychological needs do the parties have?
10. Are there constraints on your negotiations, such as time or capacity? Can these be used to either party's advantage?

PTSD or not PTSD?

My client had had a death occur in a group home. Like so many social-service and volunteer agencies, they just couldn't believe that a coroner's court would convene a hearing into the case. They were used to helping people. They couldn't get their minds around the fact that media and politicians might expect them to be convincing on the topics of responsibility and even blame.

In one round of rehearsing for the coroner's court, I thought I'd surprise the witnesses with a line of questioning that showed empathy for the care-givers, rather than for the victim or his family. I asked if the worker who was on duty during the death had been offered counselling for Post-Traumatic Stress Disorder.

The caregiver said he'd asked for counselling but had not heard back from his bosses yet. In another room senior management of the group home were going through the same questioning with one of my trainers. They were asked why they hadn't provided PTSD counselling for staff who had seen a client die in care.

"No one asked for counselling," was their response.

We got both groups back together and pointed out that this kind of miscommunication would end up giving the impression of a poorly run facility.

That's the value of full rehearsal. People see what it will be like to have to live with the statements they make and the recollections they have.

CHAPTER 8: WITNESS PREPARATION

Event: *Union Carbide Chemical Disaster, Bhopal, India*

Date: *3 December 1984*

Summary: *Methyl isocyanate leaked out of the plant and into the camp and town nearby. Some reports said the accident was caused by sabotage, and others suggested that workers had gone on a long tea break after hearing multiple and confusing alarms. The American CEO was arrested when he went to India. The company's sister plant in Institute, West Virginia had a highly publicized leak some months later. A flock of lawyers went to the scene to initiate lawsuits and seek clients, as often happens at crisis. As many as half a million Indians claimed damages, about half of whom provided no physical evidence. Three quarters of the claims came from areas the Indian government did not designate as affected by the event.*

Result: *Perhaps 4,000 dead and 11,000 injured.*

Lessons Learned: *Your crisis may occur thousands of miles away from your head office. There may be rumours about the causes for years afterwards. Having the CEO or chair go to the site is not always the best approach. The shanty town around the plant may have grown up because plant officials installed a pipe providing potable water as a humanitarian gesture. Note the hubris and irony of the release at Union Carbide's plant in Institute, West Virginia some months after, even though company officials had stated that a similar accident couldn't happen there. That leak sent 135 area residents to hospital and injured six workers.*

Witness Preparation: Testifying as a Skill

Witness Preparation is more a subject for a book than a section of a book. But here are highlights to get you started, with more information in Appendix 5: "Witness Preparation."

Some clients balk at witness preparation. Some say they want to be "natural" or just want to "be themselves." I agree with LeGrande and Mieraue, writing in the *Georgetown Journal of Legal Ethics*: "Lawyers who fail to conduct jury research or engage in other trial preparation techniques could leave themselves open to malpractice claims."[11] The authors also say that "poorly prepared witnesses are the greatest weakness in any case." For those who just want to be themselves, I point out that good writers and speakers, such as Winston Churchill, spend an hour writing, rewriting, rehearsing and practising for every minute they spend speaking. So do actors and athletes, watching game tapes and making notes about what worked in a given performance. Proper rehearsal rarely makes a witness worse, unless it's rushed and done just minutes before the hearing. As for becoming too 'slick,' LeGrande and Mieraue have had the same experience I have: "rarely have we seen a witness who was too smooth due to witness preparation."[12]

Many of the techniques used in speaking to the press and public also work in witness preparation. Witnesses and spokespeople share many of the same responsibilities and challenges. The SOCKO™ system is particularly helpful in a hearing featuring a question-and-answer format. In court, your core message is that you are helpful, expert, cooperative and willing. Before a tribunal your message may be all these things, plus the fact that there is an urgent need for action, that you are caring, sensitive to landowners' concerns, well prepared, have a respect for the process, are open to other parties' participation and so on.

Your behavioural objective is simple. You want the board/court to thank you for your participation. You want them to recognize your expertise. You want an enhanced reputation. You want to be known as caring, cooperative and prepared.

Certain challenges are usually the same regardless of the venue or the dollar amount involved. Memories are poor, participants have vastly different accounts of what happened, files are all over the place, documents are incomplete, emotions are high and the psychological and financial cost can be staggering.

This book is not offering anything remotely resembling legal advice. It won't take the place of your own research on how much witness preparation is allowed in your jurisdiction. In some jurisdictions, for certain types of cases, it's restricted. In Germany, for instance, an expert witness who talks to a lawyer before a case is usually not allowed to take part in the actual court proceeding—that's because under the German system it's the judge who's in the fact-gathering business, not the lawyer. In England barristers don't prepare witnesses: solicitors do. Some types of cases present special challenges for witnesses. These include child sexual abuse, rape and expert scientific and medical testimony designed to bolster lay evidence. You'll need to do your own research into what is allowed and will work in your jurisdiction. In all cases, it is you, not your consultant or the author of a book or article, who is ultimately responsible for your testimony.

It's important to work with people who really know the judge, venue, procedures, panel, interveners and all other relevant details needed to fine-tune testimony. In the end, a person called to testify in court, at a tribunal, in legislative or other legal proceedings is telling a story. The witness who tells the most compelling, believable story helps win the day.

"The thought of submitting to a verbal inquisition can be terrifying and this fear alone can be thoroughly exploited by opposing counsel if a witness is not properly conditioned to the pitfalls of testifying under cross examination."

— A.M. Selkirk Jr. (1992)

Story Rules

Like any good short story, testimony involves a plot, six or fewer characters and momentum. The story can be consumed and understood in one sitting. The main characters in a regulatory hearing are often the utility or resource-sector applicant, its customers, the neighbours, the environment (including flora and fauna), aggrieved parties, parties that will benefit and so on.

Keep the story simple, brief and clear. Complex stories don't fare well.

Good story-tellers put their audience at ease. In a hearing, this starts with the opening statement. Comfortable, confident body language, including eye contact, gestures, leaning forward and a deliberate and authoritative tone, all help. A good story offers a bit of suspense and occasionally a surprise. This can be achieved with rhetorical questions, pauses to refer to exhibits and varying intensity as the story progresses. A good story usually includes some metaphors and colourful language to describe the scene. There will be anecdotes and examples to illustrate points.

Marcus Boccaccini, writing in *Behavioral Sciences and the Law*, has a unique perspective on testimony as story. He advocates "powerful speech…narrative testimony" normal language and "simultaneous speech."[13] Powerful speech avoids what I call 'weasel words'—'I think,' 'feel' or 'hope' rather than 'I know.' Narrative testimony calls for telling a story in a clear and logical way without continued prompting from counsel. Narratives may also contain longer sentences than just what's needed to respond literally to counsel's questions. I often imagine a fellow guest at a party trying to have a pleasant conversation three words at a time like some answers to questions in court. Normal language means not trying to imitate a lawyer or the phrases in a legal contract. Research shows that even university graduates have trouble understanding sentences that are longer than 18 words, but that's not a reason to resort to "Yes" and "No" answers.

The judge, jury and lawyers in court may only be listening with half an ear, just as many of us do at dinner parties. So they need repetition. Sometimes they can refer to a transcript later, but best grab their attention the first time. Plain language means no jargon and your normal vocabulary. Simultaneous speech just means that the lawyer and witness appear to be having a natural exchange, with one beginning to speak when the other appears to have ended his or her turn.

Expert Witnesses

> *"Before a witness becomes a witness, he or she is just a vulnerable person."*
>
> — ***S. Hamlin (1985)***

It seems the most natural thing in the world to find the most eminent researcher or lecturer about a topic to bolster your case. Regrettably, judges, juries, politicians, regulators and tribunals make decisions in complex ways and are influenced by many more factors than academic publications and professorships. In fact the local person often has more credibility than the academic from a prestigious institution. Moreover, it is often practical experience, rather than laboratory experiments, that carries the day.

Experts can be painted as aloof and dealing with the hypothetical.

Celebrated cases of experts who were wrong can undermine testimony. Engineers can be challenged with the collapse of the Quebec City Bridge or the failure of the Tacoma Narrows Bridge or the Second Narrows Bridge in Vancouver. Sometimes a riveter or welder can bolster an engineer's testimony.

One of the problems with rules is that they can suggest completeness. For some, a list of rules can take the place of thinking. The lists in this section may be incomplete, may not always apply or may include elements that shouldn't be used in certain circumstances. Nonetheless, here's a fairly complete list of rules for witnesses, expert or not:

Dos and Don'ts for the Expert and Non-expert Witness

DO

- ✓ Dress appropriately.
- ✓ Respect the seriousness of the proceedings.
- ✓ Prepare yourself.
- ✓ Project authority.
- ✓ Speak clearly and breathe.
- ✓ Be thorough.
- ✓ Be sincere and positive but don't sugar coat.
- ✓ Listen to the questions and answer them specifically.
- ✓ Deliver positive messages that move your case forward.
- ✓ Ask for clarification.
- ✓ Question assumptions.
- ✓ Ask to explain an answer.
- ✓ Use supportive and open body language and gestures, moving slowly.
- ✓ Lean slightly forward to engage.
- ✓ Use open, double hand gestures.
- ✓ Look at the person you are speaking to (judge, panelist, lawyer, intervener) rather than sweep the room with your eyes.
- ✓ Divide large audiences into quadrants and linger on one at a time.

DON'T

Available on the Companion DVD

- ✓ Don't argue.
- ✓ Don't feel obliged to answer only "yes" or "no".
- ✓ Don't get flustered or angry.
- ✓ Don't shift.
- ✓ Don't read for more than a sentence or two when accuracy is paramount.
- ✓ Don't apologize unless you've made a serious error or offended someone.
- ✓ Don't lie.

A confident witness, though, might purposefully shift in her chair to transmit discomfort with a topic. Reading can work if you pick a short passage and read to emphasize, for instance, that the environmental commitment was put in writing and signed by every board member or that the police at the scene had certain observations. If the question doesn't provide an opportunity to get out important information, you might just add something beyond the literal answer. A witness should never argue but might be adamant about her role or the science of the matter. Naturally there are exceptions to all rules.

Out of nervousness, many witnesses apologize for losing their trains of thought. The board may not know anything is going wrong with the witness's mental processes, so the apology is unnecessary. This is not to say that there isn't a therapeutic value in careful apologies, vetted by lawyers. Apologizing for being late, not having documents handy or other minor matters can work just fine too. Just follow up with an offer to obtain the documents or information—often called an 'undertaking.' You don't want to do this too often, because you're generating lots of work for your team, but you occasionally have to dignify a question with a commitment to find an answer.

We often apologize or transmit further information with a facial grimace. If we make a mistake, we often also make a face. First of all, facial expressions burn up energy. If you are going to use them, they should support your verbal message, not cancel it out. The facial expression that says "I goofed" is not helpful. I think many people make this face to show that they know they goofed and hope that, if the adjudicator noticed the error, s/he didn't notice anything that the witness didn't already know. That doesn't help. Most of the time the small error isn't noticed, so making a face just draws attention to it. Correct it smoothly with words, not a grimace.

> You can't simply tell a witness to follow the rules for testifying and expect a good outcome ... any more than you can tell someone the rules for football and then send him out on the field to play .... It's only through practise that the techniques of testifying will become comfortable and automatic.[14]

Witness Preparation

Discussion Points:

1. What are the likely jurisdictions where this organization might need to be represented?
2. Are there laws, codes or customs we should become familiar with?
3. What is the status of our knowledge of the impact we have on our neighbours and other third parties?
4. Have we codified our efforts to inform our neighbours?
5. How do our actions compare with those of our competitors, the industry and the jurisdiction?
6. What is new in other jurisdictions?
7. What guidelines from international agencies might pertain to our activities?
8. Do we have a great lead witness?
9. Have we rehearsed, videotaped and trained our technical experts to work as a team with the lead?
10. Can we harness third-party support?

Dead Parrot

Excellent legal advice can be to avoid saying anything at all. The reason is that counsel doesn't want public statements in the file when the court case arrives 18 months after the incident. Fair enough.

But the flip side is the need to communicate and perhaps take a hit on the contents of the file at a later date.

I was making a presentation to a law firm and making this point. A lawyer interrupted to tell me the story of her client who had called about 5 a.m. one day a few months before.

"My client called from about an hour out of town," he began.

"There had been a bad fire in the plant overnight, and they wanted me to look over a press release. Well, I'm not in the business of writing press releases in the first place and didn't want them issuing one in the second."

I asked, "Why not issue a press release?"

"Liability" I was told. "Why admit the event had even happened?" the lawyer asked.

I pointed out that if the plant had burned down, it would be completely evident to all who drove by. The fire would still be smouldering and fire-fighters would still be on the scene. The fire marshal would be investigating.

"In fact, your client now has a former plant, an ex-plant, a plant that's singing in the choir invisible, a plant that's gone to meet its maker, like the dead parrot in the Monty Python sketch.

"How about the liability in having dozens of workers needing to be driven to work by spouses, kissed goodbye and left at the gate of the former plant in cold weather? They might freeze to death."

A press release that asked workers to stay home, suppliers to hold off on deliveries and customers to be patient during these tough times might have reduced liability, improved logistics and protected reputation.

It would sure have beaten dealing with angry customers, freezing workers and a traffic jam of suppliers' trucks at the plant gate.

CHAPTER 9: LEGISLATION

Event: *Hurricane Hazel*

Date: *12-16 October 1954*

Summary: *The hurricane had taken 500 lives as it crossed Haiti and the eastern US. But Toronto's weather forecast for the 15th and 16th said the storm had weakened and would only bring light rain. Although most people in Ontario associated hurricanes with the tropics, there had been 25 tropical storms in the province since 1900. Hazel was the worst. Nine inches of rain fell on the Humber Valley in two days. Homes and bridges were washed away, and rivers overflowed their banks. Among the responders was Molson's Brewery Mobile Emergency Unit from Montreal, which gave typhoid shots to hundreds.*

Result: *81 dead in greater Toronto and a billion dollars' damage in the storm's path through Haiti and the US.*

Lessons Learned: *It wasn't until 1974 that the federal government formed Emergency Preparedness Canada. The hurricane was an impetus to create a conservation authority in Metropolitan Toronto and manage flood plains. Few people were prepared with their own emergency supplies. Note the private-sector response.*

Legislation

The following summary is a version contained in a crisis plan we wrote. It is provided to illustrate the complexity of overlapping laws and jurisdictions. Your plan should take into account local laws and conditions.

In Ontario, Canada, *An Act to Provide Formulation and Implementation of Emergency Plans* (The Emergency Plans Act) allows municipal governments to pass bylaws on providing services during a disaster. Municipal emergency plans written under this act deal with financial expenditures, power to take action before emergencies are declared, evacuation procedures, the designation of municipal council members and their duties during an emergency, review and training related to the plan, the distribution of supplies and other matters relating to an emergency. Specific plans should determine the roles and responsibilities of designated municipal officials.

The Emergency Plans Act states "A Head of Council may declare that an emergency exists in the municipality or in any part thereof and may take such action and make such orders he considers necessary and are not contrary to the law to implement the Emergency Plan of the municipality to protect the property, health, safety and welfare of the inhabitants of the emergency area." Many municipal plans therefore recommend that a senior police or fire official "personally assume control at the site of an emergency." This person may differ from the on-site coordinator, who may in turn be appointed by the senior police or fire official. Municipal plans usually invest these officials and the mayor with wide powers to order evacuations and otherwise deal with the emergency.

The head of the municipal council may declare an emergency and must notify the solicitor general. The premier may also declare an emergency.

You should consult the legislation in your own jurisdiction, but what follows is an example of relevant agencies and acts and responsibilities in one jurisdiction. Historic unitary states such as the United Kingdom and Holland present special considerations, as does a cultural imperative such as respect for hierarchy in Japan.

Local and Regional Governments

For large incidents, the municipal level of government may wish to call in federal or provincial assistance, besides notifying whatever federal or provincial agencies it has to.

Depending on the nature of the incident, these ministries/agencies may include the RCMP, provincial or city police; ministries of the environment, natural resources, transport and communications, community and social services or municipal affairs and housing; a medical office of health; and emergency-measures organizations. Terrorism can ring in myriad other agencies including CSIS (the Canadian security agency) or even international bodies such as Interpol. Your plan should list officials to contact (see the list forms in "Public Affairs Room" in Chapter 3 above). The following table is an example of a chart of incidents and their corresponding contact agencies. It happens to apply to Toronto, Ontario, but

Local and Regional Government Aid & Notification

INCIDENT	AGENCY
Any goods regulated under the *Transportation and Dangerous Goods Act*	Police, fire department, ambulance, in Canada call CANUTEC (Canadian Transport Emergency Centre) collect 1-613-996-6666 (24 hours) or *666 on mobile phone
Involving or requiring the disposal of explosives	Police, Provincial or State Police, fire department, ambulance
Fire	Fire department, police, ambulance
Evacuation	Police, Provincial or State Police, ambulance
Death or injury	Police, fire, ambulance service, coroner, director of emergency services Call 911
Chemical transport accidents	In Canada call CANUTEC collect 1-613-996-6666 (*666 on mobile phone), police, fire
Rail accidents	In Canada CNR and CPR service centres, police, fire departments
Civilian aircraft	Regional Flight Information, police, fire department, ambulance, hospital and health units, coroner
Military aircraft crash	Regional Rescue Co-ordination Center
Pesticides, environmental contaminant spill	MOE District Office
Floods	Conservation Authority, MNR, Dir. of Municipal Works
Pollutant discharge from ships	Coast Guard
Contaminant discharge into the atmosphere	Local health unit, MOE, MOL, Emergency Services

DVD

Customize on the Companion DVD

similar relationships exist between most municipalities and provinces or states across the country and in the U.S. Be sure to modify the form to reflect your needs and the current situation.

The Coroner's Act

The Coroner's Act gives the supervising coroner wide and general powers to act in cases involving death. The supervising coroner oversees the coroner in the district where the incident occurred. The local coroner conducts an investigation into the cause of death and is entitled to direct the police. Coroners may take possession of and identify bodies, determine the cause of death and issue medical certificates of death. They can also appoint constables to take charge of physical wreckage, seal off sites and protect evidence. In some jurisdictions, the supervising coroner has special kits located in pre-arranged facilities to assist in such operations.

Several provisions in *The Coroner's Act* and *The Occupational Health and Safety Act* become important in the event of death. *The Coroner's Act* states that anyone who believes that a death has resulted from violence, misadventure, negligence, misconduct or malpractice must notify a coroner or police officer. Failure to do so can lead to a fine or imprisonment.

The Occupational Health and Safety Act

The Occupational Health and Safety Act deals with an employer's obligations if an employee dies in the course of employment. The employer must notify one or more officials at the Ministry of Labour and the health and safety representatives of the trade union and provide a written report to a designated director with the Ministry of Health within 48 hours.

Organizations should review all relevant legislation, have it on hand and ensure they know which government officials to report to in the event of a death.

Employers and employees should know that while there is a duty to provide medical assistance to a living victim, it can be an offence to interfere with a dead body.

911

In many (but not all) jurisdictions, dialling 911 automatically alerts police, ambulance and fire officials, which will in turn ensure that the employer meets most or all the requirements of the acts mentioned above. Find out how these and other official responders are linked through 911 in your region.

When a crisis may involve crime, company Emergency Response officials and security should respect the needs of the police to preserve the crime scene. Most police forces are more than willing to discuss their requirements, and organizations should take advantage of this.

Legislation

Discussion Points:

1. Do we have all relevant legislation on hand?
2. How well do we know the laws in the other jurisdictions where we operate?
3. What does dialling 911 trigger in the jurisdictions where we operate?
4. Do we have good relations with third-party responders?
5. Are there third parties whose expertise we can harness?
6. Have we consulted with our unions or those of our suppliers, customers and neighbours?
7. When was the last time we met with police, fire, ambulance, hospital, mortuary and other officials?
8. Are there agreements we can reach in advance with outside officials?
9. Who is monitoring changes in legislation?
10. Who is calling and testing the phone numbers given in our plan, and how often?

Which Way to the Reading-Room?

A boot camp for troubled teenagers takes kids to a wilderness location to get them off drugs and alcohol. Disgruntled former clients were making charges of sexual and physical abuse.

We began reviewing policies and procedures to see whether they'd add to the controversy if they became publicly known. I imagined a legislative committee asking to review them and the contents ending up on national newscasts.

One policy caught my eye—no reading for the first month in the camp. I asked what purpose this policy served.

"Kids on drugs and alcohol are so scrambled, we need their minds clear, with no other input than our counselling," I was told.

I asked, "What about a youngster who brings Shakespeare or Catcher in the Rye, *saying s/he wants to keep up on school curriculum?"*

I received no answer.

"What about the Bible?"

No answer.

I counselled that there might be great clinical and psychological justification for this policy, but the camp would need a compelling story to tell the public.

These exchanges whetted my appetite for more policy questions.

Do you have dietary alternatives for Jewish and Muslim clients? Do you have any Jewish and Muslim clients? My client didn't know.

Do you have a policy on whether a Muslim can pray five times a day? I note lots of hugging and shaking hands. Do you have a policy dealing with some Arab and Jewish sects that frown on or forbid some touching?

There was no such policy.

These days, a policy can be your crisis, and so can not having a policy.

CHAPTER 10: POLICY

Event: Ocean Ranger *Sinking, Hibernia Oil Fields, off Newfoundland*

Date: *15 February 1982*

Summary: *A captain who had only been on board for eight days made an error trying to correct a list on the vessel on 6 February 1982. When the alarm sounded, the crew were slow to react, having been through two false alarms in two days. The men didn't know how to operate one new lifeboat, and another's engine wouldn't start. There weren't enough lifeboats to go around, and several had maintenance problems. In the weekly drills, the lifeboats weren't actually lowered. On February 14 a giant wave knocked out a porthole on the* Ocean Ranger, *causing electrical and other problems. The rig's standby ship was supposed to remain within 2 miles but was about eight miles away. When the standby ship arrived, the crew were on the ocean, in a lifeboat, bailing out water. When they climbed up the side of the boat, it capsized. The standby ship threw out ropes, but in the freezing water the crew couldn't grab them. An investigation showed valves in the wrong position on the* Ocean Ranger, *meaning crew had inadvertently contributed to the sinking.*

Result: *All 84 dead.*

Lessons Learned: *The value of realistic safety drills, maintenance and repairs. The need for experience, education and training at all levels. The need to pay attention to early warning-signs. This tragedy may have affected the decision to build a 'gravity-based' structure for the Hibernia oil fields at a cost of 2 billion dollars. Crises often affect future public policy.*

Policy

Human Resources

Organizations usually have many human-resources policies and statements that you can reproduce in whole or in part in your crisis plan.

The number of employees, dispersal over the country or a region, statistics (women, managers, hourly paid, etc.) and a host of other data may be valuable during a crisis or controversy.

You should also reproduce equal-opportunity policies and those that affect training, safety, health and the environment.

Environmental Policy

Without an environmental policy, you will have few positive statements to use during an environmental incident. Policies must be known and written in simple language, so that reporters, neighbours and the public can understand them.

The language that follows may form the basis or model for an environmental policy if your organization does not now have one:

- Our organization strives continually to lessen the impact of all its activities that could affect the environment. We take environmental impact into account when designing and planning new activities.
- Environmental protection and compliance is an increasingly complex field. There may be over 500 environmental acts and regulations requiring specific expertise to be fully understood.
- Our organization is committed to doing environmental audits, or retaining any outside experts as it requires, to ensure that even our minimum standard of performance complies with the most stringent legislation for each jurisdiction where we operate.
- We are committed to working with similar industries, governments, public groups and other stakeholders to continuously improve our environmental record. We regularly meet with employees, customers, neighbours and other stakeholders to ensure awareness of environmental issues and practices.

Business Ethics Standards

One great litmus test for business ethics is to imagine having family members in your meetings with you. Another is imagining a detailed description of your meeting and positions on the front page of the newspaper. You need your own written policy on ethics and behaviour. Consider the following:

- No one in this organization is ever to be expected to perform an illegal, unethical or immoral act, direct anyone else to do so, or overlook such an act by others.
- A minimum standard of performance is the letter and spirit of the most stringent laws in the jurisdictions where we operate. One reason why we require this is to enhance our reputation and relations with co-workers, customers, neighbours, governments, suppliers, competitors and other stakeholders.
- We act ethically.
- We value being, and being perceived as, a moral and ethical company.
- We recognize that reputation is a valuable business asset.
- All our decision-making processes should take account of any adverse effects our activities will have on anyone in both the immediate and the long-term future.
- People that our corporation interacts with should feel that we have dealt with them professionally and equitably.
- We should be able to justify our actions publicly.
- We understand that laws, ethics, morals and codes of conduct may not all be the same, and we need to explore all these in our decision-making.

King's Cross Underground Fire—1987

"...the outbreak of fire was not regarded as something unusual; indeed it was regarded by senior management as inevitable in a system of this age. This attitude was no doubt increased by the insistence of London Underground that a fire should never be referred to as a fire but by the euphemism 'smouldering'."

— D. Fennell (1988)

Preparedness Policy

Every organization should create a preparedness policy and include it in its orientation for new employees and refresher training for all. Some statements you may wish to include are:

- Our organization is committed to updating all its corporate and site-specific crisis-management plans to ensure they are current and will help to mitigate crises and controversies.
- Our organization is committed to regularly scheduled drills, seminars, training-programs and simulations to test our plans and capabilities.
- Our organization is working with others (governments, industry associations, academics) to incorporate new developments in preparedness techniques into its existing programs.
- We hope to involve official responders (police, fire, EMO and others) and a variety of other stakeholders in planning and testing our procedures.

Worker Health and Safety

In many industries, health and safety policies can have the most beneficial effects of all. Some elements of your policies might be the following:

- The health and safety of all employees is the primary business concern of any corporation.
- Risks are endemic to all personal and professional activities. Managing such risks is the responsibility of everyone working in our company.
- All workers are accountable for ensuring that activities, training and equipment continuously reduce the potential risk of any business process.
- The minimum standard of performance for all employees will be to comply with the spirit and letter of the most stringent health and safety legislation in the jurisdiction where the division operates.
- A commitment to safe operations must permeate the entire organization.

- Safety must not be solely the responsibility of a committee or someone with a title.
- All workers need to be encouraged and rewarded for using common sense, following safe practices and sharing their views with others, regardless of title or circumstance.

Post-Crisis Policy

One important aspect of professionally managing a crisis is timely and sensitive communication with all those affected. This plan offers several sample letters of sympathy and condolence for you to use as models.

Even after a false fire alarm, the senior manager should write a letter of thanks to the responding fire department. There should be similar communication with neighbours, governments and other stakeholders if they are affected by even a minor incident.

Evaluation of the effectiveness of the response should begin immediately after the crisis. Opinions should be solicited from all levels of the organization. You should set an internal communication program in motion immediately, to dispel any misinformation that may have arisen from the crisis.

Outside groups, third-party experts, industry allies and others should be consulted or retained as need be to help evaluate the response.

Notifying Family or Next of Kin

If the crisis results in an injury, serious injury or death of one or more employees, the person chosen to notify the family and/or next of kin should follow certain procedures to ease the impact of the news.

The company representative **should not**:

- give the bad news over the phone. Do it in person;
- make an appointment to see the next of kin or family;
- relay your message to anyone else except the person(s) concerned;
- hold any notes about the incident in his/her hand when approaching the house or talking to the family or next of kin;
- leave word with the neighbours to have the family return the call;
- speak quickly or appear overly sympathetic;

- make any physical contact with the family or next of kin unless they faint, need first aid or get into shock.
- needlessly go over material or ask questions that other agencies will deal with.

Your company's representative should:

Listen

Be empathetic

Give help as appropriate

Provide information

Provide technical assistance

Be available

Be in touch

Guide the grieving about their rights and the procedures to follow

When possible, facilitate a safe visit to the site of death

Sample Letters

Local customs and individual religious beliefs must be taken into account. When in doubt, senior management should obtain guidance and direction from a variety of community, religious and cultural leaders. What follows are sample notification letters and letters of condolence that you can adapt to suit individual needs and tastes. They should be vetted by counsel.

Sample Letter of Notification In The Case of Serious Injuries

Letter (to be couriered)

* Do not phone deliver

(Name and address of addressee)

The President and officers of (company/organization) have asked me to inform you that your (son, wife, father, etc.), (name), was hospitalized in (place where injury occurred) on (date) with a (type of illness and injury) due to (nature of incident and circumstances).

(Name of injured) has been placed on the (medical status) list and in the judgement of the attending physician, (name), (his/her) condition is of such severity that there is cause for concern but no imminent danger to (his/her) life. Please be assured that the best staff and facilities at (name of hospital, address of hospital, main phone number) are being provided for (him/her).

I understand you have already spoken to (name, title of notifier) and I would like to add our offer of assistance to you and your family.

Yours truly,

President's name
President (or other senior title),
(name division)
(name of city and province/state)

Customize on the Companion DVD

Sample Letter of Notification In The Case of an Employee's Death

Letter (to be couriered)

* Do not phone deliver

(Name and address of addressee)

The President and officers of (company/organization) have asked me to express our deepest regrets that your (son, wife, father, etc.), (name), died in (place where injury occurred) on (date) as a result of (type of illness and injury) due to (nature of incident and circumstances).

I understand you have already spoken to (name, title of notifier) and I would like to add our sincerest sympathy to you.

Yours truly,

President's name
President (or other senior title),
(name division)
(name of city and province/state)

Sample Letter of Notification of Condolence

*** (For regular mail delivery within one week of incident)**

(Date)

(Company/Organization Name)
(Insert address here)

(Name and address of addressee)

Dear Mrs.___________, Mr.___________ and family:

The employees and executives of (company) join me in extending to you our deepest sympathy on the death of your (son, wife, father, daughter).

We know the irreparable loss that you have suffered and realize there is little that we can say to help you in this moment of sorrow. However, if we can assist you with (list assistance activities) please do not hesitate to contact (name, title) at (telephone number) or write to (name, title) at (address).

Our heartfelt condolences are extended to you and the members of your family in your bereavement.

President's name
President (or other senior title),
(name of city and province/state)

Obituaries

In the event of the death of a high-profile employee, an obituary should be released to the media after the next of kin have been notified. The Human Resources Department should have these facts with a *signed* release granting permission to maintain and release this information in the event of a death.

In the event of a suicide you will likely be asked questions about motives, methods and discovery.

OBITUARY INFORMATION	
Given and last name:	
Home address:	
Place and date of birth:	
Place, date and time of death:	
Cause of death:	
Length of illness:	
Those present at time of death:	
Events surrounding death and location:	
Address of surviving relatives (Wife/husband, parents, brother/sister, children):	
Date and place of marriage:	
Date of immigration, if required:	Date of residency, if required:
Previous residence and duration:	
Previous occupation:	
Place and level of education:	
Membership in organizations:	
Awards and distinguished service:	
Church affiliation:	
Military record, wars, rank, honours, date of discharge:	
Place, date and time of funeral:	
Official at funeral:	
Resting place of body:	
Gifts or donations in lieu of flowers:	
The body, if lying in state, will be where, when?	
Pallbearers - active and honourary:	
Music:	
Burial place:	
Additional information:	

DVD

Customize on the Companion DVD

Policy

Discussion Points:

1. Do we have relevant, modern and appropriate HR policies?
2. Who will review the policies in other and similar industries?
3. How often should we vet our policies with our lawyers?
4. Are all our board and senior management obituaries up to date?
5. Who will update obituaries annually?
6. How will we ensure our employees are well informed of our organization's policies?
7. Do we have stakeholder groups with special ethical, religious or moral imperatives?
8. Do we have access to experts who can brief us on special needs quickly as needed?
9. Are we sure our health and safety procedures and policies are in line with current laws?
10. Who will search the web and other sources annually to ensure we are up to date?

Forever Young

Most of us who have had the privilege of attending college or university agree it was the time of our lives. But not today, in Montreal, at Dawson College. A gunman has left four kids with great potential dead, and more than a dozen visibly injured. Perhaps dozens of others will have psychological injuries that will recur for years.

We live in a violent society. Statistics are hard to come by, but as many as 5,000 North American children are buried in unmarked graves each year. They're often runaways, and nobody claims them. The dollar value of illegal drugs sold on the street is often bigger than a big-three auto-maker's profits in a really good year. Ten percent of the population is chronically poor.

In the US, 135,000 American children take handguns to school every day. Every fourteen hours a child under the age of five is murdered. Homicide has replaced automobile accidents as the leading cause of death in children under the age of one.

Boston therapist Terrance Real cites these numbers to explain how many adult males have brought forward childhood trauma into their violent adulthood. Usually these people are just garden-variety bullies and bombasts. Some, like the young gunman in Montreal, get really violent in their marriages, workplaces and schools.

What do we do? It's impossible to make any institution completely safe. Any building with multiple doors, windows and underground parking is a 'soft' target and vulnerable. Sure, inspection of backpacks, no lockers, no garbage cans, see-through classroom doors, metal detectors and private security guards in the hall can turn a school into a harder target. But a determined person can do lots of damage with knives, bottles and fists.

Crisis plans and procedures must change with the times and be revised regularly. This event will cause a spike in interest, then a too predictable return to hoping for the best.

How do we keep students safe? Ironically, the answer may be down the hall in the psychology department. We laugh at the movies made about young adult angst—the kind brought on by not getting picked by the team or not being asked to dance at the prom.

But those tectonic pressures and other forms of alienation are dangerous forces. It is worth noting the success extreme groups have had in recruiting alienated youth all over the world. It is worth studying the twisted hate that would drive someone to shoot others in school or engage in terrorism. Our colleges and universities then need to reach out to make sure students feel as great a sense of belonging as possible and be alert to those who don't seem to fit in. The feeder grades and high schools need to get rid of bullying. They say they have, but they haven't.

And what of those left behind? Grief is a very personal matter. No one can tell another when to cry and when to be over a trauma. Among the most ridiculous phrases are, "I know how you feel." Sorry, you don't.

The only good news is that Post-Traumatic Stress Disorder is far less prevalent than grief counsellors would have us believe.

The students, parents and friends of the dead and injured at Dawson certainly qualify. But the studies show that as few as 25 percent of potential victims actually get PTSD. Of those, a significant percentage just want a friendly ear for a while. Symptoms drop off quickly after a few weeks and life goes on.

But then there's the parents and siblings of the dead. Life will never be the same. There's survivor guilt over life's little pleasures. There's endless second-guessing about the small changes of schedule that could have saved a life. Years from now, a song on the radio will bring all the pain back. Occasional dreams will provide one last welcome visit.

The real danger now is for the living. There's a very real possibility that this tragedy will heap more tragedy on surviving siblings, destroying families and alienating those left behind.

Forty-five years ago, as a boy of seven, I was awakened by a commotion in my house. "Ricky's been shot," I heard my father say in a tone of voice that still cuts through time. Then it was my mother's voice pleading with the 911 operator—"What does it matter, my boy's been shot." She was being asked the stupid details that 911 operators ask in lieu of action. I lost my brother in a mindless, senseless, careless accident at home. It wasn't a crazed, angry loner or Goth with inexplicable motives, but it had much the same destructive power.

I just hope lots of parents are hugging their kids today.

—The author's commentary on the Dawson College shooting, September 13, 2006, edited and reprinted from the Montreal Gazette *and* Calgary Herald

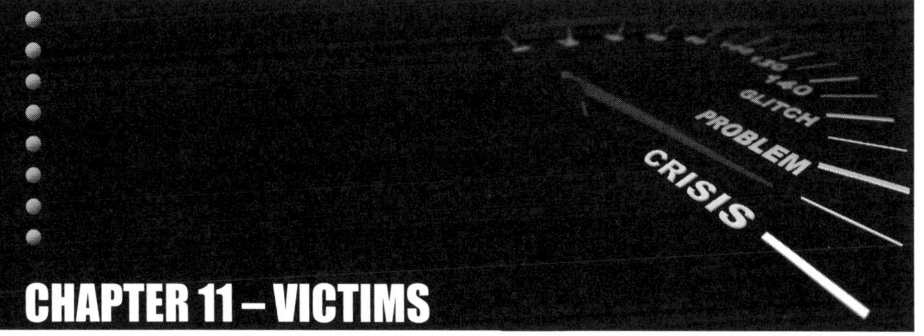

CHAPTER 11 – VICTIMS

Event: *Alaska Earthquake*

Date: *27 March 1964*

Summary: *The quake registered 8.6 on the Richter scale, larger than the 2010 quake in Haiti (7) and ten million times more powerful than the atomic bomb dropped on Hiroshima. Response came from 40,000 US service people stationed in Alaska and federal aid.*

Result: *At least 118 dead and $500 million in damage, which bankrupted the new state.*

Lessons Learned: *The power of nature. The need for volunteers and outside aid when an event destroys your ability to respond. A good crisis plan assumes that you will have fewer official responders and have to make use of volunteers. Happenstance—the* Exxon Valdez *oil spill happened exactly 25 years later.*

"... an effective disaster response will accommodate not only the needs of those directly affected (the victims) but also the needs of those indirectly affected (victims' relatives, friends, acquaintances and careers). ... [I]t is no longer acceptable that the effectiveness of a disaster response be judged only on such criteria as whether or not the perpetrators are caught, whether or not professional negligence is proved, or how quickly 'normal service' is restored. A comprehensive and holistic assessment requires that a disaster response also be judged on whether those indirectly affected are treated humanely, sensitively and with equanimity"

— Scarman Centre for the Study of Public Order

Victimization

Available on the Companion DVD

One of the most challenging aspects of crisis and disaster response involves dealing with victims. Victims include those hurt or displaced by the event and can also include responders, family members, friends and neighbours. Victims tell their stories to the courts, regulatory bodies, the media and others. You do not want them telling a story of how insensitive you were. Even when you are not in charge of the response, the incident may become known as your event, and you may appear to be responsible for all its aspects. It is in your best interests to contribute to a sensitive and effective response to victims' needs.

Besides ensuring medical treatment, you must address the longer-term emotional and intellectual damage that can also affect responders and victims. For an exploration of this complex issue see Appendix 6: "Post-Traumatic Stress Disorder and Crises."

Victim Assistance Checklist

ACTIVITY	RESPONSIBILITY	COMPLETED
Review disaster and psychological literature annually.		
Ensure that health, hygiene and loss prevention staff and consultants have incident stress and PTSD as part of their mandates.		
Establish contacts with mental health professionals who can help in time of need.		
Contact mental health associations, teaching institutions, hospitals and other groups.		
Determine if mental health students can assist.		
Develop phone trees to mobilize mental health care givers.		
Consider a series of professional development lectures by mental health professionals to educate those who will be responders.		
Build stress and PTSD mitigation activities into simulations.		
Contact volunteer groups.		
Contact victim support groups such as 'Disaster Action' in the UK.		
Review websites every six months to update additional groups and information.		
Investigate cultural and religious needs for burial and comfort.		
Contact cultural, religious and diplomatic resources.		

DVD

Customize on the Companion DVD

Caring for Extended Victims

- ✓ Activate phone trees to mobilize mental health professionals.
- ✓ Make down time and aerobic recreation available to responders.
- ✓ Communicate supportive messages to families of responders.
- ✓ Communicate daily with victims' families even if there is no news—be available and supportive.
- ✓ Don't guess at victims' needs—ask.
- ✓ Treat the dead with respect and deal with them quickly.
- ✓ Disseminate the factual information you have quickly.
- ✓ Provide concrete support—counseling, phones, transport, security, privacy, clergy.
- ✓ Consult with religious and cultural resources.
- ✓ Allow access to the disaster site.
- ✓ Do not be intrusive, but be available.
- ✓ Loved ones will want information about the time, place and cause of death.
- ✓ Don't say you "know how it feels"—you don't.
- ✓ Loved ones will want to visit the site, perhaps several times—facilitate this.
- ✓ Loved ones will want to view the body or pictures.
- ✓ Loved ones may want to speak with responders who were there.
- ✓ Loved ones may want an "artifact" from the disaster (i.e.: piece of the vehicle they were in, flower or rock from the site, sand from the sea shore, etc.).
- ✓ Remember...many victims do not recover from PTSD—they cope.
- ✓ Victims will need legal advice.
- ✓ Be honest and sensitive.
- ✓ Help victims make choices.
- ✓ Walk with, not away from victims.
- ✓ Don't force anything on victims.
- ✓ Hold a de-briefing with responders.
- ✓ Consider harnessing the knowledge of victims and survivors.
- ✓ Continue contact with victims, if productive.
- ✓ Be available—your support may be needed for longer than you think.

DVD

Available on the Companion DVD

Apologies are also crucial part of healing and reparation. For a brief discussion on effective apologies, see Appendix 7: "Apologies."

Victims

Discussion Points:

1. Who are the potential victims we will care for?
2. How far will our care reach—extended families, non-staff responders, etc.?
3. What are our current in-house resources to offer appropriate care for victims?
4. What external resources can we identify to support our own?
5. What agreements can we reach and what contracts can we sign with third-party responders, so they will be available to us?
6. Who in our employee groups may be victims?
7. Who are the right people on our team to interact with the grieving?
8. Are there physical assets we should procure right now in case of crisis?
9. Who will sign condolence letters?
10. Who will visit victims and their families?

Need Help with that Bag of Money?

A multinational had me read their crisis plan. When it came to the section on their operations in the part of the world where they were most vulnerable to executive kidnapping, the instructions included hiring a local lawyer to negotiate with the kidnappers and asking for a volunteer from staff to deliver the ransom.

I thought both directions might get several people killed. I also imagined the liability that would result if the company asked the receptionist to carry a bag of money over to the thugs holding the victim.

Because of my work with head office, I knew that they had a standing contract with a counter-terrorism company on 24-hour standby in London (former SAS, Special Branch and so on).

The only hitch in the system was that the company hadn't told that to the location that most needed to know and hadn't reviewed that local plan, which called for a response that might be more dangerous than the problem.

CHAPTER 12: SPECIFIC THREATS

***Event:** Black Death—Bubonic Plague, Europe*

***Date:** 1348-1666*

***Summary:** The disease may have come from China and was spread by merchant ships and war. Fleas carried by black rats passed it on to humans by biting people. It hit Genoa, Italy in 1348. Ships at sea drifted without crews because all had died. Half of all Italians died. Ninety percent of Londoners died, as did about three quarters of the populations of Iceland and Cyprus. People tried a series of ridiculous remedies, including praying to pagan gods, animal sacrifices and the use of toads, lizards, leeches, dead dogs, goats, human excrement and goat urine. One medical treatment that sometimes did work was using red-hot pokers to cauterize the open sores—if you lived through the pain. Governments became precarious, and anarchy prevailed in many communities. Government officials stole food, money and medicine. Royals, nobles and other wealthy people retreated to the country. There were orgies, drunkenness and 'dances of death' in which the participants literally danced in the streets until they died. The recurring outbreaks of the plague in England over the next three centuries may finally have been stopped by the London fire of 1666 or because brown rats that did not carry the virus ousted the black ones that did.*

***Result:** 25 million dead.*

***Lessons Learned:** While the bubonic plague is now extremely rare, cases do crop up occasionally, including in California in the late 20th century. Could the events of 650 years ago be a warning for what might occur in a modern pandemic? There were stories of medical workers stealing drugs and preferential treatment for professional athletes during a swine-flu outbreak in 2009-10. What would be the effects of mass migration from cities to cottages, farms and rural areas? Should officials encourage such migration?*

Reputation Equity—Attacks on the Internet

Your Reputation

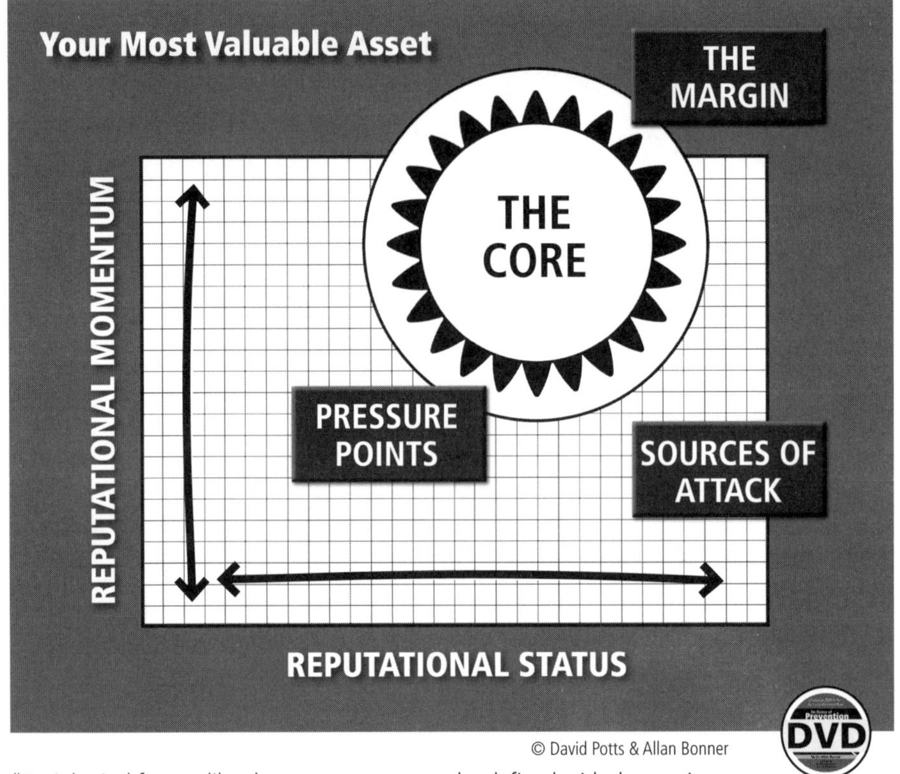

© David Potts & Allan Bonner

Available on the Companion DVD

"Sociological factors like class or power cannot be defined with the precision of concepts like weight or temperature" (**Broad and Wade,** 1982)

> It is said that your reputation is one of your most valuable assets. It's just like inventory or bricks and mortar. Reputation equity in risk management may be something like brand equity in advertising. The equity is built up over years and surpasses the economic inputs that produce the product. Reputation equity helps repel attacks and adds to brand equity. Reputation is said to enhance "customer satisfaction … employee attraction … firm equity, and investor awareness …bargaining power … [and] … new product introduction". A great reputation is said to help in raising capital and gives you a second chance in a crisis. (Highhouse et al.)

But the current studies of reputation and popular rankings of companies have little basis in scientific research. The cliché that recalling a product and saying you're sorry is the first step to retaining reputation, regaining trust and maintaining market share isn't supported by serious research. In the auto and pharmaceutical sectors the stock market reacts negatively to recalls, seeing them as a signal of financial loss. Consumers view recalls differently than investors do but may still fear problems with products that affect their health.

What about the value of a bad reputation? This sounds like an odd question until you consider how well the Rolling Stones have done from being associated with sex, drugs and the devil. The Rolling Stones have a reputation as 'evil' guys, but no one who appreciates rock and roll would say they were poor musicians. Some of the most admired companies have unsavoury pasts, including convictions for criminal conspiracy.

> *"Reputation is formed by the beliefs that people hold about an organization based upon their experience with it, their relationship to it, and their knowledge gained through word of mouth or mass media"*
>
> ***— Sims, citing various authors***

So, what do we really know about reputation? Signalling is an important concept, with your actions, recall or philanthropy being a signal of what kind of organization you are. How you frame an activity, or the context in which you put that activity, also matters. Your stakeholders will notice a 'defining moment' in their relationship with you. A discount store is supposed to have low prices and mediocre service and a high-end store is expected to have the opposite. You have to perform as advertised and expected. Third-party endorsements can help, and this is called credibility transfer. We know that people are most affected by what they hear first, most recently and most often—so-called primacy, recency and frequency.

We also know that you are judged by how people think your peers and competitors would act. Ironically, your past history may have little effect on your reputation. As in show-business, 'you're only as good as your last show.' The 'peak-end rule' means we base impressions on the most extreme event and the most recent we can remember (Kahneman in Highhouse). Being well known may make it more likely that people won't like you, while being well liked may raise expectations.

I'm convinced that reputation boils down to personal perception. I think the individual relationship that you have with stakeholders, day in and day out, is what counts. No one will know you have a great philanthropy program in place unless you tell them, and it won't likely impress unless it has something to do with your core skills and activities. But I'm also convinced that personal matters don't include who your CEO is. The notion that a prominent CEO enhances reputation and stock prices seems logical, but ask a dozen friends to start naming CEOs. I'll bet the list is short.

An attack on your reputation can come in any forum and from anyone. You can be sued for saying anything critical about anyone else, even if it's true. Then you have to defend your reputation in court, at a considerable cost. The cost can be both in money and in reputation equity.

It used to be the stroke of a pen, and now it's the push of a button that can harm your reputation. There's a lot new with the Internet that the modern risk manager needs to know about. The Internet is global, instant, anonymous, private, interactive and accessible. Unlike older forms of publishing, this raises the question of whom do you sue and where? Should you sue where you live, where your accuser lives, where you do the most business or where the web host or service provider is located? People suing you may also shop around for the best jurisdiction.

Consider how different this form of publishing is. If you have a website or email address or use the Internet at all, you may be publishing. The Internet is interactive. You may be responsible for publishing the comments of others on your blog. Anonymity sometimes gives users an unwarranted feeling of freedom and empowerment.

The Internet can also transmit images and sounds. Hypertext can link many different sites, creating comparisons and implications that even the author didn't foresee. The Internet features permanent storage and easy retrieval of messages. Your employees or an anonymous third party may be able to publish a libellous statement on your bulletin board or a private blog.

There are tens of thousands of websites and blogs that attack groups, governments or companies or advocate a boycott of goods or services. Many websites are called 'suck' sites. They usually contain the word 'sucks' in their title, as in 'Company X Sucks.'

Some groups use the Internet to raise money for victims, recruit victims and fund attacks on organizations. Some crises therefore originate on the Internet, and some only exist on the Internet, but some of those crises can then transfer over to your place of business, the news media, the courts or elsewhere. Your crisis can migrate back and forth.

Crises can also start in the real world and then transfer over to the Internet for further battles. One libel action in Britain lasted over two years and was the longest running libel action in British history.

On the positive side, you can use the Internet during a crisis unrelated to cyberspace to communicate with large numbers of people quickly. You can also refer journalists, customers and others to your website for mundane details of an event to free up staff for more pressing matters.

Several companies can help you prepare. They help counter such attacks, search for references to your company and alert you to stories about you. Some are even trying to 'stamp' websites as proof of authenticity. This is a new field that is evolving very quickly. You must begin with service providers, libel lawyers and high-tech companies to glean the latest information and techniques available. Often a libel-chill letter to a service provider will cause them to stop supporting a site, chat-room or blog containing potentially libellous comments.

TIPS

Reputation Equity Protection Tips

- ✓ Consult a libel lawyer who specializes in Internet matters.
- ✓ Consider registering your company name followed by the word "sucks" as a domain name to prevent others from using it.
- ✓ Consider registering "parody" names which resemble yours.
- ✓ Investigate ways to use the Internet and websites to fight back or lessen damages.
- ✓ Make sure your logo is trademarked.
- ✓ Be careful that your defence doesn't attract more attention than the attack.
- ✓ Identify service providers and high tech firms that can help.
- ✓ Construct a "dark" website ready to go to handle crises.
- ✓ Be prepared to post letters, facts, news releases, testimonials and other data.
- ✓ Investigate links to other information sources and third party advocates.

DVD

Available on the Companion DVD

Terrorist Activity

In the event of a real or perceived terrorist act, you may find that a variety of further responders become involved. You may find security and intelligence organizations from other countries that you didn't know were operating in your jurisdiction. For example, since 9/11, New York City has had its own agents in several foreign locations, paralleling the work of the CIA.

In Canada, the Canadian Security Intelligence Service (CSIS) becomes involved if an incident has international overtones. Its RCMP counterpart, the National Secret Intelligence Service (NSIS), concerns itself with terrorist acts that have a national or inter-provincial dimension. Both may attend the scene of the event yet work in conjunction with local or provincial police forces.

If the terrorist act is contained within provincial borders, the local police force's criminal investigations branch will investigate. If, however, the incident occurs at a federal government building or at the facility of a party that contracts with the federal government to provide 'sensitive' material, the RCMP will become involved. Companies should reflect on their products and geographical location with these facts in mind.

If several agencies and/or the government are involved, a primary concern will be coordination. When possible, crisis centres, situation rooms and media centres should be amalgamated, and all responders should speak with one voice.

An affected corporation should ask to have a delegate in a government, military or police situation room. The corporation should defer to police and government expertise in hostage negotiations, perimeter security and the like.

During a terrorist event, how you handle the news media and the release of information to the public will be greatly affected by all these considerations. You may want to let the appropriate authorities take the lead.

Bomb Threats

All bomb threats or calls dealing with sabotage or product tampering should be treated as real. The person taking the call should listen, be calm and courteous, not interrupt the caller and obtain as much information as possible. A device that tapes all telephone calls will serve as a quality-control measure and be the best source of information on a bomb threat. It will record background noises, the caller's accent, the exact words used and so on.

Each location within the organization should investigate how to trace telephone calls and, if applicable, devise pre-arranged signals to initiate tracing while the caller is still on the line.

Not everyone has recording-devices. You may take a bomb-threat call on a hand-held device. Questionnaires of the type that follow will serve to remind those who answer the phone what questions to ask of the caller and therefore should be kept near all appropriate telephones.

The building or site affected should be evacuated and the local police called.

If a device is found that appears to be a bomb, it should not be touched. The appropriate supervisor should be notified, and it should not be assumed that this is the only device on the premises. A typical terrorist technique is to explode one device to stampede people into an evacuation zone and then have another device go off there.

No one should re-enter the building until the police are satisfied that there is no bomb or it has been defused. You will need to provide floor plans and structural drawings to assist the police.

Telephoned Bomb Threats

BOMB THREAT QUESTIONS	ANSWERS
What time will the bomb explode?	
Where is it?	
Why did you place the bomb?	
What does it look like?	
How big is it?	
When was it planted?	
Did you make it yourself?	
How did you learn to make bombs?	
Where?	
When?	
Why are you doing this?	
What is in it for you?	
What do you hope to accomplish?	
Do you have a grudge against this company?	
Why?	
What is your name?	

LISTEN CAREFULLY AND RECORD THE FOLLOWING IDENTIFYING CHARACTERISTICS:
Sex: M____ F____
Accent:
Speech (fast, slow):
Estimated age:
Voice (loud, soft):
Diction (good, nasal, lisp):
Manner (calm, emotional):
Background noises:
Familiar voice:
Was the caller familiar with the area?

DVD

Customize on the Companion DVD

Rumour

Word of mouth, rumours, and stories play an important role in human communication. A great deal of what people know about any event will have come through personal human contact rather than the news media or direct experience with the event. Spokespeople must analyze and address rumours as if they were real.

Rumours can be more powerful than legitimate and accurate sources of information. The persistent rumours about President Obama's religion and place of birth are a case in point. So are old rumours about an ice cream chain being owned by a cult or a satanic symbol in a corporate logo.

Forms such as the Public Inquiry Action sheet (see "Public Affairs" in Chapter 4 above) should be used by those who staff the telephones and receive calls from the general public. This will enable senior management to gauge, track and respond to the effects of word-of-mouth communication in a crisis.

One primary task should be a thorough hunt for the source of the rumour. The credibility of the source, and what that source has to gain by spreading the rumour or lose by its being dispelled, should all be determined.

The effectiveness of the rumour can be assessed in several ways. Rumours that provide simplistic answers to complex problems are often the most damaging. Many people thrive on the confusion surrounding a crisis. Rumours can be mistaken for facts by third-party experts or the media.

Often rumours contain some truth. You need to discover whether there is a consistent element of truth in a changing rumour, whether the rumour is completely false, what damage the rumour is doing to whom and so on.

You need to identify whether the electronic or print media are contributing to the life of the rumour and whether you can stop the information flow by direct contact with them. This may also reveal whether such word-of-mouth information has changed group dynamics by turning some groups for or against your organization. Have rumours made audiences more susceptible to negative information?

Always analyze a rumour from the recipients' point of view. In the midst of a crisis, the public may be confused, and even outlandish information may seem to add meaning to an otherwise confusing event. Some damaging rumours make audiences feel better about desperate situations.

Effective rumour control involves providing the audience with alternative positive information.

You should treat rumours seriously, but not support them, until your spokespeople are able to dispel them. You should recruit a spokesperson who will carry out this task with the same dedication with which others deal with the media, the public or government agencies. You can employ third-party experts to help dispel rumours, and you must take care not to give credence to substantially untrue statements. Do not repeat themes within rumours or try to use humour to deal with them.

Incident or Rumour Checklist during Crisis

ACTIVITY	RESPONSIBILITY	COMPLETED
Contact Public Affairs/Communication for guidance and information regarding current issues or rumours.		
Survey those with regular public contact for persistent rumours (security, reception, press officers, phone operators).		
Compile information to counter rumours and distribute to public through Public Affairs.		
Provide copies of Public Inquiry Action sheet for all those with public contact (Public Affairs, reception, security, spokespeople, phone staff).		
Collate sheets and provide to Public Affairs/Communication.		
Analyze rumours.		
Determine if addressing the rumour will do more harm than good.		
Designate and rehearse spokesperson to counter rumours if going public is the choice.		
Compile counter information for distribution to reporters, public, government agencies, third party experts, employees and other stakeholders.		
Work with and brief third party experts (i.e. academics, pollsters) to dispel rumours.		
Inform employees to help dispel rumours.		
Be careful not to give credence to false rumours by repeating them.		

DVD

Customize on the Companion DVD

Planning for a Pandemic or Perhaps Other Events

Florence Nightingale made a major contribution to the nursing-profession and also to the field of statistics. In 1857 she developed a particular type of chart showing the causes of mortality among soldiers during the Crimean War. Nurse Nightingale's diagrams, known as 'rose charts,' showed that soldiers were in greater danger in the hospital than on the battlefield.

On the other side of the world, soldiers during the US Civil War knew they were often better off staying out of field hospitals because of the dangers of secondary infections and complications.

Today we need innovative statistical analysis and good guesses from lay people to prepare for a potential influenza pandemic. Will we be better off in hospitals, hiding in our homes or evacuating our cities?

If public policy is going to save lives, good research must isolate why people get sick, what might keep them safe, how to make them well, and what communication techniques will alter their behaviour.

Crisis management and risk analysis call for assessing the likelihood of an event as well as its potential impact. Prudence dictates preparing for an unlikely event with massive potential impact. A highly likely event with minimal impact does not deserve the same level of attention.

The Asian Development Bank predicts that a pandemic could cost the world economy $60 billion. That's worth an ounce of prevention, regardless of the likelihood.

Reasonable people make prudent risk decisions around the home. We use locks, bolts and alarms to keep intruders out because of the potential impact of a break-in. But we tolerate litter on our front sidewalk because it's hard to stop and the impact is limited.

So, the fact that a pandemic hasn't happened is irrelevant to proper risk analysis. Some say we are overdue for a pandemic because the last one came more than 40 years ago and they occurred more frequently than that in the twentieth century. But that's junk science—a focus on one variable (frequency) to the exclusion of countless others. Very few people died from the recent bird flu—the toll was in the low hundreds—yet the mortality rate among those affected was high. Some take solace from the fact that there were very few cases of human-to-human transmission. Others worry about the potential impact if human-to-human contact proliferates. Still others guess that it will not be any of the current strains of flu that become a pandemic but a new strain, rendering currently available drugs ineffective. The real issue is potential impact—not an irrelevant statistic on the likelihood of the event or, worse yet, the actual year in which it might happen.

Pandemic Background

We had three pandemics in the twentieth century. The so-called Spanish Flu in 1918-19 probably killed as many as 100 million people. (I say "probably" because records were not accurate and the pandemic happened during a war. The official toll is about 40 million.) The 1957-8 flu may have killed two million, and the Hong Kong Flu in 1968-9 may have killed about a million. The World Health Organization estimated that an avian flu might kill between eight and 350 million people. That's a huge range.

More troops were killed in World War I by the flu than on the battlefield. Soldiers were crammed together in troop ships, trains, barracks and the trenches. This spread the disease.

However, it is scientifically improper to extrapolate what might happen today from what happened then. Sanitation has improved, which can help. Building-codes forbid lone toilets and require washrooms to have sinks for hand-washing. There is no world war in progress. But the population travels and commutes much more, which can hinder. Communication is better, which can help. Medical procedures are much improved. There are countless other variables.

The flu virus wasn't even isolated in a lab until 1933, long after the Spanish Flu pandemic had passed. Some scientists and physicians at the time thought the virus might be spread by dusty books.

What else has changed? There were two waves of flu in 1918 and again in 1957, giving responders time to act, but there's no guarantee that a future pandemic will behave the same way. We have an aging population that may be more vulnerable but is much fitter than older people in previous generations. Those who lived through 1957 and 1968 may have developed some immunity to certain strains of flu. Studies of past flu viruses show it may not just be vulnerable populations such as the sick, very young and elderly who are at greatest risk. There can be healthy groups in their teens and twenties who have never been exposed to major outbreaks and can therefore be at even greater risk.

Even if the World Health Organization used sound methodology to estimate that up to 350 million people might die, that's still a smaller percentage of the world population than died during the Spanish Flu. In 1918 the world's population was about 1.8 billion, while today it's about 6.5 billion. It is irresponsible to quote these 'guesstimates' out of context.

Lessons from SARS

The Severe Acute Respiratory Syndrome event was statistically irrelevant. Eight thousand cases worldwide and 800 deaths is meaningless in a world where two million people die from diarrhoea each year, more than 40,000 North Americans die from ordinary flu, about 50,000 die on highways and perhaps 5,000 die from food poisoning. In years past, without 24-hour news networks, these deaths might have been missed or misdiagnosed.

The lessons of SARS are more qualitative. We know that health-care workers were at risk unnecessarily. A pandemic is both a public-health issue and an occupational health and safety issue. It can be argued that health-care workers need more protection than others because they're going to protect the rest of us. The same is probably true of the police, the military and other emergency responders.

Early in the Ontario outbreak, one Toronto police officer predicted there might be 10,000 deaths—it's not just the news media that like a good story. In what was meant to be a reassuring gesture, Ontario's premier and health minister dressed in hospital gowns and masks to tour a hospital, but that image probably compounded the fear and spread the word about SARS. Also spreading the word were daily news conferences by public-health officials announcing the latest toll. Reporters present knew that officials had been arguing about facts and perspectives behind the curtains just before the conference began—further spreading uncertainty and fear.

Risk communication with an angry and fearful public will be vital before and during a pandemic. When trying to change behaviour and perception, officials must be candid and empowering.

Another lesson was both cultural and technical. Why did it take SARS to get hospitals to install sanitizing gel and signs promoting cleanliness? One hospital CEO friend of mine tells of spending tens of thousands of dollars to install sinks for hand-washing but having great difficulty getting physicians to use them. Studies show that among the dirtiest things in hospitals are physicians' ties and pagers (ties have been banned in British hospitals). Hospital workers go for coffee breaks and meals outside their hospitals and return, wearing the same gowns and scrubs. They wear the scrubs home on public transit, even though most must know that some organisms can live on the cloth for a week. They're endangering their families and the public, and this should be banned. Even physicians don't have their lab coats washed often enough. The irony is, all these neglected precautions were standard procedure 50 or 100 years ago.

Finally, we may have learned not to be distracted by irrelevant and distracting data but instead to look to action for solutions. Take a look at an example from a hospital crisis plan I read. It contains the seeds of death, injury and loss.

The plan had one full page discussing how important water is to a hospital. Drinking, bathing, laundry, cooking and other activities were listed. The plan even cited US Navy research calculating that 246 litres of water is needed per bed, per day.

If there were an actual water shortage, none of this information would be of use, except maybe how much is needed. If you don't have any water, finding water is the issue, not wallowing in how difficult it is not to have it. There are plenty of solutions:

- Get staff to drive to the nearest stores and buy bottles of water.
- Distribute plastic jugs to staff. Have them filled at home and brought in every day.
- List tanker-truck companies able to deliver potable water.
- List methods of rationing, independent laundries that pick up and deliver and where to get portable toilets.
- List abandoned wells.
- Discharge patients early.
- Use hand sanitizers for cleaning and juice for drinking.
- Flush toilets with recycled water.
- Create mutual-aid agreements with oil refineries, waste-disposal companies or others with tanker trucks that can suck up non-potable ('white') water out of lakes, rivers, streams and the ocean to flush toilets.

A philosophical discussion of a problem does not solve the problem. A list of what a pain it will be not to have 30 percent of the workforce, no snow or garbage removal, food delivery and so on is not a crisis plan. It is just complaining and a waste of time. The other waste of time, for the most part, is job descriptions. In a pandemic 30 percent of those people will be sick anyway. A crisis is no time to be reading a sick or dead person's job description—it's a time for action, and more action until no more action can be taken! Imagine a fire-fighter at your home reading a job description.

Insurance

A pandemic is also an insurance matter. Individuals and organizations need to examine their policies. It is essential to clarify how an insurance policy will classify bird flu. Whether it's classified as a disease or an environmental hazard will affect coverage. Something transmitted from person to person is normally considered a disease, but breathing in the virus from the air could be considered pollution.

Business travellers should verify that they're covered abroad. Transport home, including flight cancellations, will be issues if they get sick.

Contamination of goods and property also presents complex problems. Insurance may cover decontaminating buildings, but what of buildings only suspected of being contaminated? If customers won't buy goods from a factory or warehouse because it's in an affected jurisdiction, will insurance pay to disinfect the facility to reassure customers, even if the procedure isn't needed? Can you insure against negative perception? There will be similar questions about suspect goods in transit, including medical and hospital supplies.

What is to be Done?

As in personal health, one doesn't need a statistic to eat better, exercise more, stop smoking and enjoy regular mental down time. There are benefits to being well prepared, regardless of whether we ever have a pandemic. Preparation for a pandemic will serve our communities well in severe weather events, terrorism, and even normal times.

Here's the worst-case scenario in a pandemic. Thirty percent of the workforce—including health-care workers—is dead, sick or pretending to be sick to avoid catching the flu. Moreover, even reasonable, rational, decent health-care workers will be stealing drugs from hospitals to give them to their loved ones. Some will be giving their hospital patients fake drugs. Hubris or familiarity with risk will cause many health-care workers to neglect necessary precautions and spread the disease in malls and on the transit system. There will be a black market in both fake and real drugs, as well as in gloves, masks and sanitizer.

Here's what all organizations can begin doing tomorrow:

1. Encourage hand-washing, because some sanitizing gel doesn't work.
2. Put hand-sanitizing gel (the kind that works) and pop-up sanitizing tissues in multiple locations in the office or plant.
3. Encourage employees to keep their homes, schools and clubs safer.
4. Promote telecommuting by funding small home offices.
5. Stockpile a small amount of food and water. Encourage employees to do the same.
6. Sign co-management and supply agreements with neighbours, competitors and anybody else who can help in times of crisis.
7. Investigate your supply chain and delivery mechanisms throughout the world to identify alternative ways of getting raw materials and selling finished products. If a channel is blocked, you will need to re-route.
8. Establish an inventory of retired workers and document their skills. If 30 percent of the regular workforce is out of the game, they'll keep the economy going.
9. Circulate a questionnaire to inventory employee skills.
10. Train workers in first aid.
11. Use the chamber of commerce, board of trade, industry associations and service clubs to lobby governments to help.

Governments need to promulgate legislation and municipal bylaws to get our communities ready. We need designated evacuation sites with stores of food, water and medical supplies, perhaps in sports stadia and shopping-malls. We need a plan to use rail lines in evacuations, because highways will be clogged. We need to know exactly where a city bus will run out of fuel as it evacuates neighbourhoods and buildings and put something in place at that spot. Investments in public transit will help, especially if we create redundant systems that can handle peak need or still move people if one system (bus, LRT, ferry, monorail, subway) is disabled.

Just in case we need to make people stay put for a while, condos, apartments, sports arenas and office towers should be required to keep some food, medical supplies and water on hand. We need to ban leaf-blowers that spread animal feces and disease. We need to ban the international trade in wild animals for pets or as meat.

Health-care facilities have the most at stake. In an outbreak they may be locked down early, but they can extend their usefulness. There's a truism in the military: "In times of war, everyone gets promoted in rank." It will be retired health-care workers, students, technicians and trained medics from the military and service groups who may be filling in for nurses and doctors who get sick. Hospitals can also extend their usefulness physically by scouting nearby sites. Perhaps a storefront can become a walk-in clinic. Schools and theatres will certainly become triage centres. Hockey rinks will store bodies.

Even if the pandemic never happens, good preparation will still make for more environmentally friendly cities, safer communities, more resilient institutions and a stronger economy—not bad unintended consequences at all.[15]

Who's in Charge?

Canada's task force on counter-terrorism identified a problem in the chain of response command. Whether it's terrorism, a pandemic or a severe weather event, multiple agencies can step on each other's toes and prevent response from taking place. That's one of the things that happened in the New Orleans hurricane.

When Canadian authorities held a news conference after arresting suspected terrorists in the Toronto area, there were at least eight different agencies represented—local police forces, RCMP, CSIS and so on. That caused my friend General Ron Cheriton, who headed that task force, to laugh and remark that not much had changed since his report.

With pandemic planning, provinces delegate the responsibility to municipalities. The mayor usually asks the deputy fire chief to write a plan. In that plan is usually a line stating that high-need people such as the elderly, sick and disabled will be the responsibility of social-service agencies. Yet there is usually no money, direction, training or extra people allocated to these small agencies. That's a secondary crisis in itself.

There's a joke among crisis managers about who is in charge. The senior public official who tours a disaster scene receives deference from responders but is a net drain on response. S/he eats a few sandwiches, gets a picture taken and maybe fills a sandbag in a flood. All response stops for about 20 minutes for the photo opportunity.

In a pandemic we need a clear chain of command. Someone needs the authority to force containers full of toys off highways and trains in order to move critical medical equipment. We will also need individual initiative. It will be individuals in condos, office towers and apartment buildings who set up the makeshift facilities that will save lives. Governments can legislate, but individuals perform.

Case studies have shown that confusion will prevail. When an El Al cargo plane smashed into an apartment building in Amsterdam, emergency responders clogged the highways trying to respond. Officials contradicted themselves on procedures and the number of dead. But an individual sports-arena manager took it upon himself to open his doors and comfort survivors. Individuals perform well in crises, organizations usually do not.

(Edited and reprinted from the author's article in *The Winnipeg Free Press* on the occasion of his chairing the first National Summit on Pandemic Planning for the International Centre for Infectious Diseases.)

Specific Threats

Discussion Points:

1. Has our IT department examined our vulnerability to Internet attacks?
2. What measures have we taken to protect our website and reputation?
3. Who is our contact with local law enforcement to learn about their procedures in the case of a terrorist threat?
4. Do we have enough media and community research to monitor potential misinformation and rumours about our organization?
5. What communications vehicles will we use to counter rumours?
6. How can we make a healthier workplace and workforce?

7. Can we institute flex time, home offices, job-sharing, full-time/part-time and other HR matters as morale boosters and crisis-planning initiatives?
8. What measures do we have in place to address staffing-shortages in the event of a pandemic?
9. Can we evacuate quickly and keep our organization running?
10. Can we stay put for a few days and keep our organization running?

Dialling for Dollars

A simulation features competent men and women diligently trying to get out from behind the proverbial 8-ball. The focus and productivity is unmistakable—quite unlike just another busy day at the office. That's why in one simulation I was running, a man sauntering around looking comfortable caught my eye.

"Hi. What's your role?" I asked casually, even though I really wanted to inquire why he wasn't working as hard as the others.

"I'm the accountant," the relaxed man responded.

"Oh, great," I began, and introduced myself. "Why not see if you can get lots of cash really quickly?"

"No problem," the confident man responded. "You don't have to worry about that."

The man didn't realize that it was he who had to worry about getting money, not I.

"Humour me, please. Let's just test how quickly you can get lots of money in a crisis." I explained that cash might be needed for sole-sourcing and single-sourcing goods and services. One might run up to a person on the street and rent or buy the pickup truck s/he's driving. One might buy up all the water in a store, and so on.

"Look," the accountant held his hand up in the universal sign of nullification, "I have a great relationship with the bank, and there won't be a problem."

I prevailed by saying, "Why not just see what we can learn about the banking-system?"

Back the same man came half an hour later.

"How'd it go?" I asked.

"Spoke to the bankers," he started. "Turns out most of them live out of town, so if there were a bad emergency in the middle of the night or on a weekend, they're pretty sure they wouldn't even be able to make it into the office."

"What if they're already in and we had a fire, earthquake, flood or other emergency at midday?" I asked.

"Well, I wondered that too," the accountant went on. "They're on a time-lock, so if we needed big money any time other than between 10 a.m. and 2 p.m., we just couldn't get it—the vault would be closed."

"Great information," I complimented. "Now the task is to find out how to get that money, if needed."

Back the same man came a while later—this time with a smile on his face. He'd just upped the limit on all senior executives' bank cards so they could get about $1000 each from banking-machines. Assuming a couple of dozen senior executives, this would keep him going for a few hours.

"Great," I congratulated. "Now the task is how to get big money when the quake disables the bank machines."

How about the old-fashioned solution—keeping plenty of cash in the main-office safe? Or, how about the new solution of emailing money?

CHAPTER 13: RUNNING SIMULATIONS

Event: *Walton Town Centre—gas tanker overturning*

Date: *11 April 1987*

Summary: *A gasoline tank truck overturned and collided with a small car. A bystander probably called emergency services, and both police and ambulance arrived at about the same time. The police officer went to a pay phone away from the scene, and medical responders went right to the crash site. Gasoline spread through the street. The liquid soaked responders' clothing. The driver of the car was trapped inside, but responders could not use the jaws of life, for fear a spark would ignite the gas. Then the driver began to have heart problems, but medical responders didn't use a defibrillator for fear of igniting the gasoline. Responders had too little foam to spread it over the entire site, and that response had to wait until more arrived. The liquid gas ran through the streets, into sewers and into the Thames River, creating a new response challenge on the water with threats to wildlife, drinking-water and pleasure craft. Gaseous fuel became an explosion hazard. One explosion occurred in a pub cellar, caused by a spark from an automatic timer.*

Result: *No loss of life. Some damage to the environment.*

Lessons Learned: *Police, fire and medical people all use different response techniques. Different response techniques are required during the same event—fire, explosion, spill, water pollution. Solving one problem with the jaws of life or a defibrillator can cause a worse problem. The definition of a problem and preferred solutions changes quickly. There is a need to coordinate responses among emergency services.*

Running Simulations

Simulations as a Learning-Tool

There's value in reading your crisis plan every now and then to get fresh ideas on what might go right and wrong in a crisis. There's value in having a neighbour, supplier or other trusted colleague give it a read too. But the best value of all is to conduct a simulation to see if you have the capability you'll need in a real event.

The other value of a simulation is to test whether your crisis plan makes sense to the people reading it. Military theory says two relevant things:

1) No battle plan outlives the first shot.
2) Everyone gets promoted at least one rank in times of war.

The first point is that you and your plan need enough flexibility to run with unforeseen events. The second point is that it will be junior and mid-level people who may be reading the plan and trying their best to implement responses.

In all cases, a simulation is the best way to see how you'll do. So what follows is some thought on just what a simulation is and how to learn from one.

Some people learn by reading, some by writing and others by speaking. Some learn through spirituality, emotions or the physical (kinesthetic) and as a result of gender, race or cultural attributes and styles. Probably most of us learn well by *doing*.

Simulations can imitate complex, expensive and dangerous real-life situations. Participants can be assigned roles or play themselves. Scenarios can be real, made-up, or computer-enhanced and are usually face-to-face experiences. Simulations can involve talking through an issue or event around a board table, acting out responses, taking on roles and even flying across the country, renting assets and mobilizing hundreds of responders.

One of the best justifications for simulations is that "the classroom is a great place to show you blew a million dollars"[16] in a game with high (but simulated) expenditures. Some simulations aren't complex enough, because real life is a lot messier than the static roles assigned and facts given out to participants. Part of the debate involves whether experiential learning is more authentic than learning in laboratory-like settings. There's another debate about how well responders and simulators can switch gender, race or religion. In an internal exercise, how well can your colleagues play protesters, activist preachers and so on? Good simulations also use case studies, videos, and perhaps outside speakers from companies that have had real crises.

The military use war games. Simulating creeping barrages with officers on horseback and elaborate exercises behind the lines for weeks was what won the battle of Vimy Ridge for the Canadians. Far from being a cheap alternative, military exercises are so expensive that they are often done in slow motion. In military simulations, you fire a $10,000 shell and then conduct a debriefing. Fire-fighters, the police and some in industry test their abilities to respond to myriad events with real fire, real car chases and the actual deployment of remediation gear.

It may be true that "there is no substitute for face-to-face interaction."[17] There may also be no substitute for silent reading, writing, speaking, listening, reflection, spirituality, kinesthetic activity or any of the other elements in learning. In fact in face-to-face simulation work participants often begin by listening to a lecture, reading instructions on paper, asking questions for clarification, speaking with a fellow role-player, debriefing and joining in a discussion. In other words, face-to-face interaction is only part of many educational techniques, normally in play in every simulation. Distance simulations and learning-experiences on the Web accommodate diverse styles, languages and cultures in multiple time zones. It is refreshing to engage another student or client on Web technology without necessarily knowing that person's gender, accent, clothing or ethnicity.

Whether in groups or alone, augmented with technology or not, reality is often the best teacher. I don't fabricate events in a simulation. I don't load up the instructions with complex details unless I'm purposefully trying to distract the client I'm testing. While it is true that real-life cases feature countless details, emotions and diversions, I have to consider which ones are merely tangential to the important learning-point I'm focused on.

More learning will occur if responders play themselves in new situations, as opposed to fictitious people in new and unfamiliar situations. What it is like to be another person in another occupation may be interesting but is often a diversion from the learning-goal. At best it involves speculation about that other person and his or her business dilemma or life situation.

I like to assign a realistic role, such as confidante, coach or counsel, to main characters in a written simulation. Responders wouldn't know all the background to the client's situation in real life. There are realistic roles to play in most negotiations for people with skill in tax, publicity, media, building-management, security, intellectual property and other fields.

There are other ways to achieve realism and harness expertise. I have my clients present a real case that they either were involved in or have thoroughly researched. Sometimes individuals have great experiences, perhaps from past employers, that their current employer doesn't know about but can really use. The case can be presented in sequence, in real time, in accelerated time or with time-outs for debriefing. Responders can work in small groups to discuss how the players would advise the characters in the event. The fact that the event is real and we can debrief on how it actually played out adds learning-value.

Time compression can be an enhancement as well. In reality, if one needs to prepare for a full opera house six months hence (as in the famous Sally Soprano case taught at Harvard), there is no need to order programs right now. But if urgency is built into the simulation, participants need to exercise quick judgment in real time and live with the consequences. Imperatives created by time zones, legislative hearings and media inquiries can speed things up and intensify the learning-experience. It might be the need to hold a mock news conference or write advertising-copy for next week's newspaper.

Ultimately, simulations are fake and you didn't actually blow any money at all, so getting participants fully engaged is a challenge.

Filling the Dance Card

To get the best value from my simulation exercises, I write 'action cards' to prompt responders' activities. A typical card reads:

ACTION CARD

Time:	10:30 AM
Who you are:	(name and title)
What you know:	Events to date (sometimes we don't distribute all cards to all participants to keep some responders at one level of knowledge and another group at another, as often happens in real life)
What happens:	300 displaced people begin gathering outside your building.
What you do:	______________________
What you want to do:	______________________
Comments:	______________________
	______________________

DVD

Customize on the Companion DVD

With these action cards we can drive events. We can also capture our detailed research on what would actually happen in a given situation. We research the science, politics, sociology and laws behind events. We then write up realistic scenarios at five-minute intervals to prompt responders to take action or make decisions.

We also have various stand-by action cards in case responders don't drive events quickly or properly. Failure to order and distribute food will trigger *fainting*-incidents among responders, failure to provide relief schedules for responders will trigger *chest pains* and so on. We usually give responders an adequate number of minutes or hours to deal with a challenge, and if they don't, we play a card that requires them either to deal with the matter or to pay the consequences. We judge them on how much prodding they needed to take action.

In a simulated evacuation of a building, subway or town, we present responders with several dilemmas. We simulate a lawyer or businessperson demanding access to the restricted site. If he is refused, he claims there are documents vital to his financial future there and that he will sue unless he can get them.

We try to build in tough, ethical decisions. We want to know whether they choose to hold a photo opportunity for the media or protect the environment. We want to know how much risk they will take to make or save money.

The cards and commentary enable us to keep track of all responders' decisions and efforts and analyze them at the end of the event.

Promises, Promises

Tokyo has been destroyed several times, in whole or in part, by earthquakes and once in World War II by bombing. Most citizens sleep with shoes under their beds. This is because one of the biggest dangers in an earthquake is from the glass that will cover the floors immediately after the first shock. Without shoes, you can't go far. Most also keep a backpack with a bit of food and water in it and a small bag of sand by the gas stove to smother fires that start when the quake shakes the pipes loose.

Compared to North Americans, who go for trips in the desert without water and drive through northern winters in business suits, these are very prudent and prepared people.

Most water-storage facilities in Japan, including swimming-pools, are catalogued for use in an emergency. In Kobe, the site of a bad quake some years ago, there were fights over whether water that was earmarked for fighting fires could be drunk and whether drinking-water could be used to put out fires. In the end, the issue was sent up and across the political and administrative chains of command to Tokyo and no decision was made in time.

Bad things come in threes, if not larger numbers. That's why in the Tokyo simulation we built in a bomb scare. I also did some research and learned that the second-in-command in Tokyo had a young daughter in a school across town. At dinner with my client the night before the event, I casually asked where he would be when the simulation began the next morning at 7:00 a.m.

"Oh, I've ruled myself out of the exercise for the first two hours" was the response. "In reality, I'd be looking for my daughter."

I complimented my client on his decision, which I would have imposed on him anyway. Then I asked another question: "What are the responders planning to eat during the event?"

My client said it was the rations they'd stored away for such an emergency.

"Great," I enthused as a new idea popped into my head. "Let's exercise the phone tree that you have to contact all responders in case of an off-hour emergency. We'll tell them the event is starting a half hour earlier, at 6:30 a.m. Let's also tell them that their kitchens are damaged by the quake, so they can't eat at home but have to start the day off downtown in their offices breaking out rations." We managed to reach all but one responder, reminding the client that not all resources will be available in a real incident.

We threw in a few other curves too. After playing the card announcing that a crowd of 300 displaced persons had gathered outside the office building housing my client, we allowed a few minutes to go by and then asked for details on what action they were going to take. When I was told it could all be handled on the grounds of the building complex, I became sceptical.

"Where would you put 300 people? How would you care for them?" I asked.

I was assured there were plenty of rations and serviceable tents that could be set up for sleeping.

"Who will set up the tents?" I asked, knowing most responders were fully occupied.

I was told that there was an apartment complex nearby that housed people who worked for my client's organization. I was assured that, at any given time, there would be thirty or so spouses, housekeepers and teenage children at home who could be pressed into service.

"Great," I enthused. "Let's find out exactly how many we can use to put up tents."

Off went a couple of responders with clipboards on which to list the dozens of volunteers, only to return forty or so minutes later with their proverbial tails between their legs. It had turned out they could only find three people in the whole housing-complex.

"How are you going to set up these tents now?" I quizzed.

I was told again that this would be no problem. They were all colour-coded and easy to assemble—like family tents sold anywhere in the world.

I insisted they must assemble the tents, as they would have to do in a real crisis. The one brain wave they got was to have some of the 300 victims act as volunteers. At least each tent would occupy two or so volunteers, who would not be getting frustrated in the bigger crowd. About two hours later, I was told that, for the life of them, they couldn't get one tent up. It was like a combination of Christmas morning trying to assemble toys and a dark campsite with a new tent.

I was asked whether responders could use an elevator to move a computer instead of moving it down a couple of flights of stairs. We were pretending the power was out, but they could plug the computer into an emergency generator on the main floor. But since the power wasn't really out and they didn't want to risk dropping the computer on the several flights of stairs between it and the generator, they asked to use the elevator. I said "Yes" but insisted they must keep the computer out of commission for an extra 30 minutes, to simulate the time it would take to get it down the stairs safely.

However, a satellite phone didn't get the special treatment the computer did. This satellite phone featured a big fan-like dish. That got deployed without incident, but a small connection was broken in the set-up and responders had to do some amateur soldering to make it work.

At one point, I asked about the 300 victims, whom I'd not thought of for a while.

"They're all fine," I was told. "We're handing out food and water in the courtyard."

I asked to be taken there for a look. There weren't really 300 victims hanging around. These were fictitious displaced people from the neighbourhood—clients, relatives, business contacts and so on. There was a little water and foot on hand, simulating a relief station.

But this was also the exact location being used to set up the satellite phone. What was being simulated was the set-up and use of a valuable, fragile and cumbersome satellite-phone station in the middle of 300 hungry, scared, grieving, displaced people. I told my client the satellite phone was broken for the duration of the event. They made notes to change their plans and set up the phone in a more secure place on the roof of their building.

Simulations

Discussion Questions:

1. Are there neighbours or industry colleagues who can comment on your simulation?
2. What scenario should we test?
3. Can we get students or others to play third parties cheaply?
4. How much secrecy do we need in our simulation?
5. What kind of learners do we have in our organization?
6. Who from our organization needs to be involved in our simulation?
7. Can we involve third-party responders such as police and fire?
8. Who will observe and write up the results?
9. Who will conduct research to see what has happened to similar organizations elsewhere?
10. What lessons can we learn from others—even dissimilar organizations?

Appendix 1: Learning from Past Disasters

Busy managers have many activities they can undertake to lessen risk or manage disasters. The data contained in the study of past disasters are of special value. There is an authenticity to the learning not offered by modelling, simulations or other means.

But with busy schedules, how do you access appropriate data and keep people and assets safe? How and when should you look for appropriate lessons? These are challenging questions for the loss-prevention professional. The answers involve the timeliness of the search, where and how to search, and decisions about what time periods to investigate.

"To extract valuable lessons after the fact, you may have to take into account how geographically remote the event was, how long ago it occurred, your own culture or your cultural perception of the responders."

Any number of factors may impede learning from past disasters. Cultures, eras and the changing perception of both time and distance vary greatly among disasters. Other variables include the expertise of responders, construction techniques and zoning in natural disasters, gender relations and linguistics.

Isomorphic Learning

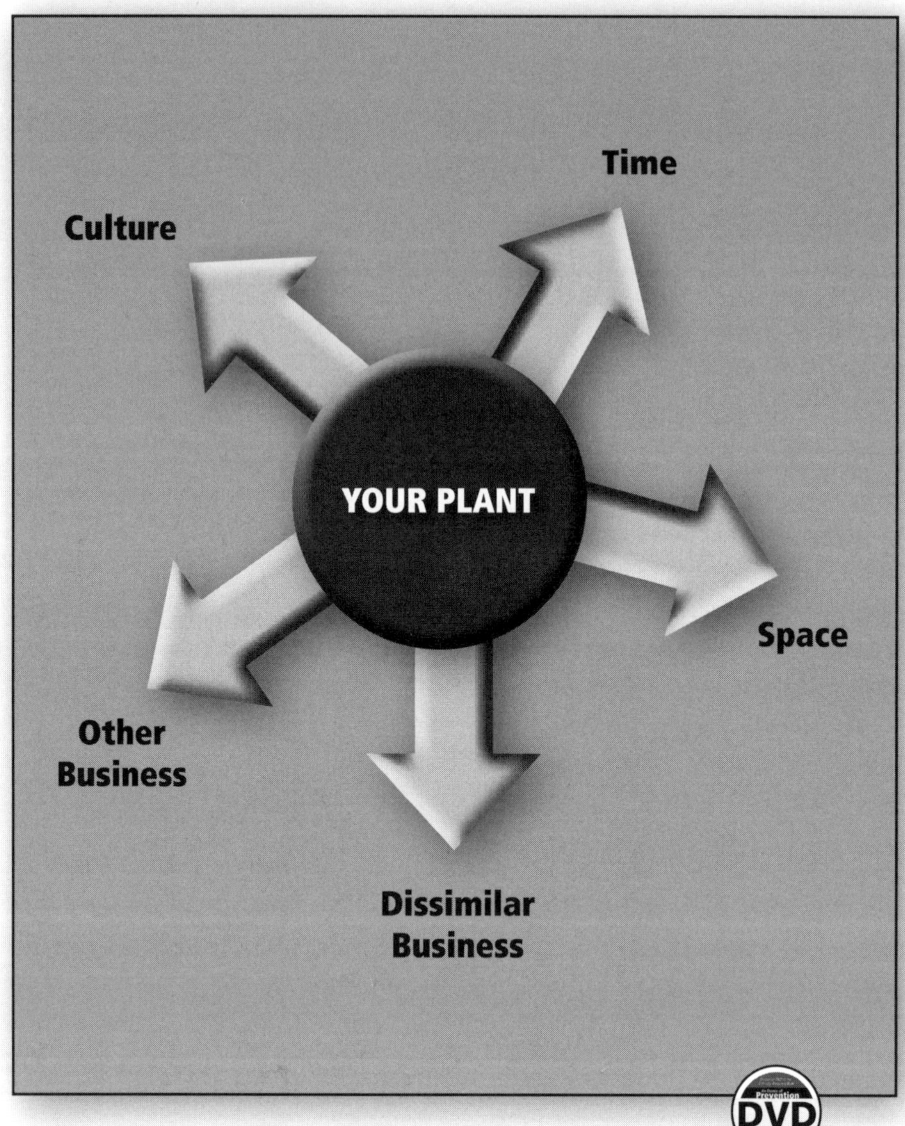

DVD

Available on the Companion DVD

Disaster

"an event, concentrated in time and space, in which a society or a relatively self-sufficient subdivision of a society undergoes severe damage and incurs such losses to its members and physical appurtenances that the social structure is disrupted, and the fulfilment of all or some of the essential functions of society prevented." (**Fritz, C.E.** "Disasters.")

Origins and Generic Impediments

Isomorphic learning has evolved from biology and systems theory. The biologist von Bertalanffy postulated that "different systems may possess common properties."[18] Systems researchers suggested there are similarities among what may appear to be unrelated organizations. For example, an airline and a shoe factory both feature division of labour, hierarchy and so on. A shoe factory employing only human labour and a manufacturing-plant that only uses robots still have things in common—inventory, quality control, supply-chain issues and so on. These similarities suggest that examining past disasters is a potential benefit, even if those disasters happened in what was a far removed culture, time, space or system.[19]

Some might argue that no two disasters are exactly alike and that looking at one might not help in managing another. Case studies of fires show the countless variations possible in what might appear to be disasters of quite similar origin: combustion. Debris under an old wooden escalator exacerbated the King's Cross Underground fire in London. An electrical spark ignited fumes in a pub cellar when a petrol tanker overturned in Walton town centre in England. Either smoking or open cooking-flames probably caused the Happy Valley Racecourse fire in Hong Kong at the beginning of the twentieth century. The use of flammable bamboo 'mats' as building-material exacerbated that situation. Despite these apparent differences, the principle of isomorphic learning suggests there are enough similarities that an urban fire-fighter may be able to learn not only from an underground fire but also from a petrol tanker overturning in a rural area or a racecourse fire from a century ago. There is a great deal to learn from other times, cultures and places.

Learning from past disasters involves allowing for time, space, culture and other factors. Response speed and effectiveness may depend on tools, location, expertise, perception of time or chance. To extract valuable lessons after the fact, you may have to take into account how geographically remote the event was, how long ago it occurred, your own culture or your cultural perception of the responders. So there are plenty of barriers to learning from past disasters.

Cultural Distance

Culture can be associated with nations as well as geographical and political boundaries. Within those boundaries culture can involve organizational culture. Within organizations, group dynamics and sub-cultures, including safety culture, come into play. There may be greater cultural differences within organizations in the same country than between different countries.

Culture is related to ethnicity, religion, language and race. All can be factors quite apart from political borders. These aspects of the human condition are emotionally charged and can divide people. Gestures and other non-verbal communication can be culturally specific and misunderstood. The Western businessperson who insists on sealing a deal with a firm handshake and a bottle of champagne could outrage several religions and cultures with either gesture. Similarly, eye contact may be a mark of sincerity for many in the West but First Nations and Asian cultures can find it confrontational.

Conversely culture can also promote learning if managers view a certain group or safety culture as a model. Certain cultures, organizations and countries have gained a reputation for excellence, and this may have sparked emulation. Examples include Quantas Airlines for safety, Southwest Airlines for employee relations, Rolls Royce for quality and Israel for counter-terrorism.

The King's Cross Underground fire in London illustrates the impediments that even subtle cultural distance can offer. Once fire broke out in the station, there was virtually no time or space separation between the responses by police, London Transport staff and fire-fighters. Police training and culture had them focus on moving people upwards, to get them away from the fire. The fire service moved passengers downwards to get them away from the rising smoke. The net result was that both response groups pushed more victims into an already congested zone nearest the fire. These actions cost lives. Familiarity with fire, culture, training in crowd control and other factors influenced the actions of all three groups—seemingly from the same culture.

Culture also helps shape learning after the fact. Inquiries aren't conducted in vacuums but are affected by news reports, laws, political pressure, lobbying by the victims and other factors. Culture may impede police officers, fire-fighters or LT staffers who seek to learn from a past fire or even from a fire they all fought together. They may be reading reports that are already biased or flawed, and their own cultural biases may impede learning even as they do their reading. Students of a past disaster should consider whether their own group's culture would have dictated a different response, especially if they had arrived first. Students need also to consider whether the disaster would have unfolded in the same way if another response group's culture had prevailed. Official investigations focus on blame or providing closure. Police seek to 'close' cases by laying charges, the caring-services seek to comfort and politicians seek to radiate calm and control. Each mindset can affect the analysis of data after the event.

Even impeccable investigations are only as good as the flawed information they receive. Eyewitnesses are notoriously unreliable. Responders, students and eyewitnesses subjectively interpret time, their life experiences and their culture. So whether the definitive or final account came from the culture of a coroner, the police, journalism, a bystander, a legislative committee, a royal commission or an organizational investigation will shape its reliability for years to come.

Paradigms, or ways of looking at events, are partly a reflection of organizational culture. Evidence that supports a particular paradigm tends to be highlighted, while facts that contradict it tend to be downplayed.

Paradigms

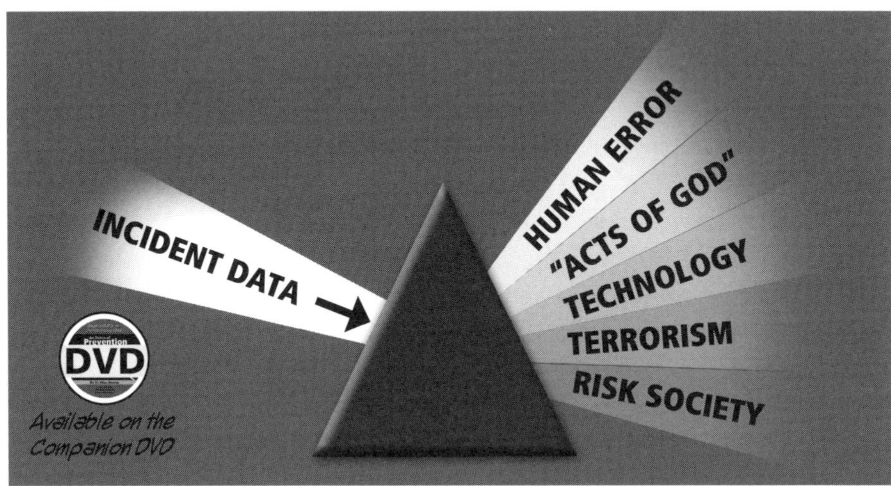

"In a situation with no alternatives, then the level of safety associated with the only course of action is by definition acceptable, no matter how disagreeable the situation ....acceptable risk is the risk associated with the best of the available alternatives, not with best of alternatives which we would hope to have available." (S.L. Derby and R.L. Keeney, 1981)

Paradigms may support a particular organization's political, economic or power interests. Which investigating agency benefits if an event is explained as a result of terrorism, commercial expediency or a design fault in technology? Police and counter-terrorist agencies' budgets and prestige expand after suspected terrorist events. Airplane manufacturers hope to disprove allegations of design flaws. Pilots try to blame their equipment, and lawyers blame those with the deepest pockets.

In one airline crash that I was involved in, the pilots' union immediately began doing a survey of its members, asking whether any had had difficulty trying to land the type of plane in question—hoping to create doubt about the aircraft and relieve pressure on the pilot. By the time the official transportation board report came out, there had been months of news stories questioning the reliability of the airplane. In fact, the pilot had made a mistake in trying to land with a low ceiling and should not have let the co-pilot attempt the landing. But once doubt has been created or investigating agencies have embarked on a course that supports a particular paradigm, the die is cast.

Spatial Distance

Ethnocentrism, by which we impose our own cultural norms on others, can make remote events appear odd, unimportant or inapplicable. Some will even dismiss the experiences of another culture because of the remoteness, race, religion or other characteristics of its members.

Greater distance compounds communication difficulties. Differences of geography, architecture, climate and many other factors can affect learning. Different legal systems across political borders can impede learning. Laws develop over time and in a cultural context. As one looks back to an event that happened under different laws, or no applicable laws at all, one must question whether the lessons apply to the present day. Security managers have to consider whether response techniques from other jurisdictions are applicable, effective or even legal.

Oil spills in American waters receive more media attention than larger and more frequent ones in Nigeria or Mexico. A perceived 'pristine' location can magnify the damage. So can proximity to media markets.

The distance between continents can hamper studies of disasters. A manager in Europe might have a difficult time understanding the Happy Valley racecourse fire in Hong Kong. If nothing else, it is hard to imagine how people could use bamboo in construction (as they still do there for scaffolding) or what a mat shed is if you haven't seen one. Similarly, North Americans or Australians might find it hard to understand how an escalator could catch fire in the King's Cross Underground station if they haven't seen an old wooden one in the London Underground or in an old department store. These challenges are like the great difficulty war correspondents had in explaining 'hedgerows' to a North American audience during World War II. The correspondents wrestled with explaining how a hedge could stop a tank. Not having seen the high mounds of earth, rock and trees hampered the audience's learning.

We have a large world in which to learn. If you're studying stadium safety in Texas, you'd have to know that those British soccer crushes and the Happy Valley fire had occurred in order to learn from them. You don't know what you don't know, and spatial distance impedes finding out.

Temporal Distance

Both the time a disaster took to occur and the 'times' in which it occurred affect our ability to learn from it. The former refers both to the length of time it can take for a disaster to take hold (e.g. fire to engulf, disease to spread) and the length of time it takes for mitigation techniques to have an effect (e.g. news to spread, responders to arrive, water to douse flames). A different attitude toward human rights, safety or the environment may characterize the 'times' in which a disaster occurred. Perceptions of risks constantly evolve, and we are becoming ever more aware of the risks we all bear.

Not only have the times changed, but time itself has changed. Events seem to happen ever more quickly these days. If your goal is to respond 'quickly,' a legitimate question becomes, "How fast is that?" When studying a past disaster in which the response was deemed quick enough, one might wonder if that would also be true today. How quick did a response to an environmental incident need to be in the 1920s, 50s or 60s, in 2000 and now?

Some suggest that time has not only changed preferred response techniques but also the definition of disaster, risk and crisis. "[T]he very nature of crisis has changed as technology, the rise of formal public opinion, and the general literacy of the masses have developed."[20] In the modern era even the nature of change is different. "What has changed about change is its magnitude, the approach it requires, the increasing seriousness of its implications, and the diminishing shelf life of the effectiveness of our responses to it."[21] So modern crisis managers must 'translate' the learning they glean from past disasters and assess how that learning will fit our times and response techniques.

Instant communications and 'media time' have affected the nature of crises and the need for a communications response. Media deadlines affect reporters' abilities to gather and distribute information. Media reports influence responders and the actions they take. The news media affect people's perception of an event and the time within which they expect officials to respond and explain their response. Managers may wonder how to learn to handle a modern event by studying similar events that happened before these media factors. How do we now compare the impact of an event that was covered mainly by newspapers, radio or broadcast TV? What about the same event covered constantly by all-news cable? How has coverage by new media changed the perception of the event and the definition of timely and effective responses?

Spatial distance may actually have a positive effect if the time period becomes worthy of study. The sinking of the *Titanic* or the *Challenger* explosion may focus attention on reverence for technology and spark learning. Learning takes time. The lessons of a disaster may become more apparent and accessible several years after the event. The facts about the event may become more widely and deeply known as time goes on.

On the other hand, time often seems to impede rather than help learning. As time passes, memories fade, documents are lost, participants die and accounts become fuzzy. Certain perceived 'truths' emerge about disasters.

Perhaps the greatest influence of temporal distance is that new processes and technology have no precedents. Optimization, where a component may perform several functions, can produce unintended consequences. So can miniaturization of components or limited redundancy and limited tolerances to save space and money. 'Coupling causes' refers to the convergence of several factors that produce effects not anticipated at the design stage.

> We have produced designs so complicated that we cannot anticipate all the possible interactions of the inevitable failures .... In the past, designers could learn from the collapse of a medieval cathedral ... or the collision of railroad trains .... But we seem to be unable to learn from chemical plant explosions or nuclear plant accidents. We may have reached a plateau where our learning curve is nearly flat.[22]

Conclusion

Learning is cumulative. A by-product of a manager's learning is a greater ability to learn. Even when it is not directly or obviously applicable, the learning from past disasters can spur a modern manager on to greater learning. A more knowledgeable manager will eventually become a safer manager. The common factors in many disaster cases include an excessive trust in technology, complacency, ignored advance warnings and slow initial response. Disasters are often marked by the ignoring of valuable lay responses, by overly optimistic reports, and by neglecting the need to be forthright. The outcome of a disaster often involves a distraught public, victims, intense media attention, political inquiry, and other unwelcome features. So a crisis manager can examine the properties that most disasters share and access valuable common lessons. Despite apparent dissimilarities, disasters have enough in common to provide great learning-opportunities.

Appendix 2: Is a Crisis a Failure of Security?

Managing a crisis may involve managing many things—bad luck, mistakes, acts of God and so on. Are crises a normal part of organizational life? Is managing a crisis just part of modern management techniques? If so, what is the inventory of physical assets, skills and outside resources needed to do a good job? Managing a crisis, even successfully, may signal a difficult recovery period, declining public confidence or business failure.

Does this mean that the security system has failed? The answers deal with definitions of management, crisis and security.

We often hear the word 'crisis' used as if it meant the same as 'danger' or 'damage.' But it doesn't carry the same negative connotations. *Oxford* defines a crisis as a "[t]urning-point or decisive moment, esp. in illness; time of acute danger ...." Only the secondary references to illness and danger imply real or even potential damage.

The *Gage Canadian Dictionary* adds that the turning-point can involve acute illness, "after which it is known whether the patient is expected to live or die." An implication is that you can't endure illness without damage. If damage has occurred, then it's reasonable to assume that there was some failure of the system that was designed to prevent it. *Webster's* reference to economic crisis uses negative phrases such as "downward turning point."

Oxford defines 'security' as "[s]ecure condition or feeling; thing that guards or guarantees ... safety ... against espionage, theft, or other danger ...." Gage adds "freedom from danger, care, or fear ...." It's hard to imagine any system that can provide guarantees or total freedom when it comes to safety or fear.

Oxford defines management as "... administration of business concerns or public undertakings ...." Gage adds "control; handling; direction."

But control can't be absolute, the directions are not always followed to the letter and the directing-ability is not perfect.

All these definitions imply that imperfection is part of life and that crises will happen.

A narrow view of security can create its own problems. If security management and crime prevention mean much the same thing, then perimeter security may be the only point to worry about. Perimeter security can just mean that tighter controls will prevent trespass and shoplifting. This limited view might cut a manager off from information about the motives of criminals or other data that s/he could obtain outside the perimeter. A soft target can be an invitation to criminals. One soft target is a weak perimeter. An implication is that the security manager (retailer or landowner) is partly to blame for the crime by having allowed such a target to exist. But too much focus on perimeter security might blind a manager to the threat of sabotage from within.

A broader definition of security might include loss prevention. A loss-prevention manager would be concerned with issues both within and beyond the perimeter of the building. S/he might engage in gathering and sharing information or other efforts to prevent incidents or lessen the impact of any that do occur. This kind of security manager might work with other responders and agencies.

In many jurisdictions, private police outnumber public police. Both are part of the broadly defined security system. In an effort to make shoplifting less profitable, they investigate those who buy stolen goods. Retailers and their security managers should cooperate with the public police and even ask them to become involved with them in the interest of loss prevention. Whether the loss-prevention manager is concerned with injury, inventory shrinkage, financial loss or other matters, all information, lawfully obtained and used, is a valuable tool. Much of that information can come from well outside a perimeter.

This broader view of security could also involve what Sally Lievesley calls "risk engineering." Risk engineering seeks to make security a quantifiable science and broadens the responsibilities of the security manager.

Security is dedicated to identifying and managing risks. Some believe all risks can be identified and reduced—if not eliminated. Wise crisis managers approach events from the point of view of the beholder (stakeholders), not just with the operational knowledge they themselves happen to have. "[T]he disaster must not be seen like the meteorite that falls out of the sky on an innocent world; the disaster, most often, is anticipated, and on multiple occasions".[23]

Examinations of police roles in crowd incidents bring these issues into focus. A broad definition of security implies that the police should be concerned with more than just keeping a crowd in a certain location, moving it in a particular direction or dispersing it. The main focus should be on safety. Police sometimes misguidedly focus "on the avoidance of public disorder, as opposed to ensuring public safety."[24] Police activities and priorities should concentrate on the activities that enable them to calm a crowd and thus manage the situation peacefully. Expecting trouble and responding with rigid reflex actions designed to take control can provoke rather than prevent. This is a failure of security, and the police can be the authors of their own misfortune—and ours.

Football-stadium violence in the UK is a good example of how authorities long failed to learn from the past. There has been a history of such violence for almost 100 years, involving well over 100 killed and several thousands injured. There are documented measures that contributed to dangerous crowd behaviour, including methods and timing of ticket sales, starting-times of matches, crowd gathering-areas and turnstile capacity. Sometimes the police mistook simple overcrowding for hooliganism. Often stadium owners took the attitude that they were merely in the business of renting out facilities and not the family entertainment business as well. After selling their tickets, they seemed unconcerned with the success of the event itself. Crowd behaviour at all sporting-events reveals a tendency to symbolic violence or adolescent disorder that may become unruly, but this is insignificant compared to the deaths that can occur in riots and crush incidents.

Is some level of crisis or disorder at sporting-events inevitable? A public-policy question might be for society to decide what sort of public disorder is acceptable. Some disorder may be inevitable, and the real question may be whether an organization's management will add to, lessen or change it. Does one accept shouting, taunting, cuts and bruises in crowds? Or is one willing to accept crushes, deaths and stabbings?

These observations and definitions may seem to be a bit removed from plant operations and practical crisis-management planning. But industry is bound to have some structural problems in the same way as society does. Absenteeism, inventory shrinkage, graffiti and productivity are issues in every workplace. I worked on an offshore oil-rig construction project that had 5,000 workers building a massive platform in a remote location. Interestingly, they lost about 5,000 small measuring-tapes. The company felt the best strategy was just to replace them rather than accuse every worker of theft, even though that might well have been the truth. But when security found a two-car garage filled with big power tools, it drew the line and called in the police.

Rigid rules may even encourage improper behaviour in the workplace. Imagine an employer who searches out and punishes people who take some time off work on the day of a major sporting-event or an important family anniversary. This might encourage deceitful behaviour. On the other hand, the employer who offers all employees a few hours off on the day of the final game of the World Cup, World Series or Stanley Cup might be repaid with increased loyalty. Earned days off and a liberal policy of allowing time off for family emergencies may achieve the same. A policy of lending tools so that workers are safe at home when doing repairs might reduce pilfering. Imagine if that offshore oil company I worked for had promised to give every worker a measuring-tape when his job was done. It might have increased loyalty and prevented workers from helping themselves to tapes.

The same principle, but on a larger and more tragic level than missing measuring-tapes, involves the 9/11 airplane attack on the World Trade Center. It not only could have been predicted but was. Academics and security experts had been writing about this possibility for years.

If security were merely prevention, perimeter control or mitigation, then if any crisis happened, you could say that security failed. But being operational implies the need to deploy when things are happening, not merely prevention. Mitigation involves managing and reducing risks, but perhaps not eliminating them completely. Inevitably some risk will remain, because eliminating all threats is not humanly possible. Crises will occur, and they must be managed.

Some crises happen over long periods of time—the fifty thousand North American highway deaths each year. Death as a result of smoking takes decades. Some risks appear to be instant, such as the 9/11 tragedy. Some risks are self-imposed—skydiving, for example. The additional 1500 or so people who died in highway accidents after 9/11 may have died from risk perception. Perhaps many thought they were safer when driving rather than flying because of a generic fear of flying after the trauma of 9/11.

Whom are we to blame because people flew less after 9/11—the individuals, the police, the government, airlines, car-makers, an educational system that didn't teach the principles of heavier-than-air flight, news reports, highway engineers, Al-Qaeda or whom?

Special Cases

Some situations are special cases. You could consider storms, floods, fires and explosions so unusual that having to manage them can't be considered a failure of a security system. Your security system may reduce the effects of such 'acts of God,' but to assume you can prevent them altogether may be unreasonable. While a security manager can't be held responsible for the weather, s/he can be responsible for planning for predictable weather events.

The second unique situation involves those charged with responding to or mitigating crises affecting others. Law-enforcement, fire, ambulance, emergency-room, gas, water, electricity and sewer workers and many others have to respond to such crises. They are managing those crises, but their presence doesn't imply a failure of their own security. A partial exception would involve the responsibility that police officers and firefighters have for prevention.

So, is a crisis a failure of security? It depends on who and where you are—the context, the times and the event you're handling.

Appendix 3: Public Participation in Crises—a Prerequisite for Effective Disaster Management

Two schools of thought exist about the value of public participation in disaster management. Many responders believe that mitigation and response should be left to professionals who have appropriate training and experience. The other school argues that those affected should be involved. Average citizens' legitimacy stems from their being on the scene, being able to act fast and first, being highly motivated to respond to threats to family and property and thus being among the most appropriate people to be involved in mitigation at the time.

However, these positions aren't really absolutes. We can't dismiss trained and equipped professionals in favour of motivated bystanders whose chief qualification seems to be that they are present. But a distraught mother's knowledge about where to look for her baby in the rubble of a building is not something a professional fire-fighter should dismiss. Does expert knowledge take precedence over lay information, and if not, does lay knowledge really help in a disaster?

British researcher Brian Wynne has shown how scientists ignored Cumbrian sheep farmers' valuable local knowledge. Farmers claimed that there was a higher incidence of childhood leukaemia near the UK's Sellafield nuclear power plant. Both public-health authorities and British Nuclear Fuels denied these claims. Although lay people had been asserting their position for years, their knowledge had to be 'discovered' by scientists to gain currency. Once the Chernobyl leak finally led scientists to study Cumbrian radiation, they found that 50 percent of radiocaesium came from "other sources," which meant the Sellafield reactor and fallout from atmospheric weapons testing.[25]

The farmers knew more than the scientists about the source of the radiation and its effect on their sheep. They also knew more about soil conditions and what sheep eat. Thus the scientists' advice on how to lessen the effects of the Chernobyl radiation was not very helpful.

Those farmers might rightly discount some expert opinion as unhelpful in disaster management.

So these two approaches represent a continuum rather than an irrevocable choice between two possible options. Official responders may have a point when they cite their experience as a reason to rely on trained personnel. They might also cite cases where public actions have impeded the response. Lay citizens might counter with cases where official responders would have performed better with the benefit of their greater local knowledge. There might be cases where the lay response was both quicker and more effective than the official one.

This appendix will explore these two perspectives in three broad categories: equity, effectiveness and the notion that many members of the public are *de facto* responders regardless of their abilities or the attitudes of official responders.

It is increasingly accepted that we should be defining 'victims' more broadly, and this may mean we must involve them and their families more in our response:

> … [A]n effective disaster response will accommodate not only the needs of those directly affected (the victims) but also the needs of those indirectly affected (victims' relatives, friends, acquaintances and careers).
>
> ... [I]t is no longer acceptable that the effectiveness of a disaster response be judged only on such criteria as whether or not the perpetrators are caught, whether or not professional negligence is proved, or how quickly "normal service" is restored.[26]

Equity

For German researcher Ulrich Beck "there are no bystanders any more."[27] Modern risks are not only spread more widely through populations but also spread over time. Beck notes that "the injured of Chernobyl are … not even all *born* yet."[28] So as these risks become larger, they begin to have potential impact on people, the environment and property beyond the confines of the laboratory or the gate of the nuclear plant.

In the past, workers who had heard of or experienced accidents could roughly measure the risks of working in factories. Comparing this risk to the pay and other factors generated a personal risk/benefit analysis. Similarly, families might have worried about the risks the breadwinner experienced but also appreciated the associated benefits. Neighbours not involved with the factory might have had a less precise risk balance sheet, but they may have factored in the business they did with the factory workers or the general benefits of living in an active, prosperous community. In this era, before Beck's risk society, involving plant workers who knew the risks and how to respond to a localized disaster was no doubt equitable and effective. Now, when risk does not stop at the plant gate, the question becomes whether a similar case can be made for involving the broader public in disaster management.

The former head of the US Environmental Protection Agency, William Ruckelshaus, argues "technology may impinge upon a democratic society."[29] He cites "the chemical products and by-products of modern technology and the potential social disruption associated with the processes we have created to control them."[30] He also argues for circulating more information and better empowering the public as antidotes. He quotes Thomas Jefferson as saying, "If we think [the people] not enlightened enough to exercise their control with a wholesome discretion, the remedy is not to take it from them, but to inform their discretion."[31]

The last century's factory workers could test machinery and production techniques to some acceptable degree. Co-workers and even neighbours could informally share in this analysis and make judgments about risk and response. Today, however, "[T]heories of nuclear reactor safety are testable only after they are built, not beforehand."[32] With the risk of widespread and even global destruction as a feature of the modern age, what results, for Beck, is a society that has "suspended the principle of insurance .... The residual risk society has become an uninsured society, with protection paradoxically diminishing as the danger grows."[33] This problem may have no solution, but involving and empowering the public goes at least some way to address it.

The people who are most closely involved in crises and disasters are the victims, their loved ones and bystanders. The effects on survivors often linger for years or even a lifetime, and their needs are often quite different from those of responders. Some cultures bury people within 24 hours of death and forbid exhumation. Others require the recovery of even minute body parts, and still others forbid the mixing of different victims' body parts. The best way to obtain such sensitive data is from the public group in question, and preferably before a disaster. In this way, responders can codify standard operating-procedures in a crisis plan that is not only sensitive to diverse needs but also more effective. For these and other practical reasons, the Home Office in the UK finds many legitimate roles for the public and volunteers to play.

The Pan Am Lockerbie crash in December 1988 highlights the equity of involving those associated with victims. Responders repeatedly asked the parents of one victim to describe their daughter. The parents were not allowed to see her body. They were not told photographs of her body had been taken and were not allowed to see them, even though the film was available for sale to medical researchers and others. The family were receiving dozens of calls, letters and visits daily. They wanted information, legal advice, access to counselling, and other help. Questions about the last moment of the victim's life, the need to visit the site, the desire for a part of the plane or other objects from the site all show that "simply guessing at the emotions of others is not good enough."[34] More openness with these victims would have been both more equitable and more effective. Disaster response involving victims is labour-intensive at the best of times. Knowing these human needs, and more closely involving the public, may help to improve the situation.

Responders who gain access to the specific data that the public can provide will be rewarded in several ways. They can respond more humanely, they will glean valuable information that they would not otherwise have and they will also become better responders.

Effectiveness

A more effective response may result from everything from letting bystanders direct emergency vehicles through to letting them help scientists identify the best mitigation techniques. Brian Wynne (citing H.J. Otway and P. Slovic), points out that "ordinary people bring more to their definitions and evaluations of risks" than experts recognize.[35] The question for those in the disaster-management business is whether they can afford to ignore this storehouse of information that the general public possesses.

Wynne's data show that even when the public passively reports trust in the emergency-response system, the government and those running the local industrial complex, this may not imply the sort of active, deep trust needed to harness public knowledge and actions when a disaster strikes. Responders dedicated to safety need to probe beyond and underneath what may be only surface trust and compliance. If responders can understand lay perceptions and knowledge, they have a better chance of conducting successful public communication campaigns. These campaigns might influence more people to be prepared for emergencies, to evacuate or to otherwise be safer in their daily lives.

After reading Wynne, one might first want to question the effectiveness of relying on traditional 'scientific' advice that may not apply locally or at all. Finally, if surveys showed general support for certain mitigation activities, the manager might want to question whether this support was firm or merely acquiescent. In this context, then, public participation seems to be essential to managing a disaster effectively.

Appendix 4: Why Risk Communication?

As Baruch Fischhoff at Carnegie Mellon University points out, risk communication is not a science.[36] It just uses scientific techniques to measure communication effectiveness when the topic is risk. Roger Kasperson points out that we know more about how individuals react to risk information than we do about how social groups react.[37] This is an important limitation, because communication theories show how peer pressure and opinion leaders can affect perception.

More research is needed on groups and group dynamics. I'd like to see more work on distinctions between men and women, rich and poor, black and white, urban and rural or young and old. Diverse people don't behave in uniform ways. Your research should take this into account.

Approaches to Risk Management and Communications

Ironically, using traditional public-affairs techniques can actually make a crisis worse. Issuing press releases and writing op-ed pieces for the newspaper may raise the public's risk perception and increase the demand for regulation, legislation or punitive damages. An organization that relies on baseline and longitudinal research conducted during normal times may know too little about the attitudes that develop during a crisis, especially if respondents feel personally threatened.

There's not much point in becoming a great crisis manager after the fact when you could have become an effective risk manager beforehand. Risk management involves identifying sources of risk and lessening them. Then there may be no crisis or disaster to manage.

Risk Communication

Risk-communication professionals have drawn up a set of rules designed to make information about risk more acceptable to a lay audience. The main ones are to make risks known and voluntary. Using hourly workers, local opinion leaders and high-school teachers as spokespeople, showing caring when disseminating facts, using positive body language and arriving early and staying late at public meetings are other recommended techniques.[38] However, risk managers who merely make a short list of such measures and assume they will address all risk issues are running a risk for themselves. Many senior managers, desperate to solve problems in their community, media or government relations, grasp at this apparently comprehensive advice, but effective risk communication does not boil down to a half dozen 'rules' that will ensure audiences accept risky situations.

The purpose of this section is to examine how psychological, sociological and cultural theories of risk differ. It will summarize the three approaches and provide an overview of how they differ.

There are three major themes in the theories—respect, openness and complexity. You may find that respect for the individual increases as each theory is described. The theories also seem to exhibit more openness as we progress. The individual's interaction with people and things becomes more important to our understanding of risk. The approach also becomes more complex or layered as we move from psychological through sociological and into cultural theories.

Value of the Approaches

Risk is not an objective, measurable entity having the same effect on people regardless of their gender, race, location and other factors. Risk can only be understood in context, including social and cultural context. We must manage risk differently in different situations. The British Royal Society's landmark study of this topic says "Risk perception is inherently multi dimensional and personalistic, with a particular risk or hazard meaning different things to different people and different things in different contexts."[39] Risk managers must take much more into account than lab results, engineering-reports, chemical reactions and similar data. You can get the science and math absolutely correct and still have frightened, angry people on your hands.

At the centre of understanding risk is the individual. It's hard to conceive of a situation where risk doesn't vary as a result of its interactions with people and groups. The age, gender, social group, cognitive skills or life experiences of the affected individuals are all major factors in risk perception. Engineers don't guess at what the bending-moment is, accountants don't guess about what the generally accepted accounting-principle is, lawyers don't guess about precedents and risk managers must not make assumptions about the measurability of risk.

A crisis has been called "a serious threat to the basic structures or the fundamental values and norms of a social system ...."[40] Can a risk, crisis or disaster exist without affecting people? If a tidal wave occurs in the middle of the ocean, where there are no ships, buildings or people, is it really a disaster, when it has no measurable effects on people? Measurable effects on living organisms in the ocean might cause the tidal wave to qualify, but normally an event would have to have some effect on property, people or the environment to be termed a disaster.

The 'Human' Approach—Psychology, Sociology and Cultural Theories

Psychological, sociological and cultural factors affect risk perception and human behaviour in different ways and with varying impact. Psychologists focus on the cognitive skills and perceptions of the individuals who experience risk. Sociologists focus on risk communication, systems theories, socio-technical interactions and learning from past mistakes. The common elements are how people interact with each of these and with technology and other risks both as individuals and in groups. Cultural theorists would have us understand risk in terms of our everyday involvement with our co-workers, family, friends and others. Risk affects our identity and vice versa.

Psychological Approaches to Risk

Many psychologists emphasize measurement. They seek laboratory techniques to provide quantifiable and repeatable results. Psychologists study how we make decisions and perceive the world around us—cognition. They use psychological studies and mental modelling under controlled conditions. The results may or may not translate into real life. In the physical sciences, serious concerns have been raised about taking data obtained in a laboratory using rats and making assumptions about how humans will react to the same substance or stimulus. These involve cross-species extrapolation (rat to human), translating short dosage times to a lifetime of exposure, correcting for weight and dosage ratios and so on.

There are similar concerns about laboratory findings in psychology. The laboratory is not the real world.

Even people's perceptions in the real world don't necessarily reflect the real world. There are differences between people's perceptions of risk and the actual incidence. For example, people prefer known, controllable and voluntary risks to the more frightening unknown and imposed risks.[41] Furthermore, lay people misunderstand probability. Psychologists conclude there is a cognition or trust problem to be addressed. However, just because people's perception of risk doesn't match the reality doesn't mean there isn't a risk involved. If people perceive a threat, they will feel a threat. The immune system can be affected by risk perception, and that is then reality.

Researchers who view risk as something concrete and objectively measurable suggest that people are irrational about risk when their perception doesn't match reality.[42] This approach, which assumes that if scientists could just inject more accurate data into the ignorant public, they would feel safer, is fundamentally arrogant. It presumes that the public is wrong, that they should understand the scientific information provided and that their feelings and perceptions are irrelevant.

In some tests, subjects are asked how likely they think a risk is to occur and how much of a threat it poses. I wonder how respondents would know the hazard posed by smallpox vaccinations unless some coincidence caused this knowledge to be in their minds. Some respondents may grow weary of trying to guess the hazard of events they've never thought about before. Surely the relevance of these perceptions has been affected by a variety of social and cultural processes. Transferring these data from the laboratory to the real world is very difficult. There is an intellectual élitism about many psychological studies. It turns out that experts are often not much better at guessing risk frequency and impact than lay people. Finally, the theorists assume that lay people wish to be informed, when in fact many don't want to digest more information, and may want to just disagree.

Another concern with many psychological approaches is the context in which the study is undertaken. This is generally a laboratory or a social setting that has been artificially constructed (focus group or lay/expert dialogue). One could argue that the methodology itself has excluded real life.

My favourite theory of how risk can change with people and context is called the social-amplification theory of risk. The Royal Society, Nigel Pidgeon and others have examined aspects of how a risk becomes more or less intense over time. But Roger Kasperson's work may be the best. My interpretation of this work is intuitive and simple. It's fine to blame the media for blowing some stories out of proportion. We've all seen the front page of the paper dealing with something less important than something on page 12 or something that didn't even make the news. That's media amplification. But there are countless other groups and agencies in society that affect our perception of events. Politicians make speeches, lawyers launch lawsuits, protestors fill the streets, clergy preach and professors lecture. All have an effect. The social-amplification theory of risk teaches that how a risk is spoken about, and how the discussion moves from group to group, changes weight and temperature. Our perception of risk also changes depending on what our friends and family say about it or how it affects them.

Sociological Approaches

Events are more than the sum of their parts. It's important to look at more than psychological factors. It is also important to go beyond explaining crises and disasters as just failures of technology. If you involve more than one person, you are embarking on a sociological approach. If culture is added, including technological or safety culture, this is a sociological approach as well.

In Britain, the Kegworth air crash of January 1989 occurred in part because a pilot mistakenly switched off his one good engine in a two-engine plane when the other one caught fire. One could view this as simply a cognitive problem involving misreading instruments or as human error. It may have been made worse by poor sight lines, which made it difficult to see the engines from inside the plane. Poor communication among crew members could have been a factor. But there are other elements. The chain of command comes into play, including flight crews' deference to captains. Captains have been known to ignore advice from junior officers. Some flight crews, and even senior officers who are passengers at the time of an incident, have failed to point out danger for fear of breaching the chain of command. Gender, age and cultural factors can play a role. Some males tend to discount advice given by females. Some people and cultures carry deference to the point of not providing advice or interrupting. Some airlines are now providing assertiveness training to counter these factors.

Coupling involves the unhappy convergence of more than one element. Couplings are relatively unpredictable and produce unintended consequences when people and technology interact. Coupling can refer to the unpredicted convergence of human foible and technical or system foible.

Systems Concepts

Systems theory looks at complex organizations as interconnected components. What constitutes a system, or what is evidence of interconnection, can be a matter of perception.[43] Systems might include all the people and institutions we interact with, because they help us create our world view or the prisms through which we view the world.

It's very difficult to control a dynamic system. It's equally difficult to predict how a system will react or evolve. Reducing a complex system to its smallest elements and examining them may tell us nothing about the larger system—"examination of an individual scaffold component does not enable accurate prediction of what a particular erected scaffold will look like or how safe it will be."[44]

Depending on your world view you may ignore data that do not conform to and support your perspective and collect and highlight data that do. This can become a great problem in police investigations, accident inquiries and risk identification and management. Investigators may only notice evidence that supports their theories and ignore other evidence. World views, prisms or paradigms may also be biases. Management systems and approaches are often built on world views. If you think poorly of people, you may design security or safety systems to match that view. You may also design supervisory and reward systems to match.

Cultural Theory

A look around some of the great multicultural cities of the world can leave an observer shaking his head over just which of the many cultures in evidence might predominate in an individual crisis response. Even within organizations there are different cultures—accounting, sales, security and so on. Any group that shares ways of doing things or thinking about things can have a unique culture. Culture can involve a shared history, laws and ways of doing things.

Working definitions of culture have changed with globalization and international trade. Now that the world is interconnected with

30 percent of GDP crossing national boundaries, I would suggest there is effectively something we could call a 'sector state.' A sector state could consist of lawyers who work in marine law in a dozen countries and speak six languages among them. It could also consist of people in six countries who all speak different languages but work on the components of a finished product for a common employer. New sector states can cross and encompass existing national, cultural, religious, professional and economic boundaries.

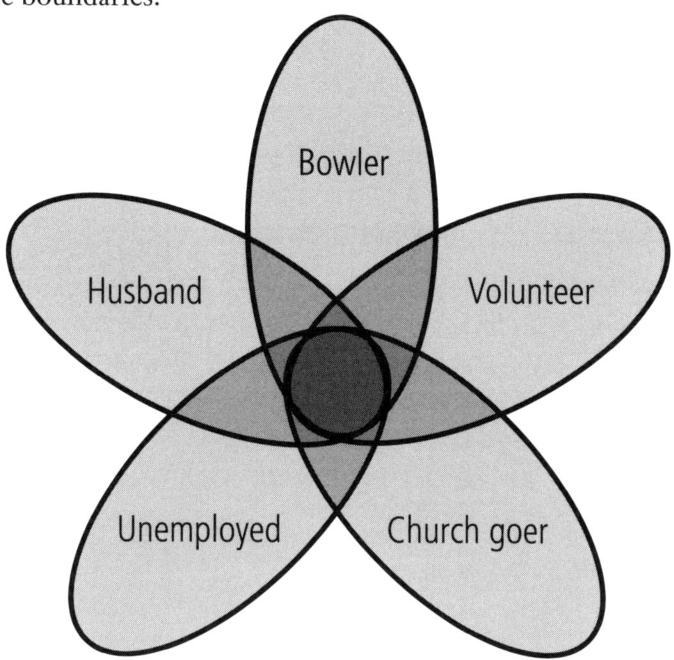

Cultural theory asks us to consider the multiple effects of our memberships. As the Venn diagram above illustrates, one may be a man, churchgoer, bowler, married, unemployed and simultaneously have memberships in dozens of other groups. Perhaps it is in the intersection or reduction that we have most in common.

Psychology studies individuals in relative isolation. Sociology studies them as they relate to other persons or groups and operate within groups or in relation to human or technical systems. Cultural theory adds complexity. It examines the texture and nuances of our multiple memberships or "patterns of interpersonal relations."[45] Many of us are pulled in several directions at once by our complex memberships and loyalties.

Quantitative Risk Assessment

Risk can't be precisely measured or defined objectively. Quantitative risk assessment (QRA) doesn't happen in a vacuum—it is conducted by people about people, and all people have biases. Risk-modelling is not independent of those causing the risk and those who are at risk. One danger of taking a strict engineering-approach that ignores the human element is that complex human foibles can't be reduced to a percentage or probability.

If we are committed to understanding risk, we must be committed to understanding the human condition. About 80 percent of "recommendations made by public inquiries ... [are] concerned with management, administration and information, and not technical matters."[46]

Risk Communication versus Risk Analysis

It's important to distinguish between risk analysis and risk communication. Risk analysts use scientific modelling-techniques to tell you that there is a likelihood of a hydrogen-sulphide release in Lodgepole, Alberta every 97 years. What these data won't tell you is whether you're in year 1 or year 96. Events with a high impact but a low probability may deserve the same attention as events with a moderate impact but a high probability.

University of Manchester professor emeritus Richard F. Griffiths points out other limitations.[47] The first and most troublesome is that risk predictions are often wrong. British experts had predicted that a release of 20 tonnes of chlorine could kill 120 urbanites and 6,000 rural people. That is 6 deaths per tonne in the country and 300 in the city. But at the time of the research a release of 361 tonnes had caused just 112 deaths. That is 0.3 deaths per tonne, and none were in the UK.

How do you model for human behaviour? Griffiths points out that current techniques lag far behind those used for physical, mechanical and chemical systems. How do you model for the possibility that an oil-tanker captain will be drinking on the job in Valdez, Alaska? How do you predict that workers will go on a tea break lasting an hour and ten minutes before responding to alarms at a chemical plant in Bhopal, India? How do you predict the behaviour of a deranged person, or what product s/he will contaminate?

If you probe Quantitative Risk Assessment techniques, you'll find guesses within the model. The model may only be as sound as the weakest guesses.

Appendix 5: Witness Preparation

Public Consultation as Witness Preparation

Credibility comes from action, not words. Credible people can speak about what they have done at least as much as about what they will do. If you haven't done anything, people may find it hard to believe that you will perform in the future. A senior executive who has hiked a trap line with a member of a First Nation to gain traditional environmental knowledge has more credibility than one who has read a book about it. The one who has read the book has more credibility than an executive who hired an anthropology professor to sit at the witness table with him.

Meet your neighbours who will help gain you permission to conduct business. Regulators and legislators know that you can't please everyone. They know a few interveners will oppose you. But those few should pale in comparison with the many hundreds you've met. You should be able to tell a simple, compelling story about having gone the extra mile to show each person maps, charts, graphs and data to support your project. Most boards can order you to do this anyway, so why not beat them to it?

There is considerable precedent on just what constitutes proper public consultation. For decades the CAER (Community Awareness Emergency Response) program in the chemical industry required member companies to communicate in a variety of ways with their neighbours. Over the years I've seen door-to-door campaigns, stickers on neighbours' phones containing emergency information, fridge magnets, brochures and community meetings. There's also legal precedent, with Canada's Supreme Court having issued two rulings on the same day about what constitutes the "duty to consult" with First Nations. One ruling was based on Maori custom in New Zealand. (By the way, the rulings were somewhat contradictory.)

We follow opinion leaders. You should know who they are in business, farming, education, the professions, the elderly and other groups and speak with them first. This is called élite interviewing and can tell you a lot about what you're up against.

Ground Rules

An athlete will do aerobic exercises to keep her heart rate above 160 beats per minute for far longer than what she might need in competition. In fact that athlete may be training for hours every day just to run the 100-yard dash in ten seconds. No one would think this was odd. But spokespeople, especially those with professional experience and credentials, often think they can get tuned up for a regulatory hearing just by reading the file or having a meeting about the issues. This is dangerous—especially when permission to do business is at stake.

Rehearsal for testifying must be tougher than real life. Successful witnesses should be secretly hoping for the toughest questions, so they can deliver the great answers they polished in rehearsal. Actual testimony should come as a relief and seem shorter than the practice sessions. Time and budgets may not allow for several days of testimony, but there must be several 30-minute segments of uninterrupted *gavel-to-gavel* questioning, so that the witnesses get used to being on the spot. There must be no stopping to discuss evidence, strategy and answers, because that will allow what could be a great witness-preparation session to degenerate into a mediocre meeting. At the end of each session, there should be a quick round of feedback and a brief discussion, but the lion's share of general discussion should happen outside the rehearsal sessions.

Witnesses should be exposed to different kinds of questioners. Some examination is dull and plodding. Some is theatrical. In many hearings, lay people are allowed to speak and ask questions. Different styles can throw a witness. To speed things up, I use a concept I call the *super-questioner.* This person may not be super in the sense of having great expertise. The term means that we usually don't concern ourselves with trying to guess which local lawyers may be at a hearing or whether a junior or the partner will appear. That's great information to have, but there usually isn't time or money to get down to that level of detail. So we simply focus on great answers, not how the question was asked or who asked it. The preparation is about the witness, not the questioner.

The person questioning is free to simulate board counsel, a neighbour, counsel for an intervener or anyone else who might legitimately ask a question. This person might change styles or topics much faster than would happen in real life. We often change questioners without the niceties of thanks and introductions, because we want to give the witnesses a workout, not perfectly simulate the procedures of a hearing. We also want witnesses to be grilled by people they've never met before, as will happen in real life.

We want witnesses to know the procedures that will be followed in a particular venue. We'll simulate two lawyers arguing over whether a line of questioning should be allowed. We want the witnesses to sit back, stay focused and wait for the ruling.

Video

There is no adequate preparation without video. Athletes watch game tapes. Actors tape rehearsals and review 'rushes' that were shot the day before. Before video, Sir Winston Churchill audio-recorded, edited and re-recorded his famous World War II speeches over and over again, as late as ten years after the war. Long before, one of the leaders of the French Revolution hired an actress to help him become a better orator. The ancient Athenian orator Demosthenes famously put pebbles in his mouth, stood on a beach and tried speaking over the roar of the surf to improve his delivery. We all need a little help.

Even if witnesses think they're so busy that they can't watch the video after the session, playing a few short clips during training illustrates points about body language and attitude that might be very contentious to raise without video evidence. Witnesses can see themselves slumping in the chair, their wandering eyes, combative looks and waffling hand gestures. They can also see that unmistakable moment when they find their voice and rhythm and start looking and sounding confident.

If witnesses will make an iron-clad commitment to watching their video, then more can get done during the session. If there's any doubt, I show more clips and freeze-frame shots right after the mock testimony. We can also edit video and email clips to witnesses in the time between the rehearsal and the actual event.

You're Always On!

These days everything is done in public. Everything is recorded, and everything is sent around instantly. At least that's the safe assumption. Although this is a given for a news conference, testifying witnesses sometimes forget it.

When I begin a witness-preparation session, I sometimes start with the question, "How many cameras are taking your picture right now?"

Groups usually see my cell phone camera, a digital camera about the size of a pack of playing-cards; my disc camera, about the size of a flattened orange; and the web camera on my notebook computer.

I can show a group that the one camera is hooked up to web page and the pictures of witnesses can be projected on the wall. This web page can be shared with anyone who has the password. The page also has a live-text box, so I can interact in real time with multiple viewers. There can be live coverage of a hearing without any participants knowing about it. So long as the board didn't object to an audience member keyboarding away, there could also be running commentary. If the board did object, the commentary could come from fact-checkers anywhere in the world.

The lesson is that as soon as witnesses get out of the hearing, they can watch their own testimony on the web. There can also be fully transcribed quotes and thoughtful commentary, rebuttals, research and clips from knowledgeable critics.

Rapport

Multiple witnesses need to support each other and to reinforce the same story line. Counsel and the applicant may have varying degrees of influence over witnesses. Some will fly in from far away for their testimony and leave. Others will be part of a panel of witnesses who sit together for the whole hearing.

A panel of witnesses presents unique challenges and opportunities. The challenges come under the general heading of teamwork. When a question is being asked of a witness, we often notice that while two members are opening their mouths to answer, another is shaking her head "No," another is nodding her head "Yes" and still another is looking perplexed. Video recording shows this in sharp relief. The tendency to answer without knowing the team's position must be trained out of the witnesses.

I recommend a 'quarterback' system, where one generalist takes most of the questions, gives a high-level response and then hands off to subject-matter experts at the table. If the quarterback has said all that is needed, no hand-off is required. Occasionally witnesses will speak up as required, without the quarterback's help. Only repeated rehearsal will smooth out the hand-offs and interjections and turn this group into a team.

Witnesses often wonder if there's a rule about whether to interject. There is. I tell my clients the following:

> "If you think that you can say what your colleague just said better, do not interject. You can't."

In our own minds we all sound much clearer, cleverer and more intelligent than the people we are listening to, but that's not true. It's a cognitive error. The best guess is that whatever our colleague said was close to the best that can be done and we should leave it at that.

But there's another part to my advice:

> "If there is a significant matter of fact that has been left out of testimony, or if there's been a significant error in the facts presented, then skilfully interject."

I recommend subtle interjection techniques: "Madam Chair, if I may add ...," "Also ...," "On that point ..." or "My field is ...."

Such phrases signal that the witness has something to add but is not contradicting the previous speaker or suggesting that s/he didn't answer fully and correctly.

Non-verbal communication is just as important as what is said. The witness should look at the person who asked the question. Whether that is board counsel, counsel to a citizens' group or the proverbial little ol' man worried about his vegetable garden—it doesn't matter. Looking at the person who is speaking to you and whom you are answering is one of the basic rules of good behaviour. Break this rule at a dinner party, and you don't get invited back. Break it at a regulatory hearing or community meeting and you might not be allowed to conduct your business.

You have many people to keep in mind. What to do? Witnesses should do the same as they do at a dinner party. Look at the person who asked you the question (counsel, board member or little ol' lady intervener), but occasionally allude to and include the others. In a short answer, fewer than 40 seconds, you might look only at the questioner. If you go beyond that, you might look to and include the board if you are saying something such as "and if we are successful" or "in order to comply with …."

In other words, if the answer involves the board, involve the board both verbally and non-verbally. However, if the answer involves the citizens in the audience, involve them: "and we've conducted seven open houses and met with 107 of our neighbours" or "and we hope all our neighbours know that we …."

The meaning of the words, and the emotional intent of the message, will dictate how you look, where you look, where and how you gesture and how you feel—just as at a dinner party. As Hamlet advised actors more than 400 years ago—"Suit the action to the word, the word to the action."

Witnesses who are not speaking have few options while they're sitting there for hours or days. They can look and nod approvingly at their fellow witness, look attentively at the questioner, take short notes, look at the board during a long answer or look at the citizens who are sitting in the audience while being spoken about. These looks should not be vacant or challenging but supportive and purposeful.

Do not pass notes around or giggle at one as if it were a note about the grade-four teacher. An exception might be made if a witness or researcher needed to pass a note about a substantial fact to one of the witnesses. The witness who takes the note should not pretend it doesn't exist. S/he should try to work the note into natural speech: "Madam Chair, I've just been reminded …" or "One of my colleagues has confirmed that the statistic is …."

Without this parenthetical explanation, board members are free to think what they want, including that your witness is being coached or was wrong about something or that the note is criticizing the board or the process.

When Confronted

You may be confronted over environmental issues or the economics of your plans. You may be confronted about your plan to include special-interest groups. Regardless of the reason for confrontation, there are a few rules that can help you respond.

Once you feel the confrontation developing, you'll probably also feel your own flight-or-fight response—the throat goes dry to allow the rapid intake of oxygen.

The mere fact we're now witnesses wearing business suits doesn't negate this instinct. Presenters, usually men, who try to pretend this programmed response isn't happening aren't fooling anyone.

Try to make your discomfort a trigger to pause and listen to what is actually being said, rather than focus on how you feel. You need to make extra efforts because the tension of the moment will mean you're not thinking clearly. Under stress, we decide how to handle a question based on the questioner's tone of voice, body language and clothing. This is very dangerous.

With practise you can also use the tension of the moment as a reminder to start exhibiting a range of positive body language. If you're not thinking clearly and you're being attacked, the least you can do is look receptive. Looking as if you're listening, processing the information you're being given and mentally working on a solution may go some way to defuse your critic. Better yet, it will improve your brain functions, and you just may come up with a solution.

Regardless of the content of the criticism and whether you have any substantial response, there's another course of action that will help you. The main strategy is to empathize. If your critic pauses and wants a response, begin with four empathetic statements. Even if you have no common ground, you can 'mirror' what is being said: "I hear you saying x," or "Let me make sure I understand your position."

Whatever you do, don't 'bite.' People make snide remarks with double meanings. Critics will try to antagonize you. Pretend you don't understand the slight and move on with the empathy and substance.

Venn to the Rescue!

Most witnesses I've helped feel overwhelmed with information. They have the history of their organization, the applicable laws, the environment, the case they need to make and lots of scientific and technical data in their minds and on paper at the table. But at any moment critics can get on the web and find esoteric details that you don't know about.

You can't get into too much trouble if you keep the following rules:

- Say only what you know for sure.
- Speak in positive language.
- Discuss only what it is your delegated responsibility to speak about, and if you're asked a question that isn't within your responsibility, hand off that question to someone else in your organization whose responsibility it is.
- Offer a clear and lucid explanation—you don't have to convince or sell, since those are tougher assignments than just explaining.
- Offer only your organization's official position on any topic.

Venn Diagram

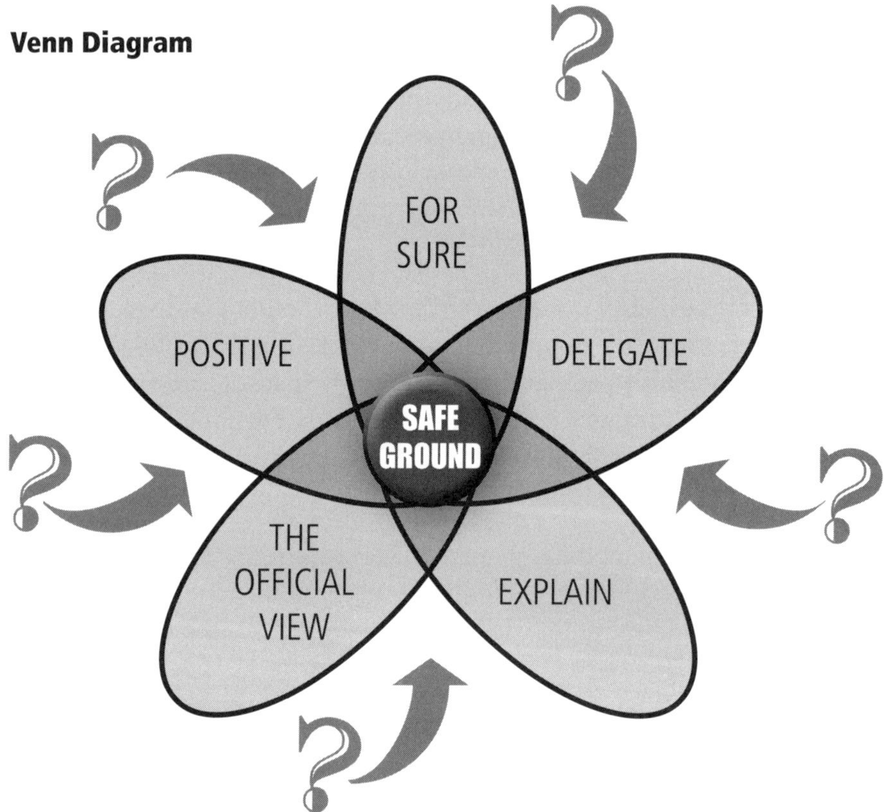

A Venn diagram, named after the mathematician, can help fine-tune your strategy. Each rule given above is a category or 'set' of information and data. If the sets intersect and the information you transmit belongs to each set simultaneously, you can't get into much trouble. But this is harder than it sounds. You need to know the facts, express them positively, know that you are empowered to speak about them, be logical and know what your organization's position is. This puts pressure on both the witness and the organization to do lots of homework so this strategy will work.

If this sounds like a tough assignment, consider the converse. Imagine speaking about something you are unsure of and in negative ways such as "We're not insensitive to environmental issues." Imagine too speaking about the economics of the deal if you're a geologist, or the compensation to local businesses if you're a marine biologist. Imagine adding a desperate sales pitch on how you have to get this project done and offering reasons that your organization doesn't agree with. Stick to your knitting.

When you reverse the rules of the Venn diagram, you will see how dangerous not following them can be.

To Tell the Truth

Many people have told me that the best approach is simply to tell the truth and be themselves. Well, on the second point, we should all be on our best behaviour when we're asking favours. It is said that poetry and drama are real life with the boring bits edited out. That's testimony too. It's a smooth, considered and lucid story that very few people can produce on the spot without rehearsal.

Truthfulness is a must, but truth needs to be contextualized. If you accept the classic definition of pollution as 'matter out of place,' then what's your truthful answer to the question of whether you pollute?

A witness needs to be, and appear to be, truthful and forthcoming. Being truthful involves not making anything up just to be helpful to the questioner. Very few male senior executives are used to admitting to others that they don't know something. It's best to be confident and definite, even if the truth is that you don't know—better still to contextualize that too, by saying your colleagues are conducting research to find out.

Being truthful is very close to being authentic. Authenticity partly means 'owning' your own story and words. So use your own vocabulary, not one you think should be used in a hearing. Being authentic also means striking the delicate balance between answering the question asked and not answering questions you shouldn't. There's also a balance between being direct and definite and not venturing off your story line or speculating. More balancing is required with skilled lawyers who want witnesses to accept a concept or use certain vocabulary. Be nice but firm, and watch out for the nice lawyer—s/he's more dangerous than the bombastic questioner.

Another balancing-act is to stick to the questions you're asked but also get out your pre-arranged messages that will convince the panel or stakeholders. What if the questioner doesn't know the right question to ask, which then triggers your delivery of the best case or vital facts? That's where judicious bridging and adding additional information can win the day.

Preparation before a hearing can seem endless, and once you are testifying, it can also seem to take forever—but before you know it, someone will say "Thank you" and you'll be done. If you follow the SOCKO™ system (see "Communicating during a Crisis" in Chapter 4), you will have:

- 3 statements, starting with the most important thing you can say;
- 3 statements including audience-centred messages, concrete evidence of the merits of your argument, statistics and anecdotes;
- 5 statements—what you know for sure, should speak about, is positive, is the official view and is a clear and lucid explanation;
- a few new facts;
- a brief history of your issue or organization—how did we get here?
- Caring, Knowledge, Action statements—what do you really care about, what do you know for sure, and what specifically are you going to do?

In rehearsal you'll find several ways to deliver much the same messages. This should be plenty of fodder for you to thrive on during several hours of testimony.

The Storyboard

One great test of how much your messages will resonate is the storyboard. Your statements should translate well into stick figures, diagrams or cartoons. If they do, they are concrete and the people you are speaking to can visualize them. If not, it's back to the drawing-board to get rid of buzzwords and jargon that people can interpret in multiple ways. The storyboard exercise also helps you speak about multiple aspects of your messages on demand. If interrupted or asked to change topics, you just pause, shuffle the Rubik's cube and start talking. (By the way I once told Mr. Rubik, the inventor of the cube puzzle, that his toy inspired me to have my clients draw three-dimensional cubes with icons on each side. He had me beat—he told me he had originally designed the toy as a teaching-tool to help architects learn about spatial concepts.)

In this set of stick figures, the drawings might serve to trigger the following thoughts:

See-saw—our choices on how to proceed or the balance struck among community needs

Bag of money—what we've spent on training or compliance

Smoke-stack—our environmental record or declining emissions

Sun shining—our commitment to the environment

Lunch pail—worker training

Clipboard—compliance

Round table—our internal quality circles

Public meeting—our regular consultation with stakeholders

Government building—regulatory and legislative compliance

Each icon should trigger a short statement. Each should have a period at the end—not a comma or a dash to invite longer sentences. In this way the icons can be delivered in any order, including last to first or diagonally. Witnesses who are interrupted won't get as flustered with this system because they can start delivering any other icon-triggered message. You never lose your place. The sides of the cube can contain further information on the same topic, so that a witness has icons and ammunition to continue speaking.

Reconnaissance

As with public speaking, you can't know too much about the venue, other presenters, interveners, panellists and the questions that you will be asked. You can't know too much about the science, engineering, environmental impact, social implications and laws that are relevant to your project. You can't focus on all these categories, but you and your fellow witnesses should divide up the topics and know them all as a group.

Team members will practise how to hand questions off to colleagues. The quarterback needs to deliver a short, helpful, sometimes substantive statement and then call on a colleague to provide more details. If that colleague has the floor and is asked a question outside her expertise, that second hand-off or hand-back needs to be smooth. The hand-off may be verbal, or involve facial expressions, body language or gestures. It will probably use a combination of all these tools.

You should visit the hearing rooms well before the event to see the panel in action. You should try to get into the room when it's empty, to size it up and hear the sound of your own voice. The acoustics change dramatically in large rooms and again when empty rooms fill with people. Get pictures taken of yourself in the hearing-room, to see how you look seated behind the actual table you'll be speaking from. If the hearing is in another town or city, then get there in good time the day before—you don't want to be rushed or tired.

Knowing your colleagues means knowing when one is reaching the end of her expertise and needs rescue. It means knowing who can add more or has done something special such as walk the full length of the pipeline. Who has special expertise worth mentioning, and who's getting testy?

Knowing the panel means knowing their regulatory record and their personal histories. I've faced broadcast-licensing panels headed by a former accountant who wanted to delve into the financial plans of every applicant. We prepared accordingly. His predecessor was a former broadcaster who didn't know or care much about accounting. He wanted to know the applicant's grand plans to make the world a better place. If the panel has voted a certain way before, that can be referenced without throwing precedent in their faces or assuming they'll vote the same way again.

Knowing your critics means thoroughly researching their positions and tactics. Google searches, including of what's going on in other jurisdictions, will give you a great start. So will asking other applicants. Critics' websites may have links to other sites or criticism of people in your industry. You can also benefit from attending critics' meetings, reading their literature and watching one of their protests.

Exhibits

There are companies that specialize in preparing exhibits for court and hearings. Often you'll be fine with your own internal communications and graphic people, but keep in mind that if your message is difficult to transmit verbally or visually, you might want outside help.

In a case before of the US Justice Department, my client had to convince the panel that they should be paid for an overrun on a defence contract. There were reasons in contract law to support their case. They came to my rehearsal session armed with a triangle diagram. This diagram showed time in months along the base line and tasks on a vertical line on the right side of the triangle, rising with the number of unforeseen tasks the company undertook. The witnesses kept referring to the diagram to explain an $80-million cost overrun.

For me, this was neither a clear explanation nor a supportive document—it was just a triangle. I finally broke the logjam with my client by asking whether I could increase my fee by 30 percent if I supplied a similar triangle diagram. This made the point that the diagram didn't explain why the tasks were undertaken, whether they were approved and so on.

We then got into a good discussion about what the additional tasks had been and why they had been needed. In contract law there are the concepts of full disclosure, special expertise and impossibility. If one party didn't disclose important aspects of a situation, or if one party had special knowledge that the other party lacked, that can nullify the contract. The same holds good if one party can show that it was impossible to fulfil its obligations under the contract.

With this knowledge, we then worked on our story rather than the diagram. Our story was that we had not been fully told of the condition of the US Defense Department property that needed refitting. We didn't know that the property had been used and stored in diverse conditions, including Arctic cold, rainforest damp and desert dryness. No one except the Defense Department knew this, and we had found it impossible to use the same refit techniques with each item. They needed vastly different approaches.

That was our story, and a diagram alone wasn't going to express it. Simple pictures of the condition of the equipment might, and so might a clearly told story.

Jargon

There is more jargon in business than in government or universities. There are many problems with jargon. First, are we sure that everybody agrees what such terms as 'value flow,' 'dashboard,' 'customer touch points,' 'value proposition,' 'propagated metrics,' 'performance gap' and 'opportunity scope' actually mean? In my sessions I've had several good discussions about what 'silos' and 'transparency' mean. Even if the management team agrees on the meaning of these terms, that's no guarantee that the average customer, neighbour, regulator or other audience members will have the same idea or any idea of what their definition is. Clarifying during testimony is not a good tactic.

The other problem with jargon is that it's not how normal people speak. The best litmus test for whether to use a piece of jargon is the 'coffee-table' test. If you wouldn't use the jargon with family members sitting around the coffee table at home, don't use it with your stakeholders. Legal journals refer to 'hyper-correct' speech, and they advise against it. There's no point in using 'at this point in time' for 'now.' Phrases such as 'pursuant to,' 'in respect of,' 'with regard to' or 'said document' are all either legal jargon, phrases from over-formally written documents or just poor syntax. They're also not how regular people who are telling the truth talk.

Non-Verbal Communication

American humorist Will Rogers was right—you don't get a second chance to make a first impression. You are judged in seconds. Witnesses must remember that a panellist or intervener may be watching how you get out of your car and judging you on the joke you are telling a colleague. Audience members and panellists are certainly judging you as you walk into the room. Lawyers are sizing you up too.

There's worse news about how you get sized up. Whenever you are doing or saying something that can't easily be understood, observers will interpret your actions or statements negatively. You need to be on your best behaviour just to elicit a neutral response. So, please review earlier sections and checklists in this book about positive and appropriate body language.

The Transcript

In some proceedings, how you look and sound is of less importance, because the panel may only be interested in reading the transcript of testimony and interventions after the hearing session. But it's hard to believe that the overall impression you give won't have some effect on panellists, and it certainly will calm or inflame interveners.

Still, to focus on just the transcript, here are some guidelines. Unnecessary commas are the enemy of clear communication. Although the eye can take in a longer and more complex sentence than the ear, short sentences are still more powerful than long ones. Variety in sentence length is good, but shorter is the goal. Commas mean there's a list, parenthetical remark, subordinate clause or other complexity in the transcript, and that makes it harder to read.

Keeping it simple in print means having three key SOCKOs™, supported by facts, figures, anecdotes and examples. Because the eye can go back and re-read the transcript, you need more variety in this document than you would in testimony where you are heard and seen. So while you still have three ideas in the transcript, the repetition needs more variety to sound emphatic but not monotonous. Robotic repetition can sound unimaginative and disrespectful, and this becomes worse in print. Your positive and empathetic statements will have the desired impact. Negatives will probably have more impact in print. If you read from a supporting document or quote someone, you should signal this by saying "quote" and "end of quote" at the beginning and end. If you show a document in the hearing, this will not show up in the transcript, so you need to describe it fully. You may also want to reference 1-800 phone numbers, websites, email addresses and so on. You might want to imagine you're on the telephone, so the phrase "as you can see..." won't make sense.

Some anecdotes are better listened to than read. If you're in a hearing where the transcript is paramount, you must consider how your stories and images will translate into print. Without intonation, facial expressions, gestures and other non-verbal elements, including 'para-linguistics,' you may find your story doesn't have the desired impact.

Depending on your rate of speech, it takes about three seconds to deliver one line of text. Assuming some blank lines between paragraphs, there may be 40 lines to a page of transcribed testimony. This means your 15-minute presentation can fit on about seven pages of paper. It can be read a little quicker than you can speak it. So you're producing a document that the panellists can read over a cup of coffee.

Hearings often go on for days, but any one witness may only speak for fifteen minutes before another takes over. Statements or questions by panellists or lawyers can also create breaks lasting a minute or two, and that can lengthen the time you use to make an effective presentation. If you are sure you will have to be the main speaker for hours on end, consider ways of carving your presentation up. Can you ask the panel to allow a supporting presentation from colleagues or technical experts? They may let you show a short video and submit a copy for them to review in private. Still pictures, charts, diagrams, models or other exhibits can serve the same purpose. These can be punctuation marks and pauses in your presentation that allow panellists to focus on your content in another way, refocus or just rest.

Speaking through Translators

Simultaneous translation puts enormous pressure on the translators. The task can only be done effectively for short periods of time. Translation can be just as challenging for those who perform signing for the deaf while the hearing is underway or captioning (closed or open) on the video of the proceedings.

Imagine trying to explain idiomatic expressions such as 'It's another kettle of fish,' 'A stitch in time saves nine' or 'such as it is' to someone who's first language isn't English. Now imagine translating that into another language. Now imagine doing it for hours at a time. You're better off keeping your testimony simple. You can help yourself and the talented people who translate, sign and caption by providing a text of your remarks or a glossary of technical terms that you'll be using. Arrive a little early and offer to discuss technical terms with these professionals.

In the Regulatory System

It's absolutely mandatory to know your regulators. Governments find tribunals particularly good instruments to implement the changing will of their political masters and the public. The tribunal may give the final word on doing a certain type of business, or there may be appeals to the political level or courts. Regardless, a tribunal can start taking stated public policy into account within days of hearing about it and in their next ruling.

There are two strategies for influencing public policy. One is to try to change the policy. In this scenario you march into a legislative committee or regulatory hearing and announce that the political régime is incorrect. You argue that the legislation and regulations are deficient and proceed to tell the regulators how matters should be. In front of a board this is futile, since a body of legislators made the regulations, not the regulatory panel. In the long term you might succeed in changing regulations through negotiations with administrative officials. But, if you haven't come to a deal with officials, and you're at the panel, you're best to show how your actions will comply with the relevant regulations and enhance their intent. In this way you can often bend the rules a little and still look compliant.

In the Parliamentary System

American politicians rarely face their accusers; rather they intone a message to a neutral speaker and then sit down. Without audience feedback, interruption or the adrenalin rush of debate, this can get you in a rut. That's why many a senator who is really passionate about a topic ends up sounding static and boring.

In the parliamentary system on the other hand, the head of government and the cabinet face their accusers every day the House or legislature sits. Members of the loyal opposition stand up during question period and demand answers or even resignations. This is great practice for stump speaking and debating during elections.

The parliamentary system also presents opportunities to question and speak in committee. A politician may be speaking to advocate a position, as a witness might, or may be questioning a witness in committee. It's crucial to decide what your goal is. Parliamentary committees have been criticized for not getting to the facts or the truth. Some lawyers criticize committee members' lack of legal training and the relaxed rules of evidence. But that's often beside the point—the purpose of a committee hearing is often political, not legal, and the facts take a back seat. A politician may be creating a clip for the evening newscast or a quote for a newsletter to constituents.

Speaking and questioning in the House is an art in itself. I conducted research into public attitudes to politicians' behaviour in legislatures before helping install television in the Ontario legislature (the second in North America) and again before training all sides of the House in

Newfoundland when TV was installed there. First of all, viewership is remarkably high. It's sometimes hard to measure, because the parliamentary proceedings are on obscure cable channels. But older viewers watch—and they also vote. The main feedback they give is that they don't understand why the serious issues of the day are hysterically funny to politicians.

Viewers can be forgiven for having this impression when they see members of the House making serious pronouncements and then doubling up with laughter when they sit down. This happens because members are also performing for their own caucuses. When they deliver what they think is a great zinger, they can't help showing how pleased they are. But this is unproductive for the television audience.

I acknowledge that members have several audiences. They need to show their skills to cabinet and caucus colleagues. They need to show partisan zeal for the party workers watching on TV and staffers watching live in the House. They need to show the members of the other parties that they are tough and not to be trifled with. There's a lot at stake in questions and answers in the House—budgets, appointments, travel and even the continued ability to ask or answer questions.

But the most important audience is the large one—the TV watchers at home. That's why I advise all members who are likely to be in the background on TV to look sharp and pay attention to the person speaking. For the persons asking or answering questions, I remind them that they are on long before they begin speaking and long after they have finished. They must be in character and stay in character for the duration. Speakers should wait until they are standing before beginning to speak. They should look at the speaker of the legislature, to whom they are literally speaking. If their question or answer lasts longer than 40 seconds, they can also glance at the members across the aisle and specifically at the one who asked the question. The gaze should be a little higher, even over the heads of the members opposite. This is because the cameras in the legislature are a little higher than head height. Gestures should be bigger but slower for TV, and neither questions nor answers should be read. If there's a document to quote, hold it up and make a big deal of having it, instead of pretending it isn't there.

Above all—practise. Remember, you're trying to make clips for radio and TV and headlines in print.

Political Debate

Most political debates aren't actually debates. You're not at the Oxford Union supporting or criticizing a resolution. You're often trying to avert a crisis in your campaign, or highlight one in your opponent's. I've worked on all-candidates debates with just a few souls in the high-school gym, local cable debates and right up to nationally televised leaders' debates in English and French. I treat them much the same.

We often don't know the exact format of the debate until the TV networks negotiate that with party officials. But I advise preparing an opening and closing statement, both of which ask for the vote and give a reason for voting. We also prepare opening statements for segments on the economy, leadership, health care, the environment, education and so on. It's not hard to guess what topics will come up. But we also prepare two or three dramatic attacks or counter-attacks. We expect an attack or two and prepare a vigorous and personal response.

I liken the task to the production of a successful TV show (which is what it is). I want to see smooth delivery, interesting policy, emotional content, friction and empathy. In an hour there's room for all of this and the candidate who touches these bases and doesn't stumble will be declared the winner.

There are two more analogies I make for politicians. I point out that a politician is really just applying for a job. The résumé is often contained in speeches and statements on TV—including in the debate. Job experience, reasons for picking this career, likes and dislikes and even hobbies are all relevant and part of the job interview. They are the jumping-off point to discuss policy. I ask politicians to complete these sentences:

"When I was a kid, I…"

"I got into politics because…"

"The reason this is high on my agenda is…"

"I recently met a woman who…"

"When I visit a school I'm reminded of…"

It is only after the personal anecdote that the politician has bought the attention of the constituent and the right to rattle off the policy in question.

The other analogy I make also deals with job applications. I tell politicians that they are really asking citizens to invite them into their living rooms (via TV) three to five nights a week on the evening news. If a voter is going to make that invitation, s/he has to be comfortable with the personality and personal behaviour of the politician. It's through personal, authentic stories that the politician achieves comfort.

Words Matter

My first testimony was at an arbitration many years ago. I was a unionized newscaster with Canada's public broadcaster, the CBC. I was in my mid-20s and had applied for a vacancy at the top of my field—anchor of 'The National.' The CBC had made several mistakes in the posting for the job. First, they posted three jobs at once—anchor of 'The National,' host of 'Newsmagazine' and host of special-events coverage. At the time it was against union rules to name more than one job in one posting. The next problem was that I was the only applicant apart from senior manger Knowlton Nash, who, the union claimed, essentially hired himself. Finally, I was only interviewed by telephone.

All this led to a multi-day arbitration at the network headquarters in Toronto. I was flown in from the prairies to testify. Just before I did, I was taken into a Four Seasons Hotel room, where union officials asked me when I had arrived in town and how long I was staying. They did some quick calculations and peeled off $800 in expense money for me on the spot. This focused my attention.

After my examination, I was cross-examined by the formidable lawyer Roy Heenan of the Montreal law firm Heenan, Blakie. Mr. Heenan tried to discredit my experience in private broadcasting by saying that I'd "read the news." Union jurisdictions were rigid in those days, and in the CBC the people who wrote the news couldn't read it and vice versa. But in the private sector, a journalist could do both. So I gently corrected him by saying, "I wrote and read the news." He kept focusing on my role as a news-reader, not a writer, because Mr. Nash had some writing- and reporting-experience that most CBC staff announcers lacked. I was nervous but held my ground and stuck to emphasizing my news-writing background.

Mr. Heenan tried again by referring to my private-sector broadcasting-experience as "announcing" or repeating that I'd been a news "announcer." I pointed out that this term was not really used outside the CBC. The people who spin records at a private radio station are 'disc jockeys,' and the people who read the news are 'news-readers,' or 'anchors' if it's a major newscast. We moved on.

At one point Mr. Heenan was summarizing, and he referred to my understanding of the "job" that had been posted. I kept using the word 'jobs' and spoke of the interview I'd had on the phone, which outlined the three jobs in question. Mr. Heenan tried to convince me and everyone else that I'd used the singular word 'job,' not the plural. I stuck to my guns again, although I wasn't actually sure and was understandably nervous. When I insisted that I remembered using the plural, Mr. Heenan asked around the table, and naturally the union lawyer said I was correct. We finally got the court reporter's opinion and may have even played back audio tapes. Luckily I had indeed said 'jobs'—the plural.

If I'd misremembered, I could still have said I'd meant to say 'jobs.' If I'd used both the singular and plural during my long testimony, I'd have been in pretty good shape. But caving in and letting Mr. Heenan tell me what I'd said would not have helped my cause.

In the end, the union lost. Knowlton Nash read 'The National' for many years, while, ironically, I was transferred to the network and anchored the radio version—'The National News,' or 'Night Nats' as it was affectionately called. I took some solace from the fact that Lorne Greene, "the voice of doom," had anchored the same newscast during World War II, before TV and Hollywood turned him into Pa Cartwright on 'Bonanza.' There was a further irony in that my two sons ended up playing in a band with Knowlton's two grandkids. It was nicknamed "the all-CBC band." Both Knowlton and I found this an amusing coincidence and ended up together in many seedy bars watching our boys play.

Well, on to other words—some of which seem picayune. 'Some' is a quantity. It's not very precise, but the word is used to express an amount. An actual number is precise. A dozen is twelve, a couple is two and several are three or more—pretty obvious. But 'decimate' refers to the Roman technique of punishing enemy prisoners or a mutinous legion by killing every tenth person. Most natural disasters don't just destroy 10 percent of a town, so 'decimate' is not appropriate.

Precision can work for or against your side. If you ask, "Did you see the stop sign?" the strong implication is that there was one. If the question is whether you saw a stop sign, there could be doubt. Plan your questions and answers accordingly.

There is good research on the merits of grabbing the semantic high ground. A protestor might “pop up,” but a government official might “arrive” on the scene. These descriptors make a huge difference in the way panels view the person being described.

Appendix 6: Post-Traumatic Stress Disorder and Crises

There is considerable debate about how widespread critical-incident stress and post-traumatic stress disorder (PTSD) are and how long they last. This section will survey some of this discussion to help readers gauge appropriate response techniques. What is not in question is the impact of victims on the disaster site. Many responders criticize the media for being intrusive and demanding. The fact is that victims will be more so. The injured will require medical attention. Triage will be required. There will be a pressing need to move the dead to a temporary morgue. This process requires special skills and extra responders.

Physical injuries are more obvious than psychological ones, but invisible injuries are just as profound and require equal attention. While the broken arm may be on the mend in a few weeks, psychological damage to victims may actually have increased a few weeks after the initial trauma.

Some disaster victims report that PTSD "is not a sickness from which, in time, we will recover."[48] However, given their finite resources, responders, courts, regulators and others may wonder whether we are in danger of over-reacting to disaster-related post-traumatic stress. If responders over-react to PTSD, they may be diverting much needed resources from other important mitigation activities.

There is an expectation that something can and should be done for a broader range of victims of disasters:

> ... an effective disaster response will accommodate not only the needs of those directly affected (the victims) but also the needs of those indirectly affected (victims' relatives, friends, acquaintances and careers).
>
> ... [I]t is no longer acceptable that the effectiveness of a disaster response be judged only on such criteria as whether or not the perpetrators are caught, whether or not professional negligence

> is proved, or how quickly "normal service" is restored. A comprehensive and holistic assessment requires that a disaster response also be judged on whether those indirectly affected are treated humanely, sensitively and with equanimity.[49]

Victims are not only those who were affected at the time but also (potentially) those who suffer later.[50] Those with PTSD are not just those who lost loved ones but may also include those who witnessed others suffer or die or simply feared for their own well-being.[51]

But where does victimization logically stop? Is there a certain point away from an event past which someone cannot be deemed a victim? Do all victims bear the same burden after the same trauma, and should they be treated the same way? Is there a familial or emotional distance from the killed or injured at which one is not likely to be affected, at least as badly, by witnessing the event? Do second-hand reports on radio, on TV, by word of mouth and in newspapers lessen the impact of an event?

Defining Post-Traumatic Stress Disorder

The three words 'Post-Traumatic Stress Disorder' denote a disorder or complex of symptoms that people experience after a traumatic event and which are associated with the stress that event engendered. But what types of disorders fall into the clinical definition of PTSD? How much stress and what type of trauma can bring on PTSD? The levels and kinds of stress that bring it on can differ for different people, and thus different types of disorders can fall within the definition. Is PTSD a product of modern life, or has it always been with us?

After watching news reports about veterans' and responders' experiences with PTSD, you might conclude that the disorder is either a new phenomenon or a more pronounced one than ever before. News programs and websites report the efforts of some war veterans to obtain recognition for what they say is PTSD. Some sites seem to promote PTSD and recruit new 'victims,' seemingly in the hope of obtaining greater settlements.

But the reality is that this syndrome, or versions of it, have been with us for a long time. PTSD can result from a wide variety of disasters and traumas and can afflict many types of victims:

> ... a clearer understanding of trauma began to develop after observing soldiers in the First World War (Salmon, 1919) and concentration camp survivors (Chodoff, 1963). It is now

> recognized that war and conflict can affect civilians as well as soldiers (Lewis, 1942), and that natural disasters (Freedy et al., 1993), technological failures (VandenBos and Bryant, 1987), violent crime such as sexual and physical assault (Kilpatrick et al., 1989), torture (Basoglu, 1992), accidental injury (Scotti et al., 1995) and refugee status (Eisenbruch, 1991) may also lead to the development of PTSD symptoms.[52]

From studying Hiroshima seventeen years after the nuclear bomb was dropped at the end of World War II, Lifton documented five characteristics of the survivors. The clearest way to define PTSD involves the symptoms. He lists "indelible imagery of the encounter with death … feeling guilty … psychic numbing … being suspicious of offers of help [and]… seeking a meaning for the experience."[53] The American Psychological Association has tried to provide identification criteria and separate PTSD from other disorders, such as Acute Stress Disorder. These criteria state that the person "experienced, witnessed or was confronted with … actual or threatened death or serious injury … [to] self or others."[54] The symptoms discussed include "fear, helplessness … horror … flashback episodes …avoidance of stimuli associated with the trauma … anger … difficulty concentrating …hyper-vigilance … exaggerated 'startle response' and sleep disorders."[55]

The American Psychological Association puts two important limitations on its definition. First, the symptoms must persist for "more than one month." Second, the patient must suffer "clinically significant distress or impairment in social, occupational or other important areas of functioning." The father who lost his daughter in the Lockerbie crash reports having had to leave his job and feeling "an unwillingness to face hassle or to make even small decisions."[56]

The courts recognize PTSD but put limits on who they believe qualifies for damages. There are many cases where survivors have been awarded damages for psychological injury, but relatives of victims have seldom if ever succeed in claiming PTSD damages after watching television reports of events. Some claims come from people who are quite remote from the disaster in question. In 1966 in the Welsh town of Aberfan, a school and homes were destroyed by a sliding heap of debris from the mining-process. Twenty-eight adults and 116 children were killed. One witness claimed she suffered a nervous breakdown 12 years after the event and that this was triggered by a newspaper report of another tragedy. The courts reserved judgment.[57]

The major point of the court cases is the issue of psychological, temporal and spatial proximity. Those seeking damages must prove close ties of love or affection to the victims, and they must have been near the disaster. They must also show damages. The British House of Lords has stated that claims can be made by those involved in disasters if:

1. their relationship to the primary victim was close enough for it to be reasonably foreseeable that they might sustain nervous shock;
2. their proximity to the accident was sufficiently close in time and space;
3. they suffered nervous shock through seeing or hearing the accident or its immediate aftermath.[58]

The courts have further ruled that "[f]ear itself cannot give rise to damages, only pain and suffering."[59] But other courts in other jurisdictions have taken different views, and crisis managers should know how events will be viewed in their locations.

Discussion

Crisis mangers need to address PTSD as they would any other damage or injury. If an organization is responsible for property damage, it has to make restitution. If that organization is responsible for physical injury, courts often award compensation. The same is logically true of PTSD. Without intruding, mental-health professionals should form part of proper disaster response. Support can include information, sensitivity, access to the site of the event, legal help and counselling, if required.

The physical symptoms of PTSD include more measurable amounts of norepinephrine and cortisol in the victims' bodies.[60] Studies of exposure to shock in animals show "the depletion of certain neurotransmitters (e.g. dopamine) which produces symptoms similar to PTSD [and] … a state of analgesia caused by the release of endogenous opiates which may become addictive so that when the opiate stressor is removed, withdrawal symptoms (anxiety, startle response and hyper vigilance) arise."[61] In other words, the victim's brain seeks the physical sensation that is brought on by the startle response, triggers it regularly, and then suffers the negative effects.

The effect on behaviour can also be pronounced. Victims may change routines to avoid reminders of past trauma. "Bank cashiers involved in armed raids often avoid returning to jobs involving face-to-face work with the public and many (female) rape victims avoid being alone with men."[62] Some become detached, and some feel guilt for enjoying life's pleasures. It seems legitimate to err on the side of support. Thus some researchers advise that treatment should be accessible to virtually all those involved in a trauma.

It's easy to see how quickly whole populations could be diagnosed as victims of PTSD. By some definitions, a potential victim is virtually anyone in any location who experiences a wide variety of events with any level of intensity or degree of proximity.

However, just because academics, the courts, mental-health professionals and others agree that PTSD exists, that doesn't mean that its source is easy to identify or that it is easy to diagnose or prevent. Proving the syndrome's existence and source may be a greater burden than with the common complaint of lower-back pain in industry. A worker may seek compensation or time off work and blame the physical labour s/he had to undertake on the job, but the real cause might be recreational activities or genetics, and how much the worker is really incapacitated might be debatable. Some PTSD cases may be equally moot.

Stress has always been with us. Our ancestors suffered from the stress of having to find food and shelter. Hunting animals and being hunted brought on stress. Even disasters have always been with us, in that humanity has always been at risk from natural disasters, which the ancients often termed 'acts of God' (or the gods). Besides the threats of pre-industrial society (plague, famine, natural catastrophes and wars) there were also magic, gods, and demons.[63] Our ancestors seem to have coped with this stress without treatment.

As perhaps with the injured worker's back, there is a certain 'background' stress, fear and trauma that we all suffer in daily life.[64] So one dilemma for the courts, responders and others is whether the symptoms in evidence stemmed from the disaster or from general background stress in the person's life. Was the disaster or trauma the prime cause of the stress disorder or merely one in a series of life events, whose cumulative effect was a stress disorder? Do the symptoms of *a* stress disorder stem from unknown or various causes or, specifically, PTSD? If PTSD, then which trauma was the prime cause?

It's hard to judge how many victims you may encounter. Lewis Aptekar's study of earthquakes has shown low reporting of PTSD in victims.[65]

Aptekar verified Smith's older findings that "less than 25 percent of disaster victims experienced any post-traumatic stress during the year after the disasters."[66] While Vaughan J. Carr et al. found higher levels of PTSD, these levels appeared to decline sharply as time elapsed after the event.[67]

Many disaster victims either don't want or don't need to participate in group therapy.[68] Studies of callers to help lines following an earthquake show that most only want to know they're doing the right thing.[69] Today victims may be more willing to identify themselves as victims than they were when this research was done. But you may find that the vast majority of victims attend only one counselling-session, with just 15 percent seeking or needing further help.[70]

Who are likely to experience symptoms? A major factor in whether PTSD exists or persists in victims seems to be the victims themselves.[71] Karen Anderson has suggested a gender correlation, and Aptekar has speculated that a wide variety of demographic variables come into play.[72] Job descriptions play a role, in that those who expect to come into contact with stress in their work may not be as severely affected as lay people who are not expecting to experience stress.[73] People may be more affected by their pre-existing view of an event than by the event itself.[74] The cause of the disaster may affect whether PTSD occurs. Aptekar has examined several factors in disasters, including "unpredictable onset (earthquake) versus its known onset (hurricane) and … indefinite duration (earthquake) versus … limited duration (hurricane)."[75]

Conclusion

Over and above legal limitations, mental-health professionals have put limits on the definition of who is victimized and what causes PTSD. "Significant" impairment must occur in "important areas of functioning."[76] Not all events cause PTSD, and people are not equally susceptible. With most victims' symptoms diminish over time, and treatments vary by cause, the type of symptoms and the individual. What the individual does for a living can reduce the likelihood of contracting the syndrome, especially if that person expects to encounter trauma as an emergency responder. Mediating agents such as the news media, as well as temporal, spatial and emotional distance, can lessen the impact of PTSD or, for most practical purposes, eliminate its impact. There is also at least mixed opinion on whether every disaster—'natural,' technological or otherwise—will cause similar levels of PTSD.

Just because there are serious limits to the prevalence of PTSD doesn't mean that responders shouldn't provide support services unless acute and prolonged symptoms persist. Responders should be sensitive to the various legitimate responses to trauma. Effects may occur early or late, as a result of obvious proximity or in persons who were remote from the scene. The effects may stem only from the trauma, or the trauma may be a trigger that causes a reaction to various earlier life experiences. Showing sensitivity, openness and flexibility may be the best course of action.

Appendix 7: Apologies

Riding out the crisis often means apologizing. Just what constitutes an effective apology is a moving target, changing with social values and customs. But here's what seems to work at this moment.

First, there can't be another transgression hidden in the apology. "I'm sorry you misunderstood what I said" is a not-very-subtle accusation that the person you're apologizing to isn't very bright. A sincere apology also has to occur right on the heels of the offence. The longer you wait, the more you have to do to be forgiven.

A sincere and fast apology should also show that you've learned a lesson. State the lesson and the changes you've made to your thinking, processes or staff to prevent another offence.

It's always a good guess that people are not well informed on public issues and might not be familiar with the original offence. So don't dwell on the negative. Focus on the changes you've made and any positive statements you can make. It's also a good guess that people aren't paying a great deal of attention to your apology. If you want them to get the message, repeat it.

Then there's the dilemma of addressing the actual people you've offended, not just apologizing to everyone in general. When people are offended or outraged, they stop receiving messages. Eighty percent of anything you give offended people to hear or read will be filtered out or not understood.

Here's where the magic number 4 comes into play. First of all, the apology needs to have four times the weight and temperature of the offence. How about the spouse who asks, "How do I look in this?" If the response is, "Have you gained a little weight?" there's some repair work to do, and it will take longer than the original six-word response.

Four is also the number of empathetic statements you need to make to open up the eyelids of offended parties and raise their metaphorical earlids. Empathy doesn't cost you anything and does not necessarily imply responsibility or liability. How about these empathetic statements:

"I can see you are angry."

"Boy, I'd be as angry as you if I were in your shoes."

"I'm really sorry you're so upset."

"I'd like to see what I can do to help."

These are generic, and more specific empathetic statements will flow from real-life situations.

After the four empathetic statements, offended parties might be willing to hear four statements about the remedies you propose. The number four is easy to remember—one message for each eye and ear.

You need to brainstorm about the substantial remedies. What actions can you take? Your apology and remedies can go bad like rotting fruit on a grocery-store shelf. An apology delayed is an apology denied. Delay only compounds the offence. The competing advice is that there's no reason to alert the world to your transgressions if you don't have to and narrow room to manoeuvre makes crisis management an unforgiving art and science.

Here are the classic elements in an effective apology:

- The apology must have four times the weight, temperature and impact of the offence.
- The remedy must exceed the expectations of the offended.
- You must make four empathetic statements to open up the eyes and ears of the offended.
- You must make four substantial statements to try to convince the aggrieved of your good intentions, the inadvertent nature of the offence or the appropriateness of the remedy.
- You must make eye contact with the offended, the reporter or the camera lens as appropriate.
- You must recognize the impact of the offence.

- You must list the lessons you have learned.
- You must list the changes in policies and procedures to prevent future occurrences.
- Look sorry, be sorry, say you're sorry.

Conclusion

Many of the sections and chapters of this book have conclusions. Many have discussion questions. There are many checklists to help readers take action. But a book needs a final conclusion.

If there is an appropriate punctuation mark to this book, it is a comma or a dash, not a period. The craft and science of crisis management is on-going. It does not stop. The bar is always higher. Horizons recede. New goals are set. The crisis manager's work is never done—especially if there isn't a crisis to handle.

There's a great expression among some First Nations people and Aboriginals—"Now that we've shot the moose, who's going to drag it out of the woods?" This is a metaphor for the fact that this book (or perhaps manual or guide) has discussed crisis management and related issues from many perspectives that seemed helpful. Now, the task is the reader's—drag the moose out of the woods by using the companion DVD and write the best crisis plan for your organization.

END NOTES

1. Scarman Centre for the Study of Public Order (SCSPO), 1997.
2. SCSPO 1, 41.
3. Turner in SCSPO 1, 37.
4. SCSPO 2, 46.
5. Zsambok and Klein (1997).
6. Morgan et al. (1985), pp. 139-49.
7. Sir Winston Churchill in his WWII speech on becoming prime minister of the United Kingdom in 1940.
8. President John F. Kennedy, inaugural address, Friday 20 January 1961.
9. Canadian Prime Minister Pierre Elliot Trudeau, when interviewed about the October Crisis, 1970.
10. President Barak Obama, 2008 presidential campaign slogan.
11. LeGrande and Mierau (2004), p. 947.
12. LeGrande and Mierau (2004), p. 947.
13. Boccaccini et al. (2005).
14. Ellison (2007), pp.171-87.
15. Prepared for the National Conference on Pandemic Planning at the International Centre for Infectious Diseases, which the author chaired.
16. Susskind and Thomas-Larmer (1999).
17. Helsen and Starkes (1999), pp. 395-410.
18. SCSPO (1997) 1, p. 241.
19. See Toft and Reynolds (1994).
20. Barton (1993), p. 15.
21. Conner (1995), pp. 37-8.
22. Perrow, pp. 11-12 and Pauchant and Mitroff (1992).
23. Lagadec (1982).
24. Brearley (1992), p. 5.
25. Wynne (1989), (1992) and in Lash et al. (1996), p. 65.
26. SCSPO (1997), 5, 321.
27. Beck in Lash et al. (1996), p. 33.
28. Beck in Lash et al. (1996), p. 31.
29. Ruckelshaus (1984), pp. 157-62.
30. Ruckelshaus (1984), p. 157.
31. Ruckelshaus (1983), pp. 1026-8.
32. Beck (1992) in SCSPO (1997) 2, p. 158.
33. Beck (1992) in SCSPO (1997) 2, p. 151.
34. SCSPO 5 (1997): 322.
35. Otway and Slovic (1992) quoted by Wynne in Lash (1996), p. 58.
36. Fischhoff (1987).
37. Kasperson (1986), p. 280.
38. Covello (1993).
39. Royal Society (1992), 135-92.
40. Rosenthal (1986).
41. Otway and von Winterfeldt (1982), p. 101.
42. Kahneman and Tversky (1979).
43. Waring (1989), p. 172.
44. Waring (1989), p. 172.
45. Thompson et al. (1990).
46. Toft and Reynolds (1994).
47. Griffiths (1981), pp.1-19.
48. SCSPO (1997) 5, p. 334.
49. SCSPO (1997) 5, p. 321.
50. American Psychiatric Association (1997), pp. 383-5.
51. APA (1997), p. 383.
52. APA (1997), p. 377.
53. Lifton (1996), p. 380.
54. APA.
55. APA.
56. SCSPO (1997) 5, p. 334.
57. SCSPO (1997) 6, p. 329.
58. SCSPO (1997) 6, pp. 350-51.
59. SCSPO (1997) 6, p. 351.
60. SCSPO (1997) 6, p. 394.
61. SCSPO (1997) 6, p. 382.
62. SCSPO (1997) 6 , p. 386.
63. Beck in Lash et al. (1996), p. 30.
64. Maguire in Lash et. al. (1996).
65. Aptekar (1990), p.74.
66. Smith (1986), p. 74, quoted in Aptekar (1990), p. 99.
67. Carr et al., (1995), p. 540.
68. Aptekar (1990), p. 91.
69. Blaufarb and Levine (1972), p. 17.
70. Blaufarb and Levine (1972), p. 17.
71. Smith (1986), quoted in Aptekar (1990); Carr et al.
72. Anderson & Gardenio (1994), p. 726 and Aptekar (1990), pp. 75-6.
73. Neustatter (1996), pp. 34-7.
74. SCSPO (1997) 6, p. 390.
75. Aptekar (1990), p. 75.
76. APA.

BIBLIOGRAPHY

American Psychiatric Association. *Diagnostic and Statistical Manual of Mental Disorders*, 3rd edn (1980), 3rd edn revised (1987) and 4th edn (1994), Washington, DC: APA.

Anderson, Karen, and Gardenio, Manuel (1994). "Gender Differences in Reported Stress Response to the Loma Prieta Earthquake," *Sex Roles*, 30, 9/10. Plenum Publishing Corporation.

Aptekar, Lewis (1990). "A Comparison of the Bicostal Disasters of 1989," *Behavior Science Research*, HRAF, pp. 75-6.

Barron's Online. (2009). "R-E-S-P-E-C-T: Here's How They Spelled It," Dow Jones and Company. Accessed from http://online.barrons.com/article/SB123457681385686739.html on September 7, 2010.

Barton, L. (1983). *Crisis in Organizations: Managing and Communicating in the Heat of Chaos.* Cincinnati: South-West Publishing, 1993.

Beck, U. (1992). "From Industrial Society to the Risk Society: Questions of Survival, Social Structure and Ecological Enlightenment," *Theory, Culture & Society* 9. London: Sage Publications.

Beck, U., in Lash et. al. (1996), *Risk, Environment & Modernity: Towards a New Ecology*, (London: Sage Publications, Inc.), pp. 29 ff.

Bertalanffy, L. von (1971). *General Systems Theory*. London: Allen Lane, The Penguin Press, p. xviii.

Blaufarb, H. and Levine, J. (1972). "Crisis Intervention in an Earthquake," *Social Work* 4 (July 16), 17.

Boccaccini, M.T., Gordon, T. and Brodsky, S.L. (2005). "Witness Preparation Training with Real and Simulated Criminal Defendants," *Behavioral Sciences and the Law* 23.

Borodzicz, E.P. (1996). "Security and Risk: A Theoretical Approach to Managing Loss Prevention." *International Journal of Risk Security and Crime Prevention* 1:2.

Bowker, D. and Morgan, J. (2006). 'Managing Reputation', *Pharmaceutical Executive*, 26, 10: p. 127.

Brearley, N. (1991) "Riot Control—Understanding Crowd Psychology", *Intersec* 1.

Brearley, N. (1992). "Public Order, Safety & Crowd Control," *Intersec* 2:1 (May, 4 6).

Bromet, E., Parkinson, D., Schulberg, H.C. and Dunn, L. (1980). "Three Mile Island: Mental Health Findings." Pittsburgh, PA: *Western Psychiatric Institute and Clinic and the University of Pittsburgh.*

Browning, L.D. and Shelter, J.C. (1982). "Communication in Crisis, Communication in Recovery: A Postmodern Commentary on the Exxon Valdez Disaster", *International Journal of Mass Emergencies and Disaasters,* (November), 10(3):477-98.

Busch, L. (1991). "Science under Wraps in Prince William Sound." *Science*, 10 May, 252(5007):772.

Carey, J. (1991). "Getting Business to think about the Unthinkable", *Business Week* (June 24).

Carr, V.J., Lewin, T.J., Webster, R.A., Hazell, P.L., Kenardy, J.A., and Carter, G.L. (1995). "Psychosocial sequelae of the 1989 Newcastle earthquake: I. Community disaster experiences and psychological morbidity 6 months post-disaster," *Psychological Medicine* 25 (Cambridge University Press), 539-55.

Checkland, P.B. (1981). *Systems Thinking, Systems Practice*, Chichester: Wiley.

Chen, Y., Ganesan, S. and Liu, Y. (2009). 'Does a Firm's Product-Recall Strategy affect its Financial Value? An Examination of Strategic Alternatives during Product-Harm Crises', *Journal of Marketing*, 73: 214-226.

Clarke, L. (1993(. "The Disqualification Heuristic: When do Organizations Misperceive Risk?" *Research in Social Problems and Public Policy*, Volume 5, p.289-312.

CNN (1989). "The Big Spill", 15 April.

Cobb-Walgren, C.J., Ruble, C.A. and Donthu, N. (1995). 'Brand equity, brand preference, and purchase intent', *Journal of Advertising*, 24n3:25

Cohen, M.J. (1995) "Technological Disasters and Natural Resource Damage Assessment: An Evaluation of the Exxon Valdez Oil Spill" (1989 Alaskan disaster), *Land Economics* (February) 71(1): 65(18).

Cohen, M.J. (1993) "Economic Impact of an Environmental Accident: A Time-Series Analysis of the Exxon Valdez Oil Spill in South-Central Alaska", *Sociological Spectrum*, 13(1): 35-63.

Comfort, L. (1990). "Turning Conflict into Cooperation: Organizational Designs for Community Response in Disasters", *International Journal of Mental Health*, 19(1):89-108. M.E. Sharpe, Inc.

Conner, D.R. (1995). *Managing at the Speed of Change*. New York: Villard Books.

Covello, V.T., Menkes, J. and Nehnevajsa, J. (1982). "Risk Analysis, Philosophy, and the Social and Behavioral Sciences: Reflections on the Scope of Risk Analysis Research", *Journal of the Society for Risk Analysis*, 2(2): 53-57.

Covello, V.T. (1983). "The Perception of Technological Risks: A Literature Review", *Technological Forecasting and Social Change* 23, 285-297.

Covello, V.T., Sandman, P.M., and Slovic, P. (1988). "Risk Communication, Risk Statistics, and Risk Comparisons: A Manual for Plant Managers," (Washington, D.C.: Chemical Manufacturers' Association), in Roth, Emilie, (1990) "What Do We Know About Making Risk Comparisons?" *Journal of the Society for Risk Analysis*, Vol. 10, No. 3, pp. 375-87.

Covello, V.T. (1993). Industry video.

Covello, V.T., Butte, G., Thorne, S. and Walsh, J. (1993). *A Process for Community Dialogue and Outreach for the Canadian Chemical Industry: A Workshop for the Members of the Canadian Chemical Producers' Association*, The Canadian Chemical Producers' Association. (Video and Manual).

Crow, P. (1989). "Exxon Valdez spill spawns a batch of legislation governing tankers," *Oil and Gas Journal*, (July 31).

Cumming, R.B. (1981). 'Is Risk Assessment a Science?', *Journal of the Society for Risk Analysis*, Volume 1, Number 1: 1-3.

Dahlin, J.A. (1989). "Oil Shock", *Business and Economic Review*, 35(4): 3-7.

Daley, P. and O'Neill, D. (1991). "Sad is too mild a word": Press Coverage of the Exxon Valdez Oil Spill, *Journal of Communication*, Autumn, 41(4): 42(16).

Davidson, A. (1990). *In the Wake of the Exxon Valdez: The Devastating Impact of the Alaska Oil Spill*, Vancouver/Toronto: Douglas & McIntyre.

Derby, Stephen L. and Keeney, Ralph L. (1981). "Risk Analysis: Understanding 'How Safe is Safe Enough?'", *Journal of the Society of Risk Analysis*, Volume 1, Number 3: 217 - 224.

Dev, K. (1994). "Tanking Up", *Far Eastern Economic Review*, (April) p.34.

Dombrowski, W.R. (1995). 'Again and Again: Is a Disaster what we call "Disaster"?', 'Some Conceptual Notes on Conceptualizing the Object of Disaster Sociology', in: Module 1, Unit 2 ('A Theory on Crisis') of *M.Sc. in Risk, Crisis and Disaster Management*, Leicester: SCSPO: 43.

Douglas, M. and Wildavsky, A. (1982). 'How can we know the risks we face? Why Risk Selection is a Social Process', *Journal of the Society for Risk Analysis*, Volume 2, Number 2: 49-51.

The Economist (1995). "The flowers of Kobe", January 21st, 35:2.

Ellison, L. (2007) "Witness preparation and the prosecution of rape," *Legal Studies* 27, pp.171-87.

Etkin, D. S. (1997). "Oil Spill Intelligence Report," *International Oil Spill Statistics: 1996*. Cutter Information Corp.: Arlington, MA.

Etzioni, A. (1967). 'Mixed-scanning: A 'Third' Approach to Decision-making.' *Public Administration Review* 27(5), 385-392.

Exxon Valdez Oil Spill Trustee Council (EVOSTC). (1992). "Summary of Injury", Alaska's Marine Resources, 7(3):2-11.

Feyerbend, P. (1975), *Agaisnt Method: Outline of an Anarchistic Theory of Knowledge*, New York: Free Press.

Fennell, D. (1988) *Investigation into the King's Cross Underground Fire.* London: Her Majesty's Stationery Office, Dept. of Transport.

Fink, S. (1986). *Crisis Management*, Amacom (U.S.) & Toronto: Prentice Hall.

Fischhoff, B. (1987). "Treating the Public with Risk Communications: A Public Health Perspective", *Science, Technology, & Human Values* 12: 3, 4 (Summer, Fall).

Fortune Magazine. (2009). "World's Most Admired Companies." Accessed from http://money.cnn.com/magazines/fortune/mostadmired/2009/full_list/ on September 1, 2010.

Frisioli, G. *Andragogy vs. Pedagogy.* Adult Learning and Technology Website. Accessed April 2010 from http://adultlearnandtech.com/historyal.htm.

Gans, H.J., (1980). *Deciding What's News*, New York: Vintage Books/Random House.

Giel, "R. (1991) "The Psychosocial Aftermath of Two Major Disasters in the Soviet Union," *Journal of Traumatic Stress*, 4: 3, pp. 382 ff.

Gottschalk, J.A. (1993). *Crisis Response Inside Stories on Managing Image Under Siege*, Detroit: Visible Ink Press.

Griffiths, R.F. (1981). "Introduction: The nature of risk assessment," pp.1-19 in *Dealing with Risk: The Planning Management and Acceptability of Technological Risk.* New York: Wiley.

Hamlin, S. (1985). "Preparing a Witness to Testify," *ABA Journal: The Lawyer's Magazine* 71, 81-4.

Hannaford, P. (1986). *Talking Back to the Media.* Facts on File Publications, New York. 132-34

Harvard Business School Press (2000). *Harvard Business Review on Negotiation and Conflict Resolution.* Boston, MA: A Harvard Business Review Paperback.

Helsen, W.F., and Starkes, J.L. (1999). "A New Training Approach to Complex Decision Making for Police Officers in Potentially Dangerous Interventions," *Journal of Criminal Justice* 27: 55, 395-410.

Henley, N. M. (1977). "Body Politics: Power, Sex and Nonverbal Communication" New York: Simon & Shuster.

Highhouse, S., Brooks, M.E. and Gregarus, G. (2009). 'An Organizational Impression Management Perspective on the Formation of Corporate Reputations', *Journal of Management* 35(6): 1481-1493.

Home Office. (1997). *Dealing with Disaster* (Third Edition), Liverpool: Brodie Publishing.

Huxley, M. (2000). 'The limits to communicative planning', *Journal of Planning Education and Research*, 19(4), 369-377.

Irvine, Robert B. (1987). *When You Are the Headline*, Homewood, Illinois: Dow Jones-Irwin.

Johnson, D. (1993). "Crisis management: forewarned is forearmed," *Journal of Business Strategy* 14:2 (March-April), 58(6).

Johnson, G. (1992). 'Managing Strategic Change: Strategy Culture and Action', in: Module 1, Unit 8 ('Introduction to Cultural History') of *M.Sc. in Risk, Crisis and Disaster Management*, Leicester: SCSPO: 333.

Kahneman, D., and Tversky A. (1979). "Prospect Theory. An Analysis of Decision Making Under Risk," in: Module 1, Unit 3 ('Psychological Approaches to Risk Management') of *M.Sc. in Risk, Crisis and Disaster Management*, Leicester: SCSPO:71.

Kasperson, R.E. (1988). "The Social Amplification of Risk: A Conceptual Framework", *Society for Risk Analysis*, 8 January, 8(2):177-187.

Kasperson, R.E. (1986). "Six Propositions on Public Participation and their Relevance for Risk Communications," *Journal of the Society for Risk Analysis*, 6(3), 275-281.

Kneale, K. (2009). 'World's Most Reputable Companies: The Rankings', Forbes.com. Accessed from http://www.forbes.com/2009/05/06/world-reputable-companies-leadership-reputation-table.html on September 1, 2010.

Koh, Y., Lee, S. and Boo, S. (2009). "Impact of Brand Recognition and Brand Reputation on firm performance: U.S.-based multinational restaurant companies' perspective", *International Journal of Hospitality Management*, 28:620-630.

Lagadec, P. (1982). *Major Technical Risk: An Assessment of Industrial Disasters*. Oxford: Pergamon Press.

Lash, S., Szerszynski, B. and Wynne, B. (edited). (1996). *Risk, Environment & Modernity: Towards a New Ecology*. London, Thousand Oaks. New Delhi: Sage Publications.

LeGrande, N. and Mierau, K. (2004). "Witness Preparation and the Trial Consulting Industry," HeinOnline—*Georgetown Journal of Legal Ethics* 17:4, 947.

Lifton, R.J. (1983). "Responses to Survivors of Man-Made Catastrophes", *Bereavement Care* 2:2-6.

Lifton, R.J. (1996). *The Broken Connection: On Death and the Continuity of Life*. Washington: American Psychiatric Press, Inc.

Lifton, R.J. (1968). *Death in Life: Survivors of Hiroshima*. New York: Random House.

Maguire, J. in Lash et al. (1996), *Risk, Environment & Modernity: Towards a New Ecology*. London: Sage Publications, Inc.

Martin, G. (2009). 'Driving corporate reputations from the inside: A strategic role and strategic dilemmas for HR?' *Asia Pacific Journal of Human Resources*, Vol. 47(2): 219-235.

Mazur, A. (1984). "The Journalists and Technology: Reporting about Love Canal and Three Mile Island," *Minerva* 22, 45-6.

Morgan, M.G., Slovic, P., Nair, I., Geisler, D., MacGregor, D., Fischhoff, B., Lincoln, D., and Florig, K. (1985). "Powerline Frequency Electric and Magnetic Fields: A Pilot Study of Risk Perception," *Journal of the Society for Risk Analysis* 5:2, 139-49.

Nelkin, Dorothy. (1985). "Introduction: Analyzing Risk", in The Language of Risk, Conflicting Perspective on Occupational Health, Dorothy Nelkin, Ed., Beverly Hills, California, Sage Publications, Inc.

Neustatter, A. (1996). "When jury service can become a trial", "You," *The Mail on Sunday* (28 July), 34-7.

Oil & Gas Journal (1993). "*Exxon Valdez* controversy revived", 26 April.

Otway, H., and von Winterfeldt, D. (1982). 'Beyond Acceptable Risk: On the Social Acceptability of Technologies', in: Royal Society, Chapter 5 ('Risk Perception') of *Risk: Analysis, Perception and Management*, London: Royal Society: 101.

Otway, H. and Slovic, P. (1992) in Wynne: 1996 in Lash: 1996, p., 58).

Otway, H. and Kerry, T. (1982). "Reflections on Risk Perception and Policy," *Risk Analysis*, 2, 69-82, quoted in "Macro-Risks, Micro-Risks, and the Media: The EDB Case,"

Palinkas, L. A., Downs, M.A., Petterson, J.S., and Russell, J. (1993). "Social, Cultural, and Psychological Impacts of the Exxon Valdez Oil Spill," *Human Organization, Society for Applied Anthropology*, Spring 52 (1:11).

Parkinson, F. (1993). *Post-Trauma Stress*, London: Sheldon Press/SPCK.

Pauchant, T.C. and Mitroff, I.I. (1992). *Transforming the Crisis-Prone Organization*. Jossey-Bass Inc.: San Francisco, CA.

Perrow, C. (1984). *Normal Accidents: Living With High Risk Technologies*. New York: Basic Books; quoted in Clarke, Lee (1993) "The Disqualification Heuristic: When do Organizations Misperceive Risk?" *Research in Social Problems and Public Policy*, 5, JAI Press Inc.

Pidgeon, N. (1991). 'Safety Culture and Risk Management in Organizations', *Journal of Cross Cultural Psychology*, 22(1): 129-140.

Pidgeon, N.F. (1992). "The Psychology of Risk," in: Module 1, Unit 3 ('Psychological Approaches to Risk Management') of *M.Sc. in Risk, Crisis and Disaster Management*, Leicester: SCSPO: 89-107.

Pidgeon, N. (1996). 'Technocracy, Democracy, Secrecy and Error' in C. Hood and D.K.C. Jones (eds) *Accident and Design: Contemporary Debates in Risk Management*, London: UCL Press.

Pierce, A. (2009). 'Managing Reputation to Rebuild Battered Brands', *Marketing News*, 03.15.09, p. 19, American Marketing Association.

Prelli, L.J. (1989). *A rhetoric: Inventing scientific discourse*. Columbia: University of South Carolina Press.

Raymond, C.A. (1985). "Risk in the Press: Conflicting Journalistic Ideologies", *The Language of Risk, Conflicting Perspectives on Occupational Health*, Nelkin, Dorothy, Ed., Beverly Hills, California: Sage Publications, Inc.

Reason, J. (1990). *Human Error*. Cambridge: Cambridge University Press.

Reischmann, Jost. (2000). 'Welcome to Andragogy.net'. Accessed April 2010 from http://www.andragogy.net.

Reischmann, Jost. (2004). 'Andragogy: History, Meaning, Context, Function.' Accessed April 2010 from http://www.andragogy.net.

Roth, E. (1990). "What do we know about making risk comparisons?", *Journal of the Society for Risk Analysis*, 10(3):375-387.

Rosenthal, U. (1986). 'Crisis Decision Making in the Netherlands', in: Module 1, Unit 2 ('A Theory of Crisis') of *M.Sc. in Risk, Crisis and Disaster Management*, Leicester: SCSPO: 41.

Rosenthal, U. et al. (1994). *Complexity in Urban Crisis Management: Amsterdam's Response to the Bihlmer Air Disaster*. London: James & James.

Rosenthal, Uriel, Charles, Michael T. and Hart, Paul T., eds (1989). *Coping with Crises: The Management of Disasters, Riots and Terrorism*. Springfield, IL: Charles C. Thomas.

Royal Society (1992). "Risk: Analysis, Perception and Management," *Royal Society Study Group*, pp. 135-92. London: The Royal Society.

Ruckelshaus, W.D. (1983). "Science, Risk, and Public Policy", *Science* 221 (September), pp. 1026-8.

Ruckelshaus, W.D. (1984). "Risk in a Free Society", *Journal of the Society for Risk Analysis* 4:3, 157-62.

Ruckelshaus, W.D., Russel, M. and Gruber, M. (1987). "Risk Assessment in Environmental Policy-Making", *Science*, Volume 236, April: 286.

Sandman, P., Sachman, D.B., Greenberg, M.R., and Gochfeld, M. (1987). *Environmental Risk and the Press: An exploratory Assessment*, New Brunswick, New Jersey: Transaction, Inc.

Scanlon, LCdr J.D. (1998). Personal E-mail, July 14, 1:02 a.m.

Scarman Centre for the Study of Public Order (SCSPO) (1997). "Distance Learning Study Notes," modules 1-6 of *M Sc. in The Study of Risk, Crisis & Disaster Management*. Leicester: Scarman Centre for the Study of Public Order.

Selkirk, A.M. Jr. (1992). "Witness Preparation: Key to a Successful Trial Strategy," *New York State Bar Journal* (February), 18-23.

Sellnow, T.L. (1993). "Scientific Argument in organizational crisis communication: the case of Exxon (Exxon Corp.)", *Argumentation and Advocacy*, (Summer) 30(1):28(15).

Sharlin, H.I. (1987). "Macro-Risks, Micro-Risks, and the Media: The EDB Case", *The Social and Cultural Construction of Risk*, B.B. Johnson and V.T. Covello, (eds.), D. Reidel Publishing Company.

Shore, J.H., Tatum, E.L. and Wollmer, W.M. (1986a) "Evaluation of Mental Effects of Disaster", Mount St. Helen's Eruption, *American Journal of Public Health* 76:76-83.

Shrivastava. P., Mitroff, I.I., Miller, D. and Migliani, A. (1988). 'Understanding Industrial Crisis', in: Module 1, Unit 5 ('Systems Ideas and Risk') of *M.Sc. in Risk, Crisis and Disaster Management*, Leicester: SCSPO: 199.

Sims, R. (2009). 'Toward a Better Understanding of Organizational Efforts to Rebuild Reputation Following an Ethical Scandal', *Journal of Business Ethics*, 90:453-472.

Smith, M.K. (2002). 'Malcolm Knowles, informal adult education, self-direction and andragogy', *The Encyclopedia of Informal Education*. Accessed April 2010 from www.infed.org/thinkers/et-knowl.htm.

Slovic, P. (1986). "Informing and Educating the Public about Risk", *Risk Analysis*, 6(4).

Slovic, P. Kraus, N. and Covello, V.T. (1990). "What should we know about making risk comparison?", *Journal of the Society for Risk Analysis*, 10(3): 389-392.

Sood, R. Stockdale, G. and Rogers, E.M. (1987). "How the News Media Operate in Natural Disasters", *Journal of Communication*, 37(3).

Stanton, A. (1989). "Management can keep a crisis from turning into a calamity," *Oil & Gas Journal*, 8 May, pp. 15-16.

Susskind, L.E. and Thomas-Larmer, J. (1999). "Conducting a Conflict Assessment," chapter 2 in *The Consensus Building Handbook: A Comprehensive Guide to Reaching Agreement*, L. Susskind, S. McKearnan and J. Thomas-Larmer, eds. Thousand Oaks, CA: Sage Publications.

Susskind, L.E. and Corburn, J. (2000). "Using Simulations to Teach Negotiation: Pedagogical Theory and Practice," Michael Wheeler, ed., *Teaching Negotiation: Ideas and Innovations* Cambridge: PON, 285.

Taaffe, Gerald (August 20, 1966) "The Great Beer Scare", *Maclean's*, Toronto: 7-29.

Thompson, M., Ellis, R. and Wildavsky, A. (1990). 'Cultural Theory', in: Module 1, Unit 8 ('Introduction to Cultural History') of *M.Sc. in Risk, Crisis and Disaster Management*, Leicester: SCSPO: 321, 322, 325, 326.

Toft, B. and Reynolds, S. (1994). *Learning from Disaster – A Management Approach*, Oxford: Butterworth Heinemann.

Turner, B. (1978). *Man-made Disasters*, London: Wykeham.

Voke, Richard, SEVESO II, How will it affect Emergency Planning, from International Disaster and Emergency Response, IDER '97 Conference Proceedings.

Waring, A.E. (1989). 'Systems Methods for Managers - A Practical Guide', in: Module 1, Unit 5 ('Systems Ideas and Risk') of *M.Sc. in Risk, Crisis and Disaster Management*, Leicester: SCSPO: 172.

Waring, A.E. (1996a). 'Safety Management Systems', in: Module 1, Unit 5 ('Systems Ideas and Risk') of *M.Sc. in Risk, Crisis and Disaster Management*, Leicester: SCSPO: 172.

Waring, A.E. (1996c). 'Practical Systems Thinking', in: Module 1, Unit 5 ('Systems Ideas and Risk') of *M.Sc. in Risk, Crisis and Disaster Management*, Leicester: SCSPO: 172.

Wheeler, M. (2000). *Teaching Negotiations: Ideas and Innovations*. Cambridge, MA: PON Books.

Wills, J. (1991). "Europe's answer to oil spills", *New Scientist*, (May), p.36-38.

Wynne, B., (1989, 1992) in Lash et al. (1996), *Risk, Environment & Modernity: Towards a New Ecology* London: Sage Publications, Inc., pp. 29ff.

Zsambok, C., and Klein, G. (Eds.). (1997). *Naturalistic Decision Making*. Mahwah, NJ: Lawrence Erlbaum.

Praise for ALLAN BONNER'S Tough *Love* at the Table

"I'm honored that you've included a column about me..."

– President Bill Clinton

"You can't fight a battle and analyze it all at the same time so this book acts as a wakeup call...an easy and entertaining read."

– Jamie Snook, Chief Executive Officer, Labrador Metis Nation

---

"I feel very honored to have been part of your latest book. I am anxious to read it and know that I will gain some new insight."

– R. Nicholas Burns, Under Secretary of State for Political Affairs, Washington

"When our clients want Million-dollar advice on dispute resolution and fascinating stories, we recommend Allan"

– Mike Taubleb, Promenade Speaker's Bureau, New York, NY

"This book is esthetically pleasing, driven by empathy and dedicated to the highest of moral, ethical and professional values. It is a generous and delicious taste of "Tough Love." Straight forward, cogent and real. The nearly lost fine art of getting people to "do what you need them to do while allowing them to believe it was their idea" is brilliantly taught by Dr. Allan Bonner."

– Detective James T. Shanahan, Chief instructor, Police Academy of the City of New York

Praise for
ALLAN BONNER'S

DOING & SAYING THE **RIGHT THING**

"Over the years, SOCKO has proven to be an effective tool for avoiding the communications pitfalls we all face in an ever interrelated and fast-moving world. In a daily ritual where people are bombarded by sales pitches and spins of all varieties, your training approach can make the difference between 20 seconds of fame and a painful, time-consuming damage control strategy. Yours is ultimately a discipline which enhances the credibility of the message and the messenger."

– Hon. Sergio Marchi, Ambassador, The Permanent Mission of Canada to the United Nations, Geneva

---

"It all comes down to messaging and THE SOCKO SYSTEM is the best single volume I have read on how to get your message across as well as what pitfalls we can avoid..."

– Colin Robertson, Advocacy Minister and head of the Washington Secretariat, Embassy of Canada

---

"I consider myself fortunate to have benefited from being trained in the SOCKO method by Allan Bonner and his team. My training occurred just after my appointment as Canada's chief negotiator for the North American Free Trade Agreement... The common-sense SOCKO approach allowed me to think much more clearly about how to communicate, and, I am convinced, led to a better result both for the government and the media and their audience."

– John M. Weekes, Chairman, Global Trade Practices, APCO Worldwide, Geneva

---

"The SOCKO system is a pragmatic, hands-on, must-read book that demonstrates how to refine, hone, and develop your personal communications skills..."

– Major-General Richard Rohmer, OC, CCM, DFC, O.ONT, K.StJ, CD, QC

"... starting with the legions of public relations and communications professionals ... they should treat Mr. Bonner's book like a religious text and return to it again and again for guidance."

– Mark Entwistle [former press secretary to Prime Minister Brian Mulroney], The Hill Times

---

"You'll come away with solid tools, techniques and processes to set you on the path to masterful communications."

– Karen Schwartz, IABC Communicator

Praise for
ALLAN BONNER'S

MEDIA RELATIONS

"Allan Bonner's wide experience as a broadcaster and consultant makes this a valuable handbook to understanding the media. It deals clearly and concisely with everything you need to know when you find yourself in the news spotlight...from organizing the press conference, to getting your message across, to answering the tough questions. Essential and insightful."

– Lloyd Robertson,
CTV News

"Bonner has taken the mystery, and I expect the fear, out of media interviews with this informative tome. By telling the reader in no uncertain terms what the reporter expects, he is making our job as a journalist all the easier. It's a must read for anyone who has to deal with the print, radio or television media."

– Harold Levy,
The Toronto Star

"Truly, a university class in media relations. It's a must-read reference source for large and small businesses, governments, schools, and non-profits. Bonner knows what he is talking about, telling the secrets that make dealing with the media easier and more productive."

– Joe Bates,
KVOS TV

"This is an entertaining, common-sense analysis of the right and wrong ways to deal with the media, by a writer who knows his subject intimately and has the war stories to prove it."

– Warren Clements, Member of the Editorial Board,
The Globe and Mail

"A simple but all-encompassing guide for those plunged into dealing with the media... The book is a valuable resource."

– Harvey Schachter, Columnist,
The Globe and Mail

Praise for
ALLAN BONNER'S

POLITICAL COLUMNS

"I feel very honored to have been part of your latest book. I am anxious to read it and know that I will gain some new insight."

– R. Nicholas Burns, Under Secretary of State for Political Affairs, Washington

---

"A pragmatic tour de force: this book is filled with insights, rich and valuable experiences and constitutes a great learning. A very interesting book on how communication skills, behavioural trends and media relations can influence one's success in politics and public governance."

– Raymond Chrétien, Former Ambassador of Canada to the United States
Fasken Martineau DuMoulin LLP

"Short. Crisp. To the point. Always interesting. My favourite: the one where he is visiting the State Department and reminds himself (and us) that seamless, effective communication flows from hard work by the principal. An excellent read for any communications professional and anyone interested in politics."

– Brian ToppNational Campaign Director, New Democratic Party of Canada (2006 Campaign)
Deputy Chief of Staff to Premier Roy Romanow

"I'm honored that you've included a column about me..."

– President Bill Clinton

"Everyman's guide to both theory and practice of the dark art—politics—with a lot of fun thrown in along the way. Wonderful!"

– Stephen LeDrew,
Toronto Lawyer and Broadcaster,
President of the Liberal Party of Canada (1998-2003)

"Could there be a more perfect lesson in getting your message across?"

– Kevin Galligher,
Principal of Link Strategies,
Former Co-Chair National Campaign Committee, PC Party of Canada

---

"Allan Bonner's astute, pungent commentary is a political education for all who believe in democratic institutions."

– George Shipley, Political Constultant,
Austin, Texas

"Like getting a crash course from Marshall McLuhan, Peter F. Drucker, Johnny Carson and Bill Clinton—all at once. Through a rich alchemy of good social science, good storytelling and easy-to-apply practical tips and techniques, Allan Bonner has revealed the secrets that have made him one of Canada's most successful media and management consultants."

– Ross Mayot, Vice President,
Learning Services Access Media Group

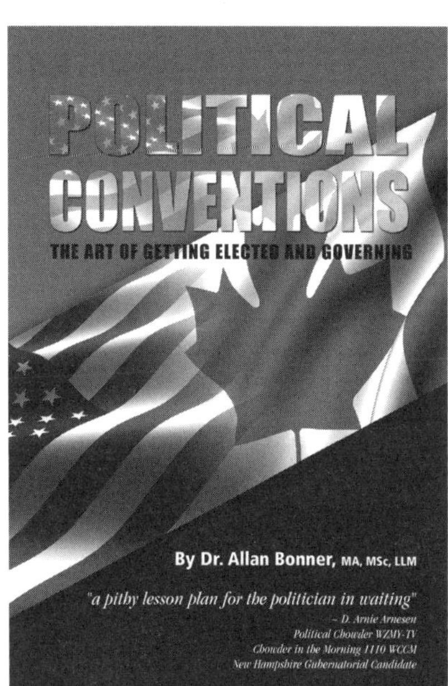

Praise for

ALLAN BONNER'S

POLITICAL CONVENTIONS

"a pithy lesson plan for the politician in waiting"

~ D. Arnie Arnesen
Political Chowder WZMY-TV
Chowder in the morning 1110 WCCM
New Hampshire Gubernatorial Candidate

"The essential primer on twenty-first century American politics. Bonner knows U.S. politics cold and has a unique ability to explain it."

~ Richard Spotswood
Political Columnist
The Marin Independent Journal
Marin County, California

"A how-to look inside the modern political process, for everyone from the nervous candidate facing his first TV interview to the undecided voter who doesn't want to be manipulated."

~ Richard Ager
New Hampshire Public Television

Praise for
ALLAN BONNER'S

AN OUNCE OF PREVENTION

"This book is an excellent piece of work. It is clear, comprehensive and articulate and provides the blueprint for establishing a culture of crisis management awareness, planning and preparation at all levels in an organization. It is a "must-read" for leaders who are serious about dealing effectively with the unexpected."

~ General (Retired) Ray Henault, former Chief of Defence Staff and former Chairman of the NATO Military Committee

---

"a content rich, solution based presentation that promotes a message vital to the critical incident response community."

Detective James T. Shanahan,
Police Academy of the City of New York

"...good, solid common sense, but it is the kind of common sense that is regularly ignored, owing to the universal guarantee that 'It won't happen here'. If we have anything to learn from the last 25 years, it's that 'it can, will and quite often does happen here'. A period of introspection, the development of some internal resilience (not much, just an ounce) can so easily and economically minimise the impact of crises."

Laurence Foster MSC
Former Head of Emergency Planning,
Greater Manchester Police.
Director of Emergency Planning,
Sakerhetspartner Norden UK.

An Ounce of Prevention DVD

$39. 95

This interactive DVD contains instructional video clips and more than 80 charts, tables, checklists, pre-written documents, forms and diagrams to help keep you safe. The checklists and diagrams can be emailed and faxed to remote locations to guide responders. Some can even be sent to hotel banquet managers so your public meeting room, public affairs desk and workspace will be as close to what you need as possible. The interactive lists and charts can be filled in, expanded and customized to suit your needs.

Imagine—your crisis plan is already more than 80 pages long just by printing out the contents of this DVD. Use this as your staff "force-multiplier" as is done in military applications. Give selected staff and colleagues a few of the forms each and get them customized in double- or triple-time.

Now is the time to list your assets, compile phone numbers, scout out resources and know how to mobilize when the time comes.

Also from Sextant Publishing:
NEGOTIATION & DISPUTE RESOLUTION
Allan Bonner Communications Management Inc.
20th Anniversary
THE SOCKO™ SYSTEM
Allan Bonner Communications Management Inc.
allanbonner.com
1-877-484-1667
Média, Présentations, Négotiations, Communications & Crises
UNFOLDING DISASTERS: THE VALDEZ OIL SPILL & OTHER CASE STUDIES
SACHEZ VOUS AFFIRMER
Allan Bonner Communications Management Inc.
allanbonner.com
1-877-484-1667
3 cours de communication pour les porte-parole
+ Vidéo + Visuels du cahier de travaille

Hear and
See the
Author in
Action...
THE
SOCKO™
SYSTEM
Public Speaking and Presentation Skills
Allan
Bonner
Communications
Management Inc.
allanbonner.com
1-877-484-1667
30 minutes of video - 90 minutes of audio - Bonus interviews and media clips
allanbonner.com
1-877-484-1667
RISK & CRISIS
MANAGEMENT
Dr. Allan Bonner
MA, MSc, LLM
Graduate Research
& Writing Skills
allanbonner.com
1-877-484-1667
Approximately 3 hours of video and 90 minutes of audio

Also from Sextant Publishing:

SATYA DAS

Satya Das

The Best Country: Why Canada Will Lead the Future by Satya Das

A #1 Best Seller! In increasingly complex and unsure times, this book explores how Canadian values, experiences and society can make a difference in a world that seems to have lost its way.

PRICE: $19.95

Dispatches from a Borderless World by Satya Das

A compassionate examination of the "human cost" in a world where entire cultures are trapped between the ebb and flow of the global economy. Quantities are limited. (Originally published by NeWest Press)

PRICE: $19.95

Also from Sextant Publishing:

Green Oil

Green Oil: Clean Energy for the 21st Century? is a number one bestseller changing the narrative around Alberta as the purveyor of "dirty oil" and showing how Alberta and Canada can become the lynchpin of the democratic world's energy security.

Co-founder and Principal of Cambridge Strategies, Satya Das, brings an expert understanding of the challenges and implications of owning the Alberta oilsands, the largest hydrocarbon deposit in the world. Sustainable development of the oil sands can play a vital and leading role in the transition from today's high-carbon economy to a clean energy future.

PRICE: $25.00

Ken Chapman

Rebooting Alberta: A Citizen's Manual

Rebooting Alberta: A Citizen's Manual delves into extensive research by Satya Das and Ken Chapman of Cambridge Strategies Inc. on the values of Albertans and their engagement in the province, their values around the oilsands and their political leaders.

The results are surprising, the implications profound as Alberta has the potential to be a world leader in energy supply and innovation, yet lacks faith in its own leadership and direction or the ability of its citizens to make a difference. Das and Chapman show how we can take this knowledge to reengage in our democratic institutions and become the best Alberta for the world.

PRICE: $25.00